1985 OUTDOOR LIFE FRESHWATER FISHING YEARBOOK

Published by
Outdoor Life Books, New York

Distributed to the trade by
Stackpole Books, Harrisburg, Pennsylvania

Copyright © 1985 by Times Mirror Magazines, Inc.

Published by
Outdoor Life Books
Times Mirror Magazines, Inc.
380 Madison Avenue
New York, NY 10017

Distributed to the trade by
Stackpole Books
Cameron and Kelker Streets
P.O. Box 1831
Harrisburg, PA 17105

ISBN 0-943822-52-1

ISSN 8756-8241

Manufactured in the United States of America

Contents

Preface

by Jerry Gibbs, Fishing Editor, Outdoor Life

Welcome to the inaugural issue of the *Outdoor Life Freshwater Fishing Yearbook*. You're holding in this single volume a collection of some of the very best fishing stories from across the nation.

Outdoor Life magazine has provided the lion's share of completely updated material, but there are also contributions from five other angling magazines as well as two book excerpts. Whatever your favorite fishing, you'll find it covered here. There are fact-packed chapters on bass, trout, pike, walleyes, muskies, and panfish designed to make your fishing more effective, and the equipment chapters will bring you up to date on the latest in fishing gear.

In Part I, Tackle and Equipment, you'll find my report on all the latest rods, reels, lures, electronics, and accessories for 1985. Bill McKeown's story, "Fishing's Newest Magic Box," explains how modern electronic wizardry can help you return to that hot-spot and keep from getting lost as well. "Trouble-shoot Those Little Outboards," by E. F. Lindsley tells how to get the most from the smaller fishing outboard engines, and keep them running faithfully.

Part II, Bass Fishing, presents in-depth fishing know-how on what may be America's favorite gamesters—the largemouth and smallmouth bass. You'll find a fascinating look at old Mr. Bigmouth's intimate feeding habits in Duke Cullimore's "Dining with the Largemouth." An eye-opening look at the largemouth's real behavioral patterns is found in "Bass Myths Debunked" by Morris Gresham. Steve Price explores the newest bass-fishing trend—homing in on fish through pH preference—and for those who like natural baits, my chapter, "Are These Bass Baits Too Good?," focuses on the premier natural offerings for big bass. Anglers who like to cast lures get an inside track on the artificials the nation's top competitive anglers use when the chips are down in Al Ristori's discussion of fishing plastic worms. Next are articles on fishing spinnerbaits and topwater plugs by Jack Lewis, on crankbaits, jigs, and jigging spoons by John Weiss, plus a lesson in deepwater trolling by Frank Sargeant. "The Bass that Thinks it's a Trout" and "How to Find Smallmouths in

Lakes" are two valuable technique stories for small-mouth lovers who fish both rivers and stillwaters.

Part III, Trout Fishing, leads off with a fascinating study of trout feeding and migration habits by Dave Whitlock. Brown-trout fanciers will want to read "Spring, Small Streams and Bruiser Brown Trout" by Doug Stange, Doug Knowles, and Lee Nelson. Ron Mitchell's "Secrets of Alpine Trout" is the best treatment on high mountain trout fishing I've read. That's followed by my story on the mysterious and often-maligned lake trout. Two good technique chapters cover the marabou jig and special casting techniques.

Part IV, Pike, Walleye, Muskie, gives fanciers of so-called cool-water species plenty to enjoy. There's an A–Z treatise on the fish that has spawned more strange legends than perhaps any other, the northern pike, and John Weiss does a top job of it in his "In Search of the Water Wolf." For walleye fans Dick Sternberg's two chapters cover the best walleye lakes, and how to hunt the species in big rivers. And finally, "Muskies Have No Virtue" by Doug Stange and Mark Windels is a complete guide to taking this freshwater trophy all season long.

Part V, Panfishing, gives every angler the kind of solid information needed to improve catches of these plentiful and tasty fish. There are chapters on crappie, big bluegills, plus an oddball weed-fishing technique that will put a smile on your face.

Part VI, Just For Laughs, is a collection of some of the funniest fishing writing that's been penned in a long while. There's a deadpan-funny profile of the lake trout, after which you'll learn how matching wits with a fish becomes an all-out survival struggle for author Joel Vance's self-respect. Pat McManus's zany satire on one of the all-time big bass tournaments is next, followed by Rex Gerlach's hilarious spoof of our often cryptic bass-fishing jargon.

All told, *OL's Freshwater Fishing Yearbook 1985* is an invaluable companion you'll find yourself turning to both for information and laid back relaxation time and again. Just open the volume anywhere and see if I'm not right.

PART 1

TACKLE AND EQUIPMENT

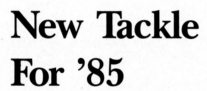

New Tackle For '85

Jerry Gibbs

Fishermen around the U.S. have an unbelievable array of new tackle to look forward to in 1985. Sparking the leading products this year are innovations that are direct spinoffs from the aerospace and microchip industries. Computer reels and carbon filament rods without attached reel seats are just two of the notable examples. Comparing the modern tackle to what was used twenty years ago is like comparing a Model A to the space shuttle.

More good news is that increased use of new materials has resulted in a price drop in top-quality

Courtesy *Fishing Tackle Trade News*

tackle. There are more mid-priced tackle items available, too, than ever before.

Though rods, reels, and fascinating new lures make up the foundation of angler needs, there are more new accessory items including electronics, tackleboxes and boat-engine aids than have been seen in some time.

Here then, are the highlights from 1985's new equipment introductions—tackle you'll want to check at your dealer or obtain more information on by writing directly to the manufacturer, whose address is listed at the end of each entry.

RODS

ABU-Garcia Inc. reintroduced the popular Conolon rod line—in graphite. Three casting and three spinning models from light through medium action are available. Features include high-modulus graphite construction and Hardloy guides. Fuji reel seat and pistolgrip handle with diamond pattern are on the casting rods. Spinning models have cork grips. Ferruling is graphite.

Six Five-Star graphite-reinforced fiberglass boat rods are also new for '85. They come in six sizes from 6–7 feet. They'll match with the firm's new big-water Ambassadeurs. There are nine spinning models in the Five-Star line, including a 13-foot model.

ABU-Garcia Inc., 21 Law Drive. Fairfield, NJ 07006.

Berkley & Company Inc. is using a unique radial construction for its all-graphite premium Lightning rods this year. The graphite fibers in this construction are interwoven lengthwise and crosswise. According to the company, the construction produces greater strength, flexibility, and finer-tuned actions. In most graphite construction, the fibers run longitudinally only, reinforced with a fiberglass screen to give hoop strength.

Lightning rods feature blank-through-handle construction and 100% graphite content. There are twenty-three actions and sizes from which to choose.

A new mid-range series of Phazer rods was launched. There are thirteen models including spinning, casting, special steelhead and fly models. Phazers also have dual graphite construction—in this case an interior wrap of bias-oriented fibers and an exterior wrap of fibers arranged longitudinally. Blank-through-handle and Hardloy guides are construction features. Phazer also carries Berkley's no-risk lifetime-replacement warranty and thirty-day trial period.

Berkley & Company Inc., Trilene Drive, Spirit Lake, IA 51360.

Browning has added a line of Telescoping Traveler pack rods of graphite. Features include six telescoping sections, aluminum-oxide guides and collapsed sizes of 16 or 18 inches depending on the model. The three models available include a 6-foot medium-light spinning rod, a 6¾-foot medium-action spinning rod and a 5½-foot casting model.

Browning, Route 1, Morgan, UT 84050.

Lew Childre & Sons Inc. now has a blank-through-handle mid-priced series of rods called Laser graphite. Weight reduction and increased strength are advantages of the Speedlite handle system, which is also available for custom casting-rod building. Spinning rods in the Laser lineup have blank-through-handle design also, with gold FPS reel seats connected to the blank with a solid arbor. Grips

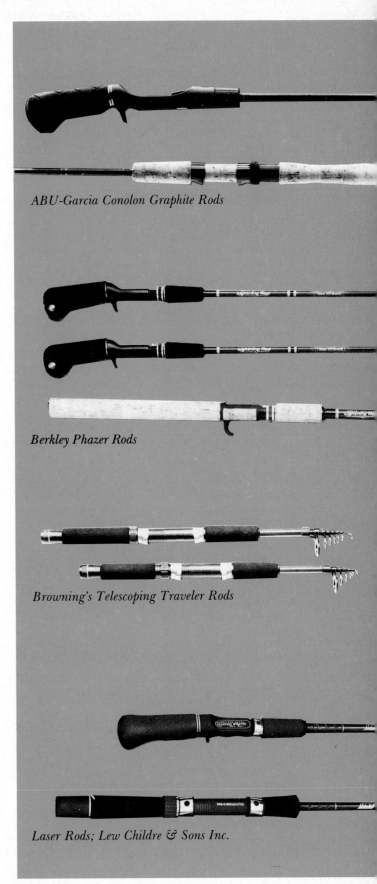

ABU-Garcia Conolon Graphite Rods

Berkley Phazer Rods

Browning's Telescoping Traveler Rods

Laser Rods; Lew Childre & Sons Inc.

themselves are urethene for the feel of cork with excellent durability.

Six casting and six spinning models are in the Laser graphite series. Action ranges from extra-light to heavy in casting and ultralight through medium in spinning.

Childre's Cobra boron and Cobra SIC graphites will come with the new Speedlite blank-through-handle system.

Lew Childre & Sons Inc., 110 E. Azalea Avenue, Foley, AL 36535.

Columbia/Bruin has switched to graphite-composite material for its Bruin 600 series, and added the Bruin 900 graphite-blend series and a Bruin 200 group of saltwater rods this year.

Three casting rods with medium-light to medium action and three spinning rods with light to heavy action make up the 600 series. All have one-piece construction with continuous graphite fibers from end to end, as well as Fuji guides with black-ceramic inserts and built-in hook keepers. Lengths range from 4¼ feet to 6 feet.

Bruin's 900 series of Bear Claw graphite-blend rods are designed to combine light weight with sturdiness. The casting rods have Fuji aluminum-oxide guides and pistol-grip handles, and the popping rod features a Fuji TFPS trigger reel seat with EVA foam handle and foregrip. The group contains two casting, four spinning, and one popping rods. All but one model, a 6½-foot spinning rod, are one-piece.

Columbia/Bruin, P.O. Drawer G, Highway 52 W, Columbia, AL 36319.

Daiwa Corporation introduced two new series of advanced-construction rods of high-tech materials. They include the K.G.X. series and Whisker rods.

In the latter, silicon-carbide microwhiskers (microscopic in size, grown to extreme uniformity and stretched into cat's-whiskers configuration) are fused in unoriented fashion with longitudinal graphite fibers in an epoxy resin. The resulting rod has a high resistance to lateral shock and flex fatigue. Whisker rods are said to be 20—40% more flexible than boron-graphite composites. They are also lighter in weight because thinner shaft diameters are possible. Spinning, casting, and fly models are available. The rods are equipped with blank-through-handle Sensor graphite systems.

In the K.G.X. rods, narrow Kevlar strips (30 strands to a strip) are crisscross-wrapped in net fashion around the outside of a graphite rod shaft. The result is great twist-resistance and exceptional

dampening power. Dampening the shaft from oscillating up and down once the casting power stroke has been completed is important for accuracy and distance in all rods, but especially in flyrods. K.G.X. rods also have Sensor graphite handles. Spinning, casting, fly and downrigger-trolling models will be available initially.

Other series and updating of rods in existing series are as follows: Sensor handles are now on the Procaster boron line. Forty-one fresh- and saltwater models with Sensor are in the Strike Gold series. Apollo Gold becomes the largest Daiwa rod series. New models are found in the Apollo graphite composite series. The Jupiter Graphite composite series of economy rods has been introduced. A new series of Freshwater Tournament rods features custom-quality appointments.

Daiwa Corporation, 7421 Chapman Avenue, Garden Grove, CA 92641.

Fenwick/Woodstream highlighted a new series of Matrix rods—composite graphite-Fenglass—designed to utilize the features of both materials. Initially there will be eight freshwater and light saltwater spinning models and four casting rods with pistol grips in 5- through 7-power action. A Flippin' Stik and a downrigger Riggerstik come in spinning or casting styles.

The popular through-blank Triggerstik handle will be available on selected boron, graphite, and Matrix models. A new blank-through-pistol-grip Triggerstik will be featured on some Boron-X and Iron Hawk graphites.

A series of Fenglas Atlanticstik was launched. There are six spinning models with one-piece and two-piece blanks, as well as one surf model and a 6¼-foot wireline-jig rod for trolling or bottom fishing. Hypalon grips, stainless/graphite reel seats and amber-color blanks are featured.

Success of the Pacificstik series has resulted in the offering of a premier Pacificstik Royale lineup. These rods feature HMG graphite butts for great pumping and lifting power. Upper blanks are Fenglass. Black underwraps, gunmetal-gray overwraps and red-and-gold trim make the line extremely attractive as well as functional. Six models for a variety of functions, from live-bait fly lining through heavy-weight jigging, are available.

Fenwick/Woodstream, 14799 Chestnut Street, Westminster, CA 92683.

Kunnan Tackle Company introduced the new line of Billy Westmorland Signature rods including three casting models in medium-light, medium and medium-heavy action; and two medium-heavy spinning models with different guide spacing and number. These are graphite rods. The spinning models have reel-seat rings and the pistol grips on the casting models are Fuji.

New models have been added to several lines as follows: a new flyrod to the boron President series; spinning, fly-steelhead spinning and casting, and salmon models to the 96% graphite Leader series; a popping model to the graphite Advantage series; a standup trolling model to the C-Striker saltwater series; saltwater spinning, two light fly, two popping, two downrigger, one flipping and two steelhead models to the graphite Competitor series.

A spin-fly combo and a fly model are new in the four-piece backpack rod series.

Kunnan Tackle Company, 9707-B Candida Street, San Diego, CA 92126.

Ryobi America Corporation unveiled a new graphite casting rod, the V-Mag Lite. Designed to complement the firm's ultralight baitcasting reels, the new rod has an 86% graphite blank, through-handle construction, and cork fore and pistol grips. It's 5½ feet and has medium action and aluminum-oxide guides. Weight is 3.8 ounces.

Ryobi's RA graphite series has three new spinning and one new casting model. The RC composite series is all new with spincasting, spinning, baitcasting and big-water spinning models. In the RS fiberglass series are one spincasting, two baitcasting and one big-water spinning models.

Ryobi America Corporation, 1158 Tower Lane, Bensenville, IL 60106.

St. Croix of Park Falls has introduced a presentation rod, a 4-in-1 spincasting, baitcasting, spinning, and fly model. It features all-graphite charcoal-gray shafts with gold-plated guides and handle appointments. Black-and-gold windings and diamond butt wrap complete the rod. Included is a fleece-lined cordura zippercase.

Combination spinning/fly model 6912-S/F features a graphite-reinforced shaft, braced stainless guides, and cork handles. Comes with cloth bag and hard plastic case.

Two flyrods with all-graphite shafts, aluminum oxide guides, and cork handles are also new. These four-section rods are joined with Ever-Fit Ferrule-S construction that allows continuous flex through the joint area. A cloth bag and hard plastic bag also come with these rods.

St. Croix also has added spinning, casting, and fly models to its Imperial Graphite XL and Pro-Graphite series.

Five two-piece rod models for medium-heavy, heavy and extra-heavy salmon and steelhead action, plus a 7-foot two-piece flyrod complete the St. Croix Imperial Graphite XL series. Spinning rods for salmon and steelhead drifting and shore casting include Fuji Hardloy single-foot guides, graphite reel seats, and cork handles. Casting rods for salmon and steelhead drifting use braced Fuji Hardloy guides, trigger-grip graphite reel seats, and cork handles.

For river drifting and shore casting, St. Croix has included a spinning rod and a casting rod for salmon and steelhead in its Pro-Graphite series. Both rods are 8½ feet for medium action. Spinning rod features single-foot aluminum-oxide guides, an anodized aluminum reel seat and cork handle. The casting rod is similar, but offers braced aluminum-oxide guides. Four flyrods in this series run from 7½ to 9

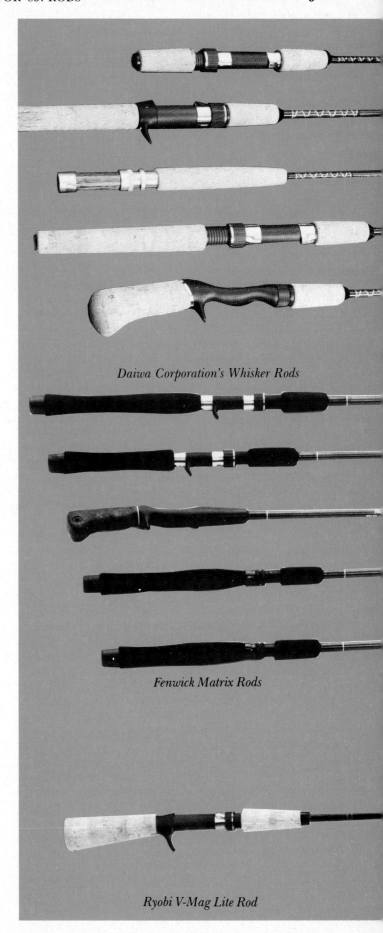

Daiwa Corporation's Whisker Rods

Fenwick Matrix Rods

Ryobi V-Mag Lite Rod

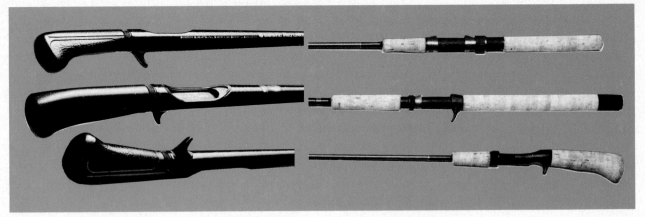

Shimano American Corporation (left); Shakespeare Fishing   Tackle Group (right)

feet in length and sport aluminum-oxide stripper guides, anodized aluminum reel seats and cork handles. The 9-foot model is recommended for salmon and steelhead.

St. Croix of Park Falls, Ltd., Highway 13 North, P.O. Box 279, Park Falls, WI 54552.

Shakespeare Fishing Tackle Group heralds a line of high-quality graphite rods with blank-through-handle construction. Called Liberty, the line is made with 98% graphite blanks, graphite or cork grips (depending on model), and Hardloy guides. Spinning, baitcasting, and popping models in a selection of actions for all freshwater and light-tackle saltwater fishing are available.

The new President series combines graphite-glass construction like the firm's popular Ugly Stik, but in this case the rods are triple-wrapped. There's an inner spiral layer of graphite covered by longitudinal fiberglass and finally longitudinal graphite. The construction results in an all-graphite tip. Other features include blank-through-handle design, cork grips, and Hardloy guides. Spinning and baitcasting models are available.

Again, using the Ugly Stik construction, Shakespeare has designed a new series of big-water rods called Tiger. The series includes casting, spinning, trolling, downrigger, jetty, jigging, and boat-bait rods. Gold-colored longitudinal fiberglass over spiral wraps of graphite in fast-taper action are the hallmarks of this line. There are seventeen models with stainless-steel guides, aluminum-oxide or roller tip tops, graphite-reinforced reel seats, and foam grips.

Twenty-three freshwater baitcasting, spinning and fly models compose the revamped 1100 series of Ugly Stiks, new for 1985.

Promotionally priced rods make up the Alpha SXG series of graphite, glass-reinforced rods for anglers on a budget. Models for spinning, baitcasting, two-handed casting, and steelhead spinning are in the series.

Additional new models are to be found in the Sigma graphite, Black Jack graphite and the Alpha-X graphite-glass composite series.

An Ugly Stik Jr. rod-reel combo is available in spincasting or spinning with a 4-foot 1-piece rod.

Shakespeare Fishing Tackle Group, Drawer S, Columbia, SC 29260.

Shimano American Corporation took blank-through-handle construction one step further with the introduction of its Magnumlite GT Fightin' rod series. With these rods, the reel mounts in the actual rod blank. When fishing, you hold the reel-fitted blank rather than a separate handle. To reinforce and strengthen the butt section into which the reel foot slips, Shimano has added titanium. Boron is used at critical points along the blank for further reinforcement. The design should make for extreme sensitivity.

Fuji Hardloy guides and hardware are used in the ten models initially available, which run the gamut from medium-light baitcasting, two-handed popping or casting, through medium-heavy and medium spinning. A new flipping model will most likely see introduction in the near future.

The superlight Fuji pistol-grip handle has been added to the firm's Magnumlite graphite casting rods.

The Triton TS rod series was newly developed to match Shimano's Triton trolling reels. These feature light tipaction with progressive taper to powerful butts for big saltwater fish. There are four models including those for medium live bait and jigging, medium spinning, heavy live bait and jigging.

Shimano American Corporation, 205 Jefferson Road, Parsippany, NJ 07054.

Wright & McGill Company boasts a new graphite backpack-rod lineup called the Eagle Claw graphite Trailmaster series. There are spinning, spin-fly combos and an eight-piece all-purpose rod that sets up five different ways to give a variety of actions and lengths for casting, fly, spinning or spincasting.

Four different flyrod models are in the Granger graphite series. Steelhead-salmon casting and spinning models have been added to this series as well.

Casting and spinning models make up the five-rod Eagle Claw Classic boron series just introduced. Other series have also had new models added.

Wright & McGill Company, P.O. Box 16011, Denver, CO 80216.

Zebco Division Brunswick Corporation offers five new Quantum boron rods including two casting, three spinning models to match their Quantum reels. Fuji Hardloy guides, cork-grip Fuji handles on casting models and graphite-reinforced cork handles on spinning rods are specialties.

There is also a graphite Quantum series called Q-Stik graphite. Three casting and three spinning rods are the introductory models in this series. Features on the casting rods include EVA pistol grips on Fuji handles, single-foot guides on light-action models and double-foot guides on heavier models.

Seven rods are in the Crossfire line of fiberglass rods. There are four spinning plus three casting models. Pistol grips are found on the casting models and EVA grips on spinning rods.

Added to the Pro Staff series are four big-water rods including three spinning and one popping model. There are two medium-action plus one light-action spinning models; the popping rod is of medium-light action. All are one-piece and have Titania guides and EVA foam grips.

Zebco Division Brunswick Corporation, Box 270, Tulsa, OK 74101.

REELS

ABU-Garcia Inc. unveiled two new Ambassadeur reels, the 4600 Plus and 5600 Plus, and also placed full lifetime warranties on the entire Ambassadeur line. The two new levelwind models feature graphite construction, traditional round shape, and Glide-lok magnetic anti-backlash control, the lever for which is conveniently located atop the left sideplate. Other features include the Fast Cast ThumBar spool release, flipping mode, and 4.7:1 retrieve ratio. The 4600 weighs 9.1 ounces and holds 150 yards of 12-pound line, while the 5600 weighs 9.8 ounces and accommodates 225 yards of 12-pound line.

Back again are the venerable, long-time-favorite ABU Cardinal 3 and 4 spinning reels with upgraded fulcrum drag system, boasting graphite-reinforced brake discs and stainless worm and brass main gears. The spools are now skirted, of course, and the reels have auto-manual internal bailtrip with either left- or right-hand retrieve. Retrieve ratio is 5.1:1. The model 3 holds 130 yards of 8-pound mono, while the 4 spools 230 yards of 8-pound test.

The Ultra Mag XL baitcasting series has been expanded to include five models. Two models have been added to the black-and-silver series of Ambassadeur Mag baitcasting reels. The old favorite 5000 Ambassadeur is being marketed again, as well.

In spincasting, the models 170GR and 290GR graphite reels come with casting thumb control and large line-hood opening. They come spooled with ABUlon mono—125 yards of 14-pound test and 110 yards of 20-pound test respectively. Both have 3.3:1 retrieve ratios.

A larger model of the Fast Cast spincasting reel has also been added, and the Comfort Touch release

ABU-Garcia's Cardinal 4

Abu Garcia's Ambassadeur Model 4600

button is now on the ABU-Matic 440 and 460.

A line of big-water Ambassadeurs called the Six-Shooters has been added. Features include magnetic braking system, adjustable handle, optional level-wind, quick-change spool capabilities.

ABU-Garcia Inc., 21 Law Drive, Fairfield, NJ 07006.

Browning launched the Mitchell Trigger Drag spinning reel that permits drag adjustment without removing your hand from the reel handle. It does not affect reeling or back-reeling. In use, the rear-drag control is set slightly less than normal. During hook-setting or fish-fighting operations, pulling up on the trigger with the index finger increases drag, and slacking off reduces drag. Four models are available: the 3510 ultralight, 3530 light, 3550 medium, and 5540 with graphite body and spool for medium-fishing assignments. All reels in the series have quick-change graphite spools.

Also new is the Mitchell baitcasting Turbo Mag reel. It incorporates a small internal air turbine with multiple blades. During casting, the turbine pulls a circular rotor disc away from the braking magnets, allowing the spool to spin freely. Braking occurs as the spool slows and the rotor draws closer to the anti-backlash magnets. Other features of this reel include single-piece aluminum-alloy frame, graphite palming sideplate and quick-change spool. Capacity is 220 yards of 8-pound test or 120 yards of 12-pound line.

Mitchell's 3530 RD

Lightning Cast trigger-bail opening has been added to the Mitchell rear-drag spinning-reel models 231 ORD and 233 ORD with graphite frames.
Browning, Route 1, Morgan, UT 84050.

Daiwa Corporation has the baitcasting reel market abuzz with the introduction of two microcomputerized models in its Procaster Tournament series. The PT 10E and PT 15E use real time-signal processing to give instant LCD readout data and audible signals on several functions. These include line capacity and diameter, casting distance, water depth, retrieve rate,

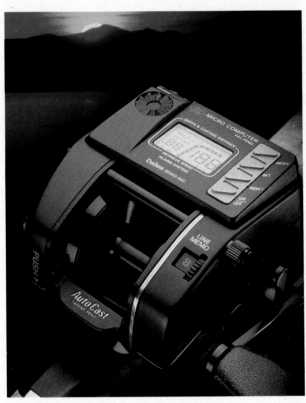

Daiwa's new reels feature LCD readout.

amount of line out when a fish is hooked, and line remaining after breakoffs. Information is continuously updated on the high-visibility LCD readout. A beep tone signals once every 10 feet during the retrieve. It also sounds once every second to aid determination of lure depth. Alternatively, you can check the LCD readout for precise depth, a great help for vertical jigging and matching lure depth to fish seen on sonar units. A bar graph on the readout indicates retrieve speed: A bar appears for each foot per second (fps) of retrieve up to 10 fps, to facilitate duplication of a retrieve that produced the last fish or strike.

Internal workings of the reel are water-shielded by O-ring-sealed covers. The reels are powered by two flat camera-type batteries.

Other features on the electronic and nonelectronic reels in the Procaster Tournament series include Autocast one-handed casting, Zero-Friction line guides, Magforce anti-backlash control, 5.18:1 retrieve ratios, pinch-proof palming-thumb protection from the line guide, and ball-bearing drive.

The AutoCast from Daiwa

Johnson Fishing's midsized model 710

All-graphite construction is now offered on the mid-priced Strike Gold series of skirted spinning reels. There are twelve models ranging from the Minisystem G 750 up through the heavy-duty salt-water GS 7050.

Daiwa Corporation, 7421 Chapman Avenue, Garden Grove, CA 92641.

Fenwick/Woodstream offers a three-model series of spinning reels with rear drag, reinforced graphite construction, auto-manual-closing bail, silent anti-reverse, and right- or left-hand retrieve. The Eagle reels feature 5.4:1 retrieve. Models 8100, 8300 and 8500 hold 230 yards of 4-, 6- and 8-pound test line respectively.

A Class I model has been added to the firm's World Class series. Like the larger Class II, the new model has perforated spool, dual pawl controls and extremely light drag capability. Both Class I and II have exposed palming rim. The Class 4 direct-drive model now has a clicker that functions as line is going out.

Fenwick/Woodstream, 14799 Chestnut Street, Westminster, CA 92683.

Johnson Fishing Inc. now markets a mid-sized spincasting reel, the model 710. Like its predecessors, the Century and Sabra, 710 boasts the tangle-free Drive-Train drag, which prevents line twist even if the reel is cranked while line is being taken out against the drag. Model 710 has a dark-green cover like the Century and Sabra, and black graphite casing. It is spooled with 80 yards of 14-pound line.

Johnson Fishing Inc., 1531 Madison Avenue, Mankato, MN 56001.

Penn Fishing Tackle Mfg. Company spotlighted the model 505HS, a high-speed addition to the well-known Jigmaster series. It's the first Penn conventional reel to have a 5:1 gear ratio and first Jigmaster with ball-bearing action. It has a lightweight die-cast black anodized-aluminum spool and newly designed reinforced sideplates.

Also new is the woven drag material that has been under development for ten years. The new material will eventually go in other conventional Penn reels. It is unharmed by water and grease, and by inadvertently leaving the drag screwed down.

Penn Fishing Tackle's 230 GR

Penn Fishing Tackle's 505 HS

The first graphite-body, rear-drag, trigger-bail spinning reels from Penn will be seen in '85. The 200 series reels have fully shielded drag components and oversized drag-control knob. Stainless-steel main shafts for strength and rigidity are standard. Retrieve ratio is 5.3:1. Three models include the 240GR, 230GR, and 220GR. They hold 150 yards of 12-pound, 140 yards of 8-pound and 130 yards of 6-pound mono respectively.

A mid-sized model, 104, has been added to the popularly-priced 100 series spinning reels.

Penn Fishing Tackle Mfg. Company, 3028 W. Hunting Park Avenue, Philadelphia, PA 19132.

Ryobi America Corporation announced a new series of baitcasting reels called the V-Mag Lite. These reels are styled after the firm's popular V-Mags, but have one-piece graphite frames and graphite spools. The smallest model weighs 5.4 ounces. All the V-Mag Lites are equipped with Ryobi's Touch 'N Trip thumb-activated freespool button for one-handed casts. Magnetic cast control, multiple pickup points and aluminum-oxide line guide are standard. Six models are available in 4.1:1 or 5:1 retrieve ratio, right- or left-hand crank, ball-bearing or bushing drive and two different line capacities—depending upon the specific model.

New in spinning are the MG and MGT graphite series. Construction consists of graphite frames, spool and rotor. Rear drags, skirted spools, and ball-bearing drives are standard. Wound line is evenly distributed on spool with gear-reduction oscillation. Six sizes are available in 5.3:1, 4.5:1, or 4.3:1 retrieve ratios, depending on models. The four models in the MGT series offer trigger-opening bails. The system is gear-operated, not merely a lever.

Middle-of-the-line DP or DPT graphite reels also have graphite body, spool and rotor with rear drag. Five models are in the MG series, while there are four in the trigger-operated DPT line.

The SL spinning reel series will appeal to value-minded anglers who still want a graphite-body reel, spool, and rotor. Four models are available to handle lines from 4- through 25-pound test. Bushing action (oil-less bearings) and retrieve ratios ranging from 5.3:1 to 4.3:1 are standard depending on which of the five models is chosen.

Ryobi America Corporation, 1158 Tower Lane, Bensenville, IL 60106.

Shakespeare Fishing Tackle Group added EZ-Cast trigger-opening bail to its series of Sigma graphite spinning reels.

High quality and low price are touted for the Alpha-X and Alpha line of spinning and fly reels. Five models in the Alpha-X spinning series and four in the Alpha spinning series cover most types of fishing from ultralight to medium saltwater. EZ-Cast is featured on some models as are several most-desired items on spinning reels, including left/right-hand retrieve, auto- or manual-closing bails, stainless-steel main shafts and more. The Alpha-X has rear drag, the Alpha has spool drag.

There is one Alpha automatic fly reel for lines numbered 4 through 8, and four single-action fly reels for lines from 5 through 9.

Five spinning models and three spincasting models round out the Omni-X series of budget-price reels. Spinning reels are made from a variety of materials, come with manual-auto or auto-bails only, and have fiberglass, graphite or aluminum spools, depending on the model. Sizes accommodate ultralight to light-

Shakespeare's Alpha X040 with EZ-Cast

saltwater fishing. The spincasting reels come spooled with Sigma monofilament.

Shakespeare Fishing Tackle Group, Drawer S, Columbia, SC 29260.

Shimano American Corporation banners their Fightin' Drag mechanism on selected baitcasting, spinning, and spincasting models for '85. Properly used, the mechanism promises to reduce breakoffs

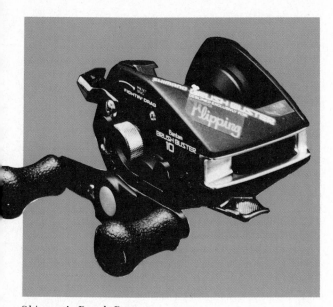

Shimano's Brush Buster

to near zero. Fightin' Drag for baitcasting reels works like this: A lever on the sideplate above the star drag is pushed forward to preset-drag position. The user then sets the star drag to proper tension to allow a fish to take out line below the breaking point. During fishing, the lever can be positioned all the way back to full-lock for hook setting and winching fish from cover. There is no drag slip in this position. In effect, you are in direct drive. If a large fish is hooked, the lever can be quickly thrust forward to shift the drag into its preset, fish-tiring position. The mechanism works similarly on Shimano's spinning and spincasting reels, but because lighter lines are normally used on these reels, the drag does not achieve full-lock, although it does increase force considerably.

Four Bantam Magnumlite GT-Plus revolving-spool models, nine GTX-Plus spinning models, and two Spincast-Plus models are equipped with the mechanism. Four rod-reel spincasting Fightin' Drag combo packs are available.

Another new entry is the Bantam Brush Buster, designed exclusively for flipping. Built around the concept that the flipping angler should not pay for advanced features primarily associated with casting ease, the Brush Buster is flagged as a powerhouse winch with 3.8:1 gear ratio. It has no levelwind mechanism and features bushings rather than ball

bearings. Brush Buster is equipped with the Fightin' Drag and has a no-backlash line stripper. Construction features graphite and titanium components.

Shimano American Corporation, 205 Jefferson Road, Parsippany, NJ 07054.

South Bend Sporting Goods Inc. has a new four-model Black Beauty series of spinning and spincasting reels. The 160 spincasting has auto anti-reverse and an aluminum hood with ceramic line ring.

There are three spinning models to handle light-freshwater through light-saltwater fishing. The spinning reels have rear drag, pushbutton skirted spools, folding bails, and most other desirable spinning reel features.

Two models in the Finalist fly-reel series have been introduced. They have lightweight aluminum spools and frames, bronze bearings, stainless-steel main shaft and permanent in-out click. They convert to left- or right-hand retrieve.

The model 110 is a budget-priced spincasting reel designed for beginning anglers. Specialties are a star-drag contoured thumb lever, corrosion-resistant Cycolac exterior. The 110 comes spooled with 8-pound line in color-coded blister packs.

A Black Beauty reel from South Bend

The Black Beauty series reels are available on matching rods as combo outfits, carded or preassembled for display.

South Bend Sporting Goods Inc., 1901 N. Nashville, Chicago, IL 60635.

Zebco Division Brunswick Corp. announced a top-of-the-line reel series (with complementing rods) called Quantum. In development the past two years, the Quantum reel series consists of two magnetic-brake baitcasting reels and seven spinning reels.

The Quantum QD 1310 baitcasting model has double-sealed stainless ball-bearing drive, while the QD 310 features polished graphite bushings. The reels have 5.1:1 retrieve ratios, Q-Cast recessed spool-release button for one-hand casting, dual cam-actuated Dynamag magnetic cast control coupled

The Quantum QD 1310, from Zebco

with a spool-tension control and U-spool to achieve the best casts with a variety of lures. Both models hold 160 yards of 12-pound line without spool arbor attached.

The Quantum spinning reels are built with the largest drag surface of any rear-drag spinning reel on the market, according to Zebco. Models QMG 20 and QMG 200C are graphite spinning reels, the latter having a trigger-opening (Q-cast) self-centering bail. Both have all the most-desirable features of better spinning reels, sport a fast 5.4:1 retrieve ratio and hold 160 yards of 8-pound mono. The five-model standard Quantum spinning reels include two

models with trigger-activated bails. The QMD 10, 100C, 20 and 200C models have 5.4:1 gear ratio, ball bearings, pop-off graphite spools. The large model QMD 50 has an aluminum spool and 4.5:1 ratio. Other features are silent, selective anti-reverse and internal bail trip.

In the Zebco lineup is a commemorative edition of the all-time favorite model 33. Called the 33 Classic, the reel boasts fancy trim on handle and housing, a graphite-composite frame, stainless ball bearing, SLD drag with two stainless-steel washers and two Pennlon washers, and 3.1:1 retrieve. All model 33s sport improvements from drag components through quieter, stronger gearing. The 33s come with 110 yards of 10-pound line.

Added to the Pro Staff spinning series are three Cam-Cast trigger-operated-bail models including ultralight, light and medium freshwater. There's also a new saltwater model, the PS 70 with aluminum spool. It handles 275 yards of 20-pound line.

Other Zebco reels to check include the affordable Crossfire spinning series; model 808 Lancer, a heavy-duty spincasting reel; model 888 Pro Staff, a big-water spincasting reel; 3/20 spincasting with Cycolac body; and model Z20, a lightweight spincasting reel available in balanced rod-reel combos.

A final reel addition is the Z300, a single-action flyfishing-type reel aimed at the heavy-duty Great Lakes trolling market. It holds 1000 yards of 15-pound, 700 yards of 20-pound line, comes with click drag.

Zebco Division Brunswick Corp., PO Box 270, Tulsa, OK 74101.

LINE

Du Pont Company unveiled a new Stren Class Line. Geared especially for record fishing, class lines are designed to break at or below the packaged rated test, unlike other premium mono which usually breaks a little higher than rated. Use of laser micrometers during processing insures consistency of the new Stren which comes in aqua-fluorescent color in 100, 250, and 2400 yard spools. It's available in 2, 4, 8, 12, 16, 20, and 30-pound test. Anglers who set IGFA records with the new line will receive 2400 yards of Stren each year for life, plus a plaque, jacket, and cap.

Du Pont, Marketing Communications Dept., Wilmington, DE 19898.

Mason Tackle Company announced T-Line monofilament in clear or soft brown finish. A premium line, it's available in 2- through 30-pound test in the following layups: 100 yards, 250 yards, ¼-pound bulk spools, 1-pound bulk spools.

Mason Tackle Company, 11273 N. State Rd., Otisville, MI 48463.

Bruce B. Mises, Inc. is introducing Maxima Chameleon in hand-tied compound-tapered leaders. Lengths are 7½ and 9 feet. One- through 5-pound test are available in the 7½-foot versions while the 9-foot leaders come in 1½- through 6-pound test.

Bruce B. Mises, Inc. 18239 S. Figueroa St., Gardena, CA 90248.

Scientific Anglers has several new fly lines. There's a Wet Tip 10 feet Intermediate—a floating line with 10 feet of intermediate density, slow-sinking tip perfect for fishing subsurface but *just* over weedbeds—especially in lakes—and in saltwater for certain bonefish and tarpon assignments. Available looped or unlooped.

There's an Intermediate Shooting line of 30-pound test, .035 diameter, in 100-foot lengths. This slightly larger shooting line will be good when hooksetting strength and line control are vital for big-fish work. This is an intermediate, slow-sink formulation.

Wet Cell Sinking/Shooting Line is the smaller diameter (.032, 20-pound test) in fast-sinking formulation for steelhead, salmon, some saltwater, and deep-lake fishing.

Air Cell Floating/Shooting Line is the standard 100 feet, 20-pound shooting line in floating formulation, now available with an end loop.

Scientific Anglers/3M Center, St. Paul, MN 55144.

Triple Fish introduced pre-packaged saltwater Perlon leaders on plastic wrist spools for easy dispensing. Size range from 15- to 300-pound test. Fifty

yards are spooled for tests 15 to 125 pound. Spools of 150- and 200-pound test come in 100-yard lengths. Spools of 250-pound and 300-pound test are offered in 90- and 70-yard lengths, respectively.

Also new are no-waste Perlon filler spools in five line tests. They're designed to fill a 4/0 Penn International to capacity. Filler spools are available in 20, 30, 50, 60, and 80-pound test, in clear, pink and green.

Triple Fish, 5755 S. Tampa Ave., Orlando, FL 32809.

LURES

Accardo Tackle Company introduced a new popping bug, the Silver Minnow, with barred-rock hackle, red mouth and silver body. The bug should be effective when bass are schooling or feeding on a variety of forage fish. The Stinger-style hook makes the lure more effective in hookups per strike.

Accardo Tackle Company, 3708 Conrad Street, Baton Rouge, LA 70805.

Acme Tackle Company has a new version of its perennial Little Cleo favorite. It's the Super-Lite Flutter Cleo. Made of solid brass, it's fitted with a stainless-steel split ring and Mustad siwash hook, and comes in the twelve most popular finishes including glow colors. The spoon bend is virtually the same as the heavier Cleo, but the new version is about half the thickness of the original. It should be super-effective when slow trolling for all salmonids and many other species.

Acme Tackle Company, 69 Bucklin Street, Providence, RI 02907.

The Fred Arbogast Company Inc. announced the Arby Hanger, a modified crankplug designed to take fish suspended around vertical cover. The Arby, a past favorite, was modified so the user can crank it down to its 12-foot maximum depth, then pause.

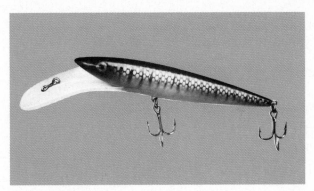

The Arby Hanger

The plug will stay at depth, slowly turning like a real minnow, until the retrieve is continued. Fish usually strike on the pause. The Arby Hanger comes in 3/8-ounce and 5/8-ounce sizes with extra-strong hooks and a wide variety of finishes.

Another new bait is the Jitterstick, a topwater plug that combines the venerable Jitterbug-lip sound and wobble, with a tail-mounted propeller. It's designed to be fished in choppy water under breezy conditions. Sizes are 3/8 ounce and 5/8 ounce. The plug comes in twelve colors.

A hot new Tiger finish, available for '85 on the Arbogast Mud Bug, Hula Diver, Arbo-gaster, and Arby, has proved extremely successful for fish that feed visually. The color combo consists of a chartreuse underside coupled with fluorescent-orange top and black tiger stripes. Walleye seem unable to resist the pattern, and largemouth bass have not been far behind.

The Fred Arbogast Company Inc., 313 W. North Street, Akron, OH 44303.

Arkie Lures Inc. has several new accessories and lures. The Shineee Hineee is a panfish jig with silver body and two strands of Mylar in the hair tail. It's available in 1/32-, 1/16- and 1/8-ounce sizes, plain or with a safety-pin-type spinner. Single-spin safety-pin-type spinner arms are now available in a variety of sizes from 00 through 3 for panfish jigs. Finally, bristle-weedguard rubber-skirted jigs, so popular for flip-

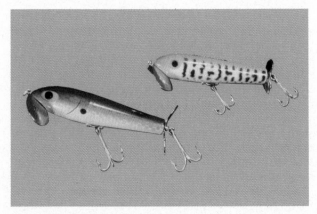

Two varieties of the Jitterstick

ping, now come in tricolor models—a variety of three color finishes in ¼-ounce and ⅜-ounce sizes.

Arkie Lures Inc., P.O. Box 1460, Springdale, AR 72764.

JIM Bagley Bait Company Inc. built its Chug-O-Lure to please the most discriminating topwater specialist. Made of imported hardwood, the plug goes through thirty-five quality control steps. The lure features the time-honored scooped-chugger face, but has a concave belly which slows forward motion. This allows the user to work a small pocket

JM Bagley's Chug-O-Lure

or other spot longer, teasing fish to strike. The ⅜-ounce plug comes with or without tailspinner in six popular colors.

There's also a Diving Bang-O-Lure, the successful topwater bait now with a diving lip and tougher construction. It'll go to 7 feet and comes in 4¼-inch and 5¼-inch sizes and six colors.

Jim Bagley Bait Company Inc., P.O. Drawer 110, Winter Haven, FL 33880.

Blakemore Sales Corporation unveiled the Double Chance spinnerbait, a unique design featuring the swivel-fastened blade attached in a central position

Blakemore Sales' Double Chance spinnerbait

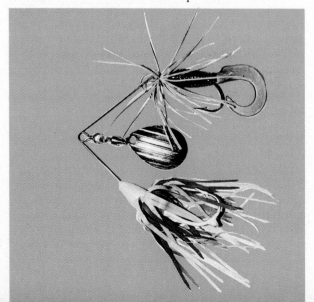

to the line-tie eye. The upper arm, which formerly held the blade, now carries a skirted curly-tail grub. This is the first version.

The second model has two blades in the usual upper-arm position, as well as a center-mounted blade. The center-blade swivel on both models is fixed to make it impossible for the blade to loop around the upper or lower arm wire. The first version should be fished to 12 inches or so while the second is for near-surface fishing.

Blakemore Sales Corporation, P.O. Box 505, North Highway 65, Branson, MO 65616.

Blue Fox Tackle Company, which is now handling the Dr. Juice fish-elixir attractants, has designed Juice Gills to fit its popular line of Vibrotail jigs. The Juice Gills are contoured to fit between the Vibrotail head and soft-plastic body. The material absorbs liquid-scent attractants and slowly leaches them into the water.

A new version of the Roland Martin spinnerbait was announced. It features a big gold No. 5 willow-leaf blade in tandem behind a smaller copper Colorado blade on the upper-wire arm. Other color combinations are available, but Martin likes this one. The blade combo produces heavy, thumping vibrations underwater and has been attractive to big bass, northern pike, and muskie.

For the trolling market is the King Aqua spoon, designed for wide-arc action at slow speeds. It's available in ⅜-ounce and ⅝-ounce sizes in fifteen patterns with regular trebles or single-siwash hooks.

A line of Firefly floats has been introduced. They glow for fifteen hours, powered by replaceable lithium batteries. The soft red glow at the top of the stick indicates a strike as it sinks at night. It may also attract fish.

Blue Fox Tackle Company, 645 N. Emerson, Cambridge, MN 55008.

Burke Fishing Lures announced an affiliation with Doug Hannon, known affectionately as the Bass Professor for his in-depth bass-fishing research. From the affiliation have come several product introductions. The Swimmin' Worm, a homemade concoction of some years ago, is now available pre-rigged with some fish-getting modifications. It has been successful for very large bass. Basically this rig is designed for use around docks and in sparse grasses because the hook is exposed. The rig comes with a special compound-bend hook, 20-pound camouflage leader and four-ball bead-type swivel. The rig also comes with two spare worms in the pack. Each worm is X-marked at the spot where the hook-point exists. The lure is simple to fish, unlike normally worked plastic worms. Just cast and retrieve slowly. When swimming, this worm's head maintains a straight attitude exactly like a water snake. Only the body undulates.

Also new are Slinker worm sinkers, which operate like a pegged cone weight to keep the sinker from sliding from the worm, but in this case the connec-

Burke's Dedly Dudly D.D. III

tion is not rigid. Instead, a stainless wire insert having an open eye at the hook end and needle shape at the line-tie end, goes through the sinker for hinged action.

Other new lures include a ¼-ounce Mini Weed-Beater weedless soft plug, a shad-shaped weedless Flex Plug called the Shadoo, a three-bladed version of the Dedly Dudly D.D. III. Compound-curve triple blades give this buzzing bait quick lift because they start turning instantly.

Burke Fishing Lures, 1969 S. Airport Road, Traverse City, MI 49684.

Cordell Tackle brings out two lure models for '85. The C.C. Rattlin' Shad is a shad-shaped diving plug with multiple rattles that help give hard-pulling ac-

tion for continuous lure contact, plus the obvious noisemaking feature. The Rattlin' Shad digs to 12 feet, and with the newly designed Platter Paddle-bill the lure can be retrieved or trolled at extremely high speed.

The new Jointed Rattlin' Spot is a ½-ounce Spot but with a v-joint body and the addition of rattles.

Cordell Tackle, P.O. Box 1452, 3601 Jenny Lind, Fort Smith, AR 72902.

Cotee Industries Inc. has a line of weedless jigs whose weedguards should not hinder hookups. Made of heavy monofilament, the guards have a concave end that slips over the hook barb. On the strike, the guard slips down rather than popping up.

Jigs are packaged in a clear reusable snap container that provides storage convenience to the retailer and angler after purchase. Called Jig Mate (a Hook Mate is also available), the unit holds four finished jigs with their hooks totally protected. An alternative to blister packages and bags, the units are made of clear K-resin with hangup slot.

Cotee Industries Inc., P.O. Box 1984, New Port Richey, FL 34291.

Crankbait Products Division spotlighted the new Super-Dawg, a crank-bait designed to imitate a water-dog. It features an elongated hard-plug body attached to a replaceable grub curly tail at the rear. Two versions—a deep diver that runs to 6 feet, and

The C.C. Rattlin' Shad

a shallow runner that swims at 3 feet—are available in eight finishes.

Crankbait Products Division, the Highland Group, 9300 Midwest Avenue, Garfield Heights, OH 44125.

Creme Lure Company, pioneer of the plastic worm, has some new styles for '85. There's a Glo Worm-finish series in blue, gold, purple and green with dark bloodline and luminescent hues. The modulated series in red-pearl, purple-pearl, blue-pearl and black-yellow have vermiculated-color renderings the length of the lure.

The popular rigged Scoundrel worms now come with one spare in the pack. There's also a new S.S.T. 10-inch Whopper Worm available in a 3-pack or 12-pack.

Creme Lure Company, P.O. Box 87, Tyler, TX 75710.

Ditto Mfg. Inc. now has five different versions of its popular three-color worm. Also new is the 2GS and 3GS Shadtail soft-plastic curly-tail shad lure in five finishes. Three sizes of a new high-action, soft crayfish—2FCC, 3FCC and 4FCC—were introduced.

Ditto Mfg. Inc., P.O. Box 222, San Mateo, FL 32088

H & H Lure Company has a buzz-bait with a unique, vertically oriented separate front blade that acts as a knocker to be hit by the main overhead buzzing blade. New also is the Magnum H Spinner lure series. These spinner-baits have heavily cupped blades. Triple-color skirts are available for this series.

The jig-head soft-body Cocahoe Minnow Jr. is now available as a tandem consisting of two, ¼-ounce jigs tied on 30-pound mono.

H & H Lure Company, 1087 N. Dual Street, Baton Rouge, LA 70814.

Hanna Lures Ltd. (Formerly Pee Wee Lures Mfg. Inc.) introduced photo-printed patterns on its Natural Shad soft-plastic swimming jig with hook weedguard. The new Laser Grub, an eel-like soft-plastic bait, also comes in photo prints. Other introductions include the Bally-Hoo, an 8-inch soft ballyhoo imitation, in white, glitter or printed patterns; the Renegade, a twin-tail swimming worm; and Pro Chunk, a soft plastic frog to be used alone or as a trailer.

Hanna Lures Ltd. 1077-H Fred Drive, Morrow, GA 30260.

Harrison Hoge Industries Inc., has the popular regular-body-style Panther Martin in-line spinners in a new copper finish. The blades are copper-plated, while the bodies are offered in the traditional colors. Model designation is PMP 2, 4 or 6, representing weights of ¹⁄₁₆-, ⅛- and ¼-ounce. Also new are two sizes of saltwater Panther Martins. PMSW models are available in 1½-ounce and 2-ounce sizes with all nickel-silver blades and silver-painted lead bodies. They come with permaplate VMC single or treble hooks, but VMC bronzed hooks are available for use on large fish in freshwater.

Harrison Hoge Industries Inc., 104 Arlington Avenue, St. James, NY 11780.

James Heddon's Sons Inc., built the Timber Rattler, a shad-shaped crank-bait of Michigan swamp-grown white cedar that is cured for one to two years. The wood has an extremely tight grain which does not absorb water like balsa can. The Timber Rattler has a hollow chamber for its rattles, traditional Heddon glass eyes, strong hook hangers. Comes in five popular finishes. The medium-running crankbait will need no tuning.

James Heddon's Sons Inc., P.O. Box 167, 3601 Jenny Lind Road, Fort Smith, AR 72902.

John J. Hildebrandt Corporation introduced the S.S.T. spoon for steelhead, salmon and trout. The ultralight spoon may be used either with weight on a spinning outfit, or alone on flyrods. Weights available are: ¹⁄₃₂-, ¹⁄₂₄-, ¹⁄₂₀- and ¹⁄₁₆-ounce in nickel, chartreuse, fluorescent red and metallic gold.

John J. Hildebrandt Corporation, P.O. Box 50, Logansport, IN 46947.

Hopkins Fishing Lures Company Inc. announced the availability of 22-k gold plating on several of its popular hammered spoons. In the gold are the ⅓-ounce No. 1 and ½-ounce No. 2 No-EQL spoons; ¼- and ½-ounce swimming-tail ST No-EQL spoons; and the best-selling 75 Hopkins Shorty, the 45 Shorty and the 75 ST Shorty.

Hopkins Fishing Lures Company Inc., 1130 Boissevain Avenue, Norfolk, VA 23507.

Johnson Fishing Inc. followed its successful introduction last year of the Chumm'n Minnow with the Chumm'n Worm and Chumm'n Beetle for '85. The lures are made of Flavorol fish by-products. The worms come in 4-packs and are available in black, purple and natural. The beetle, a Beetle Spin lookalike, is packaged spinnerbait-rigged with spare body. There are three colors available.

A new spinnerbait is the Super Beetle Twist with willow-leaf spinner and curly tail. The Super Busy Beetle also features a willow blade, but has a turned-down swimming-type tail.

The largest of the venerable Silver Minnow weedless spoon series was introduced. It weighs 1⅛ ounces, has a 4-inch blade, and should be excellent for big northern, muskie and big bass.

Johnson Fishing Inc., P.O. Box 3129, Mankato, MN 56001.

Knight Mfg. Company Inc. now has the effective King Tongs spinnerbait in ⅛-ounce size. This is the spinner-bait with a hook formed into the upper-wire blade-holding arm. Ten color combos are available. The popular Lit'l Critter soft-plastic swim-tail crayfish is now available in ¹⁄₁₆-ounce size. New stripe-pattern finishes are on the soft plastic Liv'n Fishie. Shad, perch, minnow and shiner patterns are offered.

Knight Mfg. Company Inc., P.O. Box 6162, Tyler, TX 75711.

Kwikfish Lures Inc. is marketing a new Jointed Kwikfish. Four sizes are available: 4¼, 5, 6¼ and 8½ inches.

Kwikfish Lures Inc., Ren Cen Station, P.O. Box 43014, Detroit, MI 48243.

L & S Bait Company Inc., maker of the popular MirrOlure series, has several new models. The 95MR and 97MR are floaters, 3⅝ inches and 4¼ inches long, respectively; the 96MR and 98MR are floater-divers with the same measurements as above. All have sound chambers with glass balls and MirrOlure flash and durability. The lures are aimed at the bass market.

There are two new deep-diving Shad Rattlers, the 91MR and 92MR, 2¾ inches and 3⅜ inches, respectively.

The 33MR fast-vibrating sinker is another rattle-bait addition, and three new fluorescent finishes are available on most of the company's lures. Colors include pink, chartreuse and gold with contrasting red eyes.

L & S Bait Company Inc., 1500 E. Bay Drive, Largo, FL 33541.

Bill Lewis Lures added the Rat-L Top, a ¼-ounce topwater bait with rear propeller-type spinner. The lure has rattles which act as an attractor while giving the plug a little more resistance so it can be worked in one spot longer. A variety of finishes are offered.

Bill Lewis Lures, P.O. Box 4062, Alexandria, LA 71301.

Lindy-Little Joe Inc. believes in scent attractors and has added some items that facilitate the use of such enhancements on their artificials and bait rigs. The popular Pop-Tail trolling plug may now be used with Scent-Sation Tablets placed in the hollow head. The tablets are made either of freeze-dried alewives or salmon eggs. They release their odors for 30–45 minutes.

The Little Joe Floating Spinner bait rig and the Lindy Rig now come with Whizker Hooks; the fuzz fibers permanently attached to these hooks hold your favorite liquid or paste scents.

Lindy-Little Joe Inc., P.O. Box C, 1110 Wright Street, Brainerd, MN 56401.

Luhr Jensen & Sons Inc. now offers five of its top lures in the 499 Genuine Silver Plate series. Lures available include: Krocodile Flutterspoon (a hammered version is also available), Loco Spoon, Alpena Diamond Spoon, and the Jensen Dodger. They come in new red, silver and black packaging for easy identification. Real silver is said to have a much better reflective capability than chrome or nickel plate, which often appear dark underwater.

Luhr Jensen & Sons Inc., P.O. Box 297, Hood River, OR 97031.

The Pop-Tail trolling plug

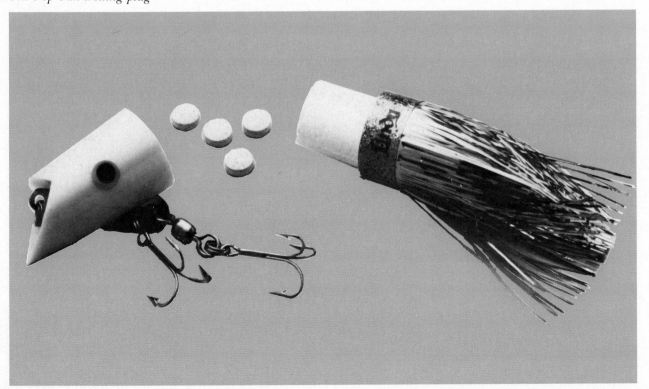

Mann's Bait Company announced a new feeding-stimulant additive to coat soft-plastic baits—especially worms. Called FS 454, the chemical is not a scent. Instead, it encourages bass, which have been enticed

The new Razorback Deep Hog from Mann's

into grabbing the treated lure, to hold on and eat. For '85, FS 454 will be available on the Augertail Worm and Cajun Crawdad. The formula was developed by a team of scientists from Duke University.

Other new introductions include: A Deep Diver Hardworm and two new colors—clear foil flake and coachdog—for the Hardworm series; a ⅜-ounce Deep Hog that runs to 15 feet in the Razorback series; blue, pink, green, silver and gold metal-flake finishes for the Jellyhoo; white-fluorescent and chartreuse-fluorescent finish for the Sting Ray, Augertail and Augertwin grubs; and Tennessee Shad, Tiger Shad and Fire Shad models for the Rattlin' Finn-Mann lure series.

New displays are offered for the Jellyhoo and an-other bin display is available for any of the other Mann baits.

Mann Bait Company, Division Techsonic Industries, P.O. Box 604, Eufaula, AL 36027.

Mister Twister Inc. offers several new lure series including the Sassy Shiner soft baits with split dorsal and action-swimming tail. The new-design dorsal allows the hook bend and point to remain plastic sheathed for weedlessness. A variety of colors and straight jighead style or spinnerbait version are available. The Mister Mino incorporates the soft-plastic Mepps minnow and plain jig head or spinner arm with new Sissor Blade to make the spinner run at different depths while altering actions.

The Curly Tail Crappie has a splash of color just

The Mister Mino with the Sissor Blade

Sassy Shiner soft bait from Mister Twister

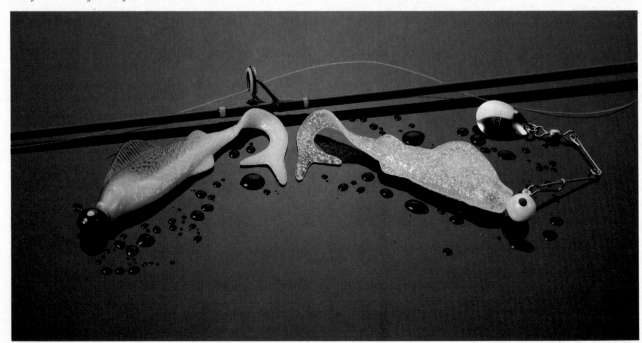

at the head. Available as a spinnerbait or plain jig lure, it's ideal for panfish.

The Mister Twister Meppster incorporates a Mepps Aglia long or standard blade and a rubber skirt followed by an action curly tail on the Keeper hook.

Mister Twister Inc., P.O. Drawer 996, Minden, LA 71058.

Norman Mfg. Company Inc. announced built-in scent on the entire line of popular crankbaits as an option. The anise attractant will last up to two weeks, at which time additional scent may be added to the absorbent finish.

A new ⅛-ounce Triple Wing Buzz-Bait was highlighted. The tri-wing design allows for ⅓-slower cranking for sound-making and keeping the lure in the strike zone longer.

The Rip-N Minnow was so popular that the company added a deep-running version called the Deep-Rip-N Minnow. It's available in over fifty finishes and the built-in-scent version as well.

Norman Mfg. Company Inc., P.O. Box 580, Highway 96 East, Greenwood, AR 72936.

Normark Corporation introduced the larger J 13 Jointed Floating Rapala model. It's 5¼ inches long and designed for Great Lakes and other larger-lure needs. A silver-fluorescent-chartreuse finish has been added to the series of Jointed Floating Rapalas.

Back in the line of vertical fishing spoons is an improved version of the Rapala Pilkki, featuring a

hook, a ⅝-ounce King Aqua with single siwash hook, and a No. 4 Super Vibrax in-line spinner.

Normark Corporation, 1710 E. 78 Street, Minneapolis, MN 55423.

Ojibway Bait Company offers a new Alewife Rig consisting of a 6-pack of freeze-dried alewifes and spinner, plus two-hook tandem rig. Hooks include a single 1/0-front and treble-hook rear model. Blade color choices include orange, yellow or green.

Ojibway Bait Company, P.O. Box 418, White Earth, MN 56591.

Producto Lure Company Inc. has a new worm accessory called the Missing Link. It consists of two barbed shafts attached to a ball-bearing swivel. The user cuts the worm in half and inserts one of the shafts in the back half and the other in the front half of the worm. The result is a jointed bogus crawler. It's said to increase action of the worm's rear section by 50% while keeping the front section running true with no twists. Hook is inserted in the usual way. An additional claim is made for more positive hook setting due to less resistance.

Producto Lure Company Inc., P.O. Box 969, Longwood, FL 32750.

Rebel Division created a unique series of medium-running plugs called the Fastrac series. A newly engineered bill allows the plugs to be retrieved or trolled at very high speeds—good news for those who

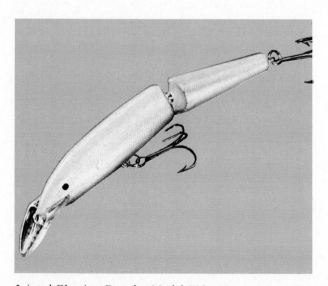

Jointed Floating Rapala, Model J13

Rebel's Fastrac plug

chain-hook attachment on the single-hook models for short-biting fish. Four weights and three finishes are available on this ice or open-water spoon.

A Salmon Trophy Kit is new for large trout or salmon. It includes a Jointed No. 11 Floating Rapala, a Fat Rap, a ⅜-ounce King Aqua Spoon with treble

use high-gear-ratio reels or practice speed trolling. Four most-popular plugs sport the new bill: the series 20 Minnows, Wee-R, Shad and Shad Jr.

In tests the Fastracs were trolled fast enough to break 10-lb.-test line, without the plugs rolling up.

Rebel Division, Plastics Research and Development

Corporation, 3601 Jenny Lind, Fort Smith, AR 72902.

Renosky Lures has a line of spoons called the Laser, made of stainless steel. One side sports a no-chip coating in photo-printed fish image, while the flip side is silver stainless. The coating is pliable and absorbs fish scents handily. There are five sizes and thirteen bait-and-gamefish patterns available. The spoon has already accounted for pike, muskie, lake trout, steelhead, browns, salmon, bass, blues, snook, and weak-fish. The spoon may be cast or trolled and features no-twist action.

Realistic photo finishes are available on the firm's various soft-plastic series of shads, minnows and sunfish.

Renosky Lures, 130 Lincoln Avenue, Homer City, PA 15748.

Sevenstrand Tackle Corporation is marketing its popular Clout in Flashtail Clout version. It comes with a tiny Strike Lite chemical lightstick insert to produce internal illumination for hours.

Sevenstrand Tackle Corporation, 5401 McFadden, Hungtington Beach, CA 92649.

Sheldons' Inc. is introducing a new tiny 00-size spinner blade on its popular Mepps in-line spinners. There will also be a unique split blade called the Sissor Blade which can be opened or closed to provide variable action and different running depths.

Sheldons' Inc., P.O. Box 508, Antigo, WI 54409.

South Bend Sporting Goods Inc. designed the new Lunker Target Eye Spoon series with prismatic-tape eyes and stripes for trout, salmon, bass and pike. Sizes from ¼ ounce to ¾ ounce are available, and the spoons are marketed individually or in kit form.

South Bend Sporting Goods Inc., 1950 Stanley Street, Northbrook, IL 60062.

Strike King Lure Company Inc. announced the new Spindance, a short-arm dropping-model spinnerbait with a Y-shaped weedguard arm. Models from ¼ ounce to ⅝ ounce are available in fourteen finishes.

A series of small soft-plastic-dressed jigs from ¹⁄₃₂ ounce to ¹⁄₁₆ ounce were introduced. Series are: Mini-King Jr., Mini-King Jig, Mini-King Spin.

The Buzz King is a new buzzing bait with plastic three-blade spinner in clear, black or chartreuse to match or contrast with the rest of the lure. Buzz King comes in ¼-ounce or ⅛-ounce sizes.

Strike King Lure Company Inc., 2906 Sanderwood, Memphis, TN 38118.

T'S Bass Lures Inc. has a new line of soft plastics called Snakey, printed-snake imitations that simulate a variety of species. They can be fished behind a spoon, jig or spinner, and rigged like worms or in any manner the user prefers. Six- and 8-inch versions are available.

T's Bass Lures Inc., 7 Timothy Lane, Somerset, KY 42501.

Tiki Lures Inc. introduced the Spoonfish line of sonic-hole spoons. There's the Stiletto, a spoon-forward spinner-aft rig for walleye in one size and twelve colors; the standard Spoonfish spoon in five sizes and twelve colors; and the Spoonfish spinner, in which the sonic-hole spoon acts as a jig head on the lower wire arm of the spinnerbait.

Tiki Lures Inc., 2272 Aragon Avenue N., Kettering, OH 45420.

Viking Lures Inc., the makers of the light-up Little Litnin' introduced last year, has a full series of lures designed around the same concept. Besides the original in shallow-and mid-depth models, there's the Fire Bug, a surface popper; Depth Seeker, a diver; and the Shiner, a floating-sinking model for suspended fish. All are available in a variety of finishes. You can also use them without the blinking red light.

Viking Lures Mfg. Inc., 24800 Northwestern Hwy., Suite 301, Southfield, MI 48075.

Weber Tackle Division has a couple of new spoon series. The Silver Streaker spoon has genuine silver plate, comes with a variety of colored stripes, and is available in ⅓-, ⅖-, and ¾-ounce sizes. The heavier Silver Bullet spoon is available in ⅞- and ½-ounce

Viking's light-up Depth Seeker

sizes. It should prove a good surfcasting tool, as well as a long-range casting lure for stripers and other species.

Mr. Champ now comes with a variety of new Wave prismatic-tape stick-ons.

Weber Tackle Division, Weber International, P.O. Box 47, 1039 Ellis Street, Stevens Point, WI 54481.

Whopper Stopper/Fliptail has a new shad-type crankbait for highspeed, deep running. Called the Shadrak (2800 series), the lure is 3 inches long, weighs ⅜ ounce and comes in five different finishes. Molded for positive alignment, Shadrak eliminates bothersome tuning.

Whopper Stopper/Fliptail/McCollum Lunker Bass Lure, P.O. Box 1111, Sherman, TX 75090.

Wilderness Enterprises, Inc. designed the Hawg Boss Super Toad and Super Toad II crankbaits in twenty-five realistic finishes to complement its Stinger series introduced last year. Super Toad dives extremely deep for a plug of its body size. It will reach 12–15 feet depths. The Super Toad II has a mid–range of 8–10 feet with a tight-vibrating action.

A series of steelhead, salmon, and trout plugs in appropriate bright colors was also introduced.

Wilderness Enterprises Inc., Spokane Industrial Park, Bldg. 18, Spokane, WA 99216.

The Worth Company added salt to the plastic formulation of its Tournament series worms, crayfish, crabs and other baits. The addition of sodium is said to cause fish to hold onto the lures a little longer.

The Coho Flasher spoons are new for lake trout and salmon. The light spoons weigh just ¼ ounce and come with a 5/0 single or 1/0 treble hook in a variety of fluorescent colors overlaid with a metallic-sparkle prismatic finish.

The Worth Company, P.O. Box 88, Stevens Point, WI 54481.

Yakima Bait Company has made several changes to baits in the Worden's Lure line. The lures include the Spin-N-Glo Walleye Rig and the Rooster Tail Medalist series. The former consists of an altered Spin-N-Glo steelhead driftbait, with slide-through snelled hook. The medalist is an in-line weighted spinner now in a variety of new body and hackle-tail dressings. Additionally, the Sonic Rooster Tail is now available in silver-finished body and blade. Last year, only brass was obtainable.

Yakima Bait Company, P.O. Box 310, Granger, WA 98932.

ZETAbait Company has a new 6-inch version of the Gillraker action-tail plastic worm. Also, for the first time, a line of Speckled Pup worm finishes that imitate salamanders will be marketed in '85.

ZETAbait Company, P.O. Box 7985, Jacksonville, FL 32207.

ACCESSORIES

DU-BRO Products has the answer for anglers troubled by nail-knotting or snelling large-diameter monofilament to bait or lure hooks. The No. 1115 Nail-Knotter Tool makes this chore a snap with difficult heavy mono up to 250-pound test.

A second tool will appeal to fishermen who use wire for any fresh- or saltwater species. The Wire Straightner is a small brass roller tool designed to eliminate kinks in single strand wire. It comes in three sizes for wire of various gauges.

Du-Bro Products, 480 Bonner Rd., Wauconda, IL 60084.

Berkley & Co., Inc. has a handy Line Stripper that makes removing line from spinning and light conventional reels fast and easy. Serious anglers who frequently change their line during the season will appreciate the tool, which is powered by two C-cell batteries. You simply insert the end of line to be removed into a hole in the unit's head, push a button, and let the mono shoot in a trash receptical. It's about five times faster than hand-pulling.

Berkley & Co., Inc., Trilene Dr., Spirit Lake, IA 51360.

The Line Stripper speeds line changing.

Cannon/S&K Products, Inc. unveiled one of the more exciting concepts in downrigger fishing in a long time. It's the Digi-Troll, a computer-operated unit with all the features of the best-selling Mag 10A, plus a built-in memory. You touch a button and the Digi-Troll lowers the cannonball weight to pre-selected depth. In fact, it can store two depths to which you can gain immediate access. You can also program the unit to oscillate, that is, raise and lower your cannonball periodically within a set area to tease fish when they're fussy. This is a top technique for lake trout.

A conversion kit is available, allowing you to turn your Magnum 10A into a Digi-Troll. Other conversion kits turn some manual Cannon's into electrics.

Cannon/S&K Products, Inc., 1732 Glade St., Muskegon, MI 49441.

Feldman Engineering & Mfg. Co., Inc. has a new hand-operated folding ice auger. The hinged drill locks for use with a sleeve that fits over the hinge.

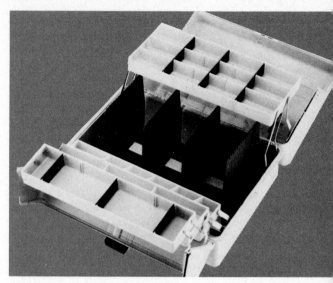

The Crank or Spin 85 Tacklebox

trays for four slotted vertical plastic dividers from which to hang plugs up to 7 inches. Four conventional trays hold jigs, other hardware, and there are two porkrind jar holders. Hand racks can be removed.

Fenwick/Woodstream Tackle Box Div., Front & Locust Sts., Lititznister, PA 17543.

Flambeau Products Corp. has two new boxes for '85. There's a 2706 Hawg Pac designed to hold twelve bottles of porkrind, four racksworth of spinnerbaits, plus other lures in three adjustable trays.

The 2734 Vented Kool Pac is a box that has three lure trays, a large storage compartment below them, plus a foam cooler with built-in reusable freeze pack to hold live bait or lunch. The main box lid is vented and the entire unit is light gray color to reduce heat buildup.

Flambeau Products Corp., PO Box 97, Middlefield, OH 44062.

This ice auger folds for convenience.

It is one-piece, so there's no danger of losing parts. It comes in three blade diameters.

Feldman Engineering & Mfg. Co., Inc., PO Box 153, Sheboygan Falls, WI 53085.

Fenwick/Woodstream has a new Crank or Spin 85 tacklebox designed by top bass-tournament fishermen Hank Parker and Rich Tauber. It solves the problem of carrying long crankbaits by trading two

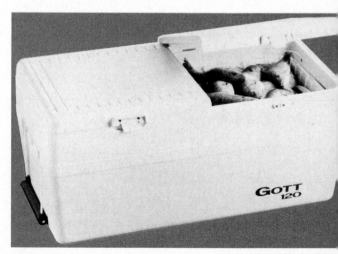

Gott's 120-quart fish box/cooler

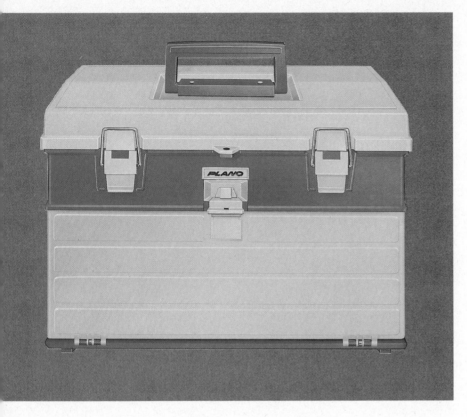

Plano's 757 Tacklebox

GCBG Products, Inc. introduced the Bass-Guard 1, an easily installed aerator that can be placed in existing livewells or turn ice coolers into live wells. The unit mounts simply with suction-cup feet to nonporous surfaces. The vertical spray-tube comes in 7- or 12-inch length. Bass Guard II comes with the two tubes, 12-volt pump, battery clips, and filter with replacement warranty.

GCBG Products, Inc., 5611 Knobby Knoll, Houston, TX 77092.

Gott Corporation has a new 120-quart fish-box/cooler. It is all white, measures 38½ × 18½ × 17¾ inches high, and weighs 34 pounds. It features a two-part lid to minimize cold loss as only half the top needs to be opened at one time.

Gott Corp., PO Box 652, Winfield, KS 67156.

Harrco, Inc. announced the new 160 Sea Lab tacklebox, a cylindrical unit that hangs 120 lures in clear view. Besides space for the hanging lures there are two trays with twelve compartments each.

Harrco, Inc., PO Box 280, Ludington, MI 49431.

MAC-JAC Manufacturing Co. has a new ball-bearing swivel base for its own downriggers and will be bringing out an adapter plate for the base to handle all competitive downrigger makes. This is an extremely smooth-operating unit.

An entirely new clutch drag system on its own downrigger units incorporates a thrust bearing that precludes the need for turning the crank handle when lowering the downrigger weight.

Mac-Jac Manufacturing Co., 1590 Creston St, Muskegon, MI 49443.

MAC-WEL Corp. has an ingenious device that permits your big engine or electric (if it doesn't have a weedless prop) to move through the thickest vegetation without fouling. Called Weed Shark, the device is a cutting tool that attaches to the motor housing close ahead of the propellor blades. As the prop turns, the weeds are drawn across the cutting edge, sheared away before they can tangle. The stainless-steel tool is epoxy-mounted to the motor. The unit comes with required glue. It fits all size outboard and I-O engines and electric motors.

Mac-Wel Corp., 6 Main St., Marcellus, NY 13108.

Pacific-Atlantic Products Ltd. has a new pulley head on its downriggers. The swivel, hooded-spool unit is designed to prevent rigger cable tangle in all situations.

Pacific-Atlantic Products, Ltd., 395 S. Pitcher St., Kalamazoo, MI 49007.

Plano Molding Co.'s 757 tacklebox is a big four-drawer model with a 3½-inch-deep well in the top under the lift-back cover. You need not lift the cover to gain access to the drawers, which provide up to forty compartments. It's an ideal box for use in cramped or small boats.

Plano Molding Co., PO Box 189, Plano, IL 60545.

Fishing's Newest Magic Box

Bill McKeown

Remember the old one about cutting a notch in the gunnel of your boat so you can find the spot again where you caught the big fish?

Now it's true—and you don't even need a knife or a wooden hull. All it takes is a little box the size of a big book. You just push a couple of punch keys on the front of it and you're in business. The gadget instantly memorizes where you are and, anytime you want to return to that exact spot on the lake, for example, to try to catch another lunker, it steers you right back to the same place—as if it had memorized the street address of the chunk of water where that fish lived.

For the first time, freshwater fishermen are learning about the mysterious numbers game that has started to become *the* secret to success on salt water a couple of years ago.

Is it accurate? "We used to dread the thick spring fogs," one Lake Michigan charter captain explained. "Now I look forward to heading out and hiding in one. I can go right where I know the fish are and, without Loran, the other boats can't follow me."

To play by the numbers is not yet cheap but every season the price goes down. Even so, fishermen's heaven still hasn't arrived because there are places where the wonder box won't work. Some canyon lakes and impoundments in the West still seem to block the radio signals you need to receive.

Like radar, sonar, and other recent, made-up words for electronic aids, Loran simply stands for *Long Range* Navigation. Radio beams are aimed out from several shore stations and the clever Loran receiver on your boat becomes a precise radio clock. It won't give you the time of day but the times it does give you—in millionths of a second—can tell you exactly where you are.

After Loran-A was developed at Massachusetts Institute of Technology during World War II, it became so successful that 75,000 ships and planes were using it by the end of the war, and commercial fishermen started buying up cheap surplus rigs. Recently, more accurate Loran-C sets have been phased in, prices have come down, and all Loran-A transmission has been suspended. The old units are now obsolete and the new, compact Loran-C packages are the wonder machines.

You don't have to understand the space-age electronics inside to let a Loran lead you to the lunkers but knowing some basics makes it easier. It's helpful to understand why you don't even need a compass sometimes to steer a course—and why even the wrong readings from your gadget can put you right on the fish.

To begin with, a master Loran broadcast station and several slave stations, often hundreds of miles apart, transmit time signals that are only microseconds (millionths of a second) different. The Loran receiver on your boat computes the time difference between the signals from the master and a slave station. The number it gives you will be this time difference (TD), and you will be located somewhere on

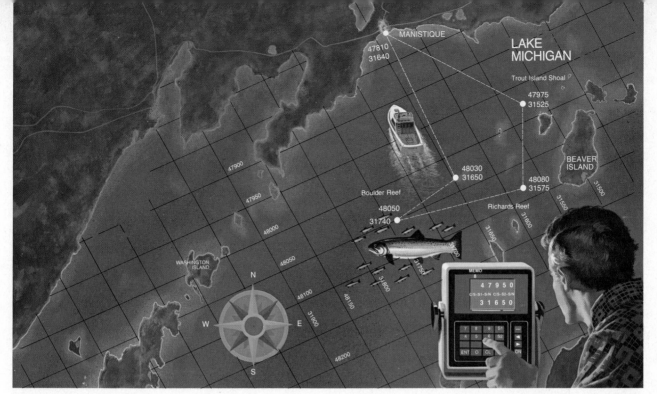

Illustration by Dean Ellis

a line of position (LOP) between the stations where this TD is always the same. But, because the Loran can tune in another slave station plus the master, it does so, and picks up a second LOP. Where these LOPs cross, you have a fix that shows exactly where you are on your chart. If your Loran set also gives you a conversion into longitude and latitude, this is an additional way to determine your fix on a chart that doesn't give Loran numbers.

Complicated? A little, but the great thing is that you don't even have to know this much to go fishing. You probably already know where you are—you're right in home harbor. What you want is to find where the fish are out in the lake. You know there is an old underwater creek bed and some submerged trees out there somewhere in the middle of the lake. They show on the chart and are real hotspots if you can only find them. You mark the spot on your chart and note the Loran coordinate numbers. Then you just steer your boat out until your unit reads the same numbers, and start fishing. Anglers who have gotten used to Loran can watch their ratings and even find a spot without using a compass.

Or, suppose you're drifting along and the fishing suddenly gets hot and heavy. You write down the two numbers of your Loran fix or punch the memory buttons on your set, if it has them. Now you can go right back to the same spot. Because you are freshwater fishing inland, your Loran radio signals must cross hundreds of miles of land and that may distort them slightly. But even this doesn't matter. What you want is repeatability, so you can go right back to the hotspot, whether the numbers correspond to those on your chart or not. One check is to sit in home harbor and see if your Loran readings are the same as those on the chart. If they are slightly different, you can correct the whole chart accordingly. All that matters is that you know how to return

to the same spot. It's the numbers on the face of the unit that count.

Experienced Loran users note down or punch into the memory the numbers for home anchorage, buoys, way points, and fishing hotspots, often right on the chart.

Multifeature sets can also calculate your speed over the bottom, speed and direction of drift, estimated time or arrival at your destination, and all the compass courses along the way. Some Loran fans will tell you it's best to have an elaborate, expensive set. Others insist that you probably won't be using longitude and latitude, plus the other refinements, for ordinary fishing and cruising, so why pay for them. You'll get arguments about various features—but not about the value of the units.

Not one of the adventurous, freshwater boatmen now using Loran that was surveyed would want to live without it again. Mike Voiland of Brockport, New York, is a regional specialist in sport fisheries for New York state and Cornell University under the Sea Grant Program. He has been studying fish management along the southern shore of Lake Ontario where, he points out, the bottom is like a soup bowl and there are no special wrecks or underwater structure to run to. Instead, fishermen must return to areas where underwater currents and thermal patterns, which don't show up on depth recorders, are holding the fish. Weather may be terrible during spring and fall when the fishing may be best, and Voiland finds that the Datamarine and Micrologic Lorans he has tested in his MerCruiser-powered Thompson are ideal for getting him out and back in a fog or when a storm comes up.

Because of the narrow angle of the baseline extension signals going out over his section of Lake Ontario, he recommends that boatmen and charter captains be prepared to spend enough for a quality set. Once they learn to use one, he reports, they swear by it.

Charter captain Lee LeBowe, with his 31-foot Bertram *El Toro,* fishes Lake Michigan out of Waukegan, Illinois. He was first sold on Loran when he delivered a boat south from Key West across 1,000 miles of open water in the Gulf of Mexico to Cozumel. He saw how the saltwater skippers of the Atlantic trusted their units, and now does the same with his Si-Tex 787C. Fishermen trailer boats into Waukegan from all over the Chicago area, particularly members of the Salmon Unlimited Club, and now he says you see more and more Loran antennas.

Capt. Burt Atkinson, also in Waukegan, takes charter customers out on his *Donna G* in the summer. Then he switches to his larger, commercial boat for finding his nets 25 miles out among the ice floes in the winter—something that would be almost impossible, he says, without his favorite "working tool," a Raynav 2000 Loran. It's also essential, he reports, because he takes his charter fishermen along the Illinois/Wisconsin border out on Lake Michigan. He could be stopped and the fishermen checked for an additional license if Atkinson didn't know exactly where the state line was and drifted across it by mistake. He finds he never needs latitude and longitude coordinates; his Loran numbers do it all with transmissions he receives from as far away as Florida, Indiana, and New York broadcast chains.

Farther north, out of Racine, Wisconsin, aboard his *New Mystery,* charter captain Ray Eggert finds lake trout and salmon along three sets of underwater ridges. He uses his Morrow/LLC 4000 Loran programmed with way points to get him to the fish, and then to tell him the speed he's trolling and if he is being wind-drifted off course. In bad weather, Loran is so accurate that Eggert feels it has made radio direction finders obsolete. By plugging in distance and course, even in a fog, he makes sure that his estimated time of arrival back in port matches the scheduled opening of the harbor's lift bridge so he can get back in without waiting.

Inland fishermen, so far, aren't as secretive as saltwater skippers are about their "special numbers," which give Loran TD coordinates to pinpoint wrecks and structure where big fish live. There is the story of a successful captain on the Atlantic Coast whose boat was broken into and burglarized. The only thing missing, however, proved to be his "book of numbers," which listed fix coordinates where the fishing hotspots could be found. A few weeks later, the word went out that copies of the book were available for $50 each. There was no way to prove that these "publishers" were the crooks, but the captain was so angry that, after he had re-recorded his Loran-fix numbers, he had them mimeographed and gave them away free—putting the fix on the fix salesmen.

At present, inland Loran transmissions cover 63 percent of our forty-eight contiguous states and 92 percent of the population. Only down midcontinent is there a strip, including North and South Dakota, Nebraska, and parts of several other states, where the signals cannot be received. The Coast Guard has proposed five new stations to fill this gap but these have not yet been funded.

Bass and striper fishermen, especially on the big impoundments across the South, should be the next to learn what they're been missing. Fishing tournament and TV-music notable Arthur Smith has used his Si-Tex for two years on the Santee-Cooper Lakes in South Carolina, to keep track of the big stripers and catfish.

"On a foggy morning," he points out, "there are no landmarks in sight. On the lower lake, particularly where the forest was bulldozed out before it was flooded, there are no stick-ups. But Loran puts you right over the underwater structure where the fish are holding."

Bass guide greats Tommy Martin and Larry Nixon of Toledo Bend Reservoir at Hemphill, Texas, and Ricky Green, of Arkadelphia, Arkansas, have tested Si-Tex Lorans on the wide waters of Lake Okeechobee, Florida, according to Dave Church of Si-Tex Marine Electronics, Box 6700, Clearwater, FL 33518 (813-535-4681). Their 787 model, the size of a desk dictionary, is called the world's smallest. Once an angler has located fish far out on a lake such as Okeechobee, he can record the precise spot and go back the next day to find out if the fish are still holding there.

Installation of a basic Loran set can now be done by the purchaser, Dave Church reports, if you follow instructions carefully and ground the Loran properly. For more elaborate receivers and for harbors where there are high-power lines and interference that require notch-filter correction, the help of a licensed radio technician is recommended.

New talents are continually being programmed into the remarkable gadgets. Now some models can be interfaced with a SatNav computer or an autopilot to steer your boat. Texas Instruments makes a Loran that will talk to you to give readings. Micrologic packages its ML-5000 with a portable powerpack so you can take it along on any boat. King Marine's new 1350 Recorder interfaces sonar with its Loran 8001 and prints the TD numbers or LatLong on its depth-finder chart.

Yet, Loran doesn't have all the answers. As several captains have pointed out, it can get you to the fish but it still doesn't catch them for you. Noted West Coast fisherman Willard Cravens, of Port Angeles, Washington, notes that when fall fogs cover the Straits of Juan de Fuca, Loran can steer you home but it's not radar and won't warn you of freighters heading through the mist to Puget Sound. But after fishing many years without Loran, Cravens advises that now he wouldn't want to fish without his Si-Tex 787C. Loran was remarkably easy to learn to use, he recalls, after he remembered he wouldn't be using it to navigate around the world and didn't need to memorize the complete instruction manual.

Ten years ago, you didn't need Loran, Cravens states, but now, with all the fishing going on, he considers it a necessity.

New Electronics For '85

Jerry Gibbs

BH Electronics announced the new Z-series Sonic Wave microprocessors with CRT type Video display. Two models are in the series: VS2020Z and VS2040Z. The key-panel-controlled units offer full-screen or split-screen display, zoom, white line, programmable depth in 1-foot increments. Freeze, numeric depth display, line display, instant recall of last programmed function and variable sweep speed are also featured. The TV-type screen is 6 inches. Options include constant boat speed and surface temp display. The VS2040Z comes with dual transducers (9-degree and 32-degree cone angles) for separate or simultaneous (split screen) readings for navigation, fish-finding, or downrigger ball tracking.

BH Electronics, Inc., 331 Bremer Building, St. Paul, MN 55101.

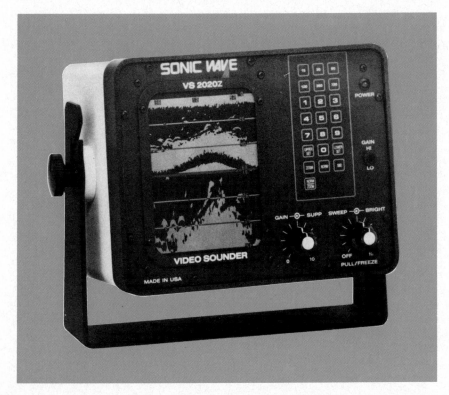

BH Electronics offers two new video sounders. Pictured is the Sonic Wave Model VS 2020z

Eagle Electronics now offers a number of quality accessories to compliment their flashers and graphs. A total of nine transducers are available. Styles are available for mounting on electric motors, through hull or on the transom, in three different cone angles.

Eagle flashers can be converted to portables with the PPP-1 Power Pack. SB-1 and SB-2 switch boxes allow operator to switch between transducers or units.

A kick-up transducer mounting bracket for small boats and a handy 10-foot transducer extension cable are available.

Eagle Electronics, PO Box 669, Catoosa, OK 74015.

Fish Hawk has a new Thermo-Troll unit to monitor temperatures to 200 feet when downrigger trolling. You attach the sensor unit to your downrigger cable and via telemetry the temperature information is received and displayed continuously on a meter inside your boat. The universal model works with all Riviera, Big Jon, Mac Jack, Walker, Cannon downriggers and others.

Fish Hawk Electronics Corp., PO Box 340, Crystal Lake, IL 60014.

Ray Jefferson has a new surface temperature instrument called the Seawater Temperature Indicator, Model 290. It displays surface temps to within .1 degree F.

Ray Jefferson, 2213 Locust St., Philadelphia, PA 19103.

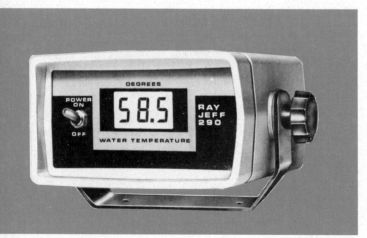

Ray Jefferson's Model 290.

Johnson Fishing, Inc. announced the first electric fishing motor with adjustable shaft to fit different size boats and conditions. The telescoping shaft extends from 15 to 30 inches. The Adjustable Model RJ-3 is a 3-speed motor with 15-pound thrust for small fishing boats and inflatables.

Johnson Fishing, Inc., 1531 Madison Ave., Mankato, MN 56001.

King Marine Radio Corp. introduced a simple-to-operate Loran-C in a mini-compact case that mounts separately or stacked over its already popular tiny VHF radio. The 8001 has large easy-reading LCD display. Its memory stores ninety-nine waypoints with instructions on how to reach them. Beginners can quickly learn basic functions and operate the unit on "page" 1 showing latitude, longitude, waypoint number, distance to destination (waypoint),

King Marine Radio's mini-Loran, Model 8001.

bearing to steer and speed achieved. There are three other "pages" of additional information and functions for advanced operation.

The unit can interface with King's 1350 Recorder to print Loran numbers on the chart paper so you can return directly and exactly to a particularly interesting fishing spot.

King Marine Radio Corp., 5320 140th Ave., North, Airport Industrial Park, Clearwater, FL 33520.

Lowrance Electronics announced the X-16 Computer Graph which follows the now-famous X-15 and X-15A. The new model measures depths to 8000 feet (with a special transducer). It measures in 1-foot increments. The model 15 measured in 10-foot increments. Through an add-on box controlled by its keyboard, the new unit can use both 192 and 50 kHz transducers for cone angles from 8 to 45 degrees. The X-16 remembers functions last programmed before turning off the unit, so there's no need to reprogram each time you shut off and turn on.

The unit prints Loran-C coordinates, interfacing with a forthcoming Lowrance Loran-C unit, and some which are presently available. Most programmed functions are printed on the chart bottom. There are seven paper speeds and a new processor doubles the printing capacity of the unit to provide

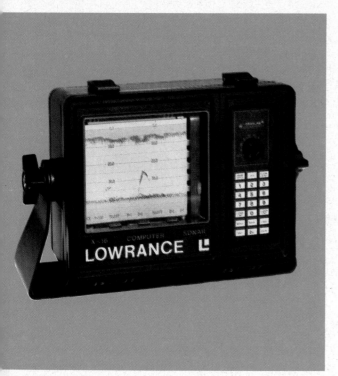

The X-16 Computer Graph, newest in Lowrance's line.

finer target resolution (separation). There are eight levels of surface clutter control, an automatic suppression system, optional light, medium, or dark chart-image selection. Range and scale settings plus other information will be printed evenly, not jammed or expanded with varying paper speed. Other features of the X-15 series will be retained.

In other news a new digital unit, the 3100, has been introduced. The small unit has 200 watts of power, sells economically, is ideal for running navigational channels or skirting reefs and rocks.

Lowrance Electronics, Inc., 12000 E. Skelly Dr., Tulsa, OK 74128.

Shakespeare Fishing Tackle Group launched a new series of 12-volt electric fishing motors. They include the Sigma 20, 25, 30, 35. The model numbers also designate pound thrust. Design has produced high thrust at lower overall motor weight. A three-blade weed-free prop provides peak efficiency at lower amp draw. One-Stik control eliminates the need to check switches: push in the handle for 5-speed forward selection, pull it for reverse. You can also bypass lower speeds and go directly to high. There's a quick-release system for removing the motor while leaving the transom mount attached. The engine stores up in a safe, 90 degree position from the running attitude. Recessed vents in the head assembly disperse heat buildup allowing the unit to run cooler and draw fewer amps.

Two new economy motors, the Sigma 10 and 15, were also introduced for small boats and canoes. They, too, have weed-free props, a new transom

mount. The 10-pound-thrust model has two speeds while the 15 has five.

Shakespeare Fishing Tackle Group, Drawer S., Columbia, SC 29260.

Si-Tex still has its standard size units but has launched new series of compact chart recorders, flasher, and a Loran-C. Notable is the HE-203 microprocessor chart recorder about the size of an average flasher unit. It has five depth scales from 0–20 through 0–120 feet. Paper is cassette loading. Two different pulse lengths may be selected. Twenty-foot expanded scale areas can be selected. Operating frequency is 107 kHz.

The ultra-slim SH series of flashers offers per-

The Si-Tex HE-203 chart recorder is a new compact.

formance at an economical price. The SH-1 has three depth scales from 0-30 to 0-120 feet , while the SH-2 has five scales down to 0-480 feet plus an audible adjustable alarm.

The Model 787 is a super-small Loran-C measuring just $5\frac{3}{4} \times 6\frac{5}{16} \times 3\frac{1}{4}$ inches. It has course steering, 8-position memory, backlighted displays, draws less than ½ amp, has autopilot steering output, elapsed time counter. A 787C version is available for a slightly higher price. Besides the features of the former model, it shows current position, bearing to next waypoint, distance to go, heading in degrees, time to go, velocity made good. Also featured are fifty waypoints, ten instant-position memories, auto waypoint sequencing for up to ten positions.

Si-Tex Marine Electronics, Inc., PO Box 6700 Clearwater, FL 33518.

Techsonic Industries unveiled four models of Humminbird LCR (Liquid Crystal Recorder) depth sounders that bridge the gap between flashers and

Techsonic has four new depth sounders. The LCR 3000 is the deep-water version.

paper chart recorders. LCR's are automated sonars with computer circuitry. Images of bottom, structure, and fish are formed by pixels or dots on the display screen. No paper is used. Features include: four to five depth scales, depending on model; zoom with added information; auto sensitivity control; stop action; forward and reverse; liquid crystal display; night light; high-speed operation; waterproof case; automatic noise rejection; STC to eliminate surface clutter; lifetime-guaranteed service policy.

In use, if you're on the 0–30 feet scale and switch to the 120 feet, the memory shows you what you missed. If you set the cursor to zoom in on an area, the selected area will cover the entire screen, not just a larger version but with more detailed information plucked from the stored information in the computer memory. In zoom, target separation is 1½ inches. The depth scale is automatically changed as you go from shallow to deeper water. You can adjust the sweep speed of the unit for fast running. Many more features are included. Automatic operation may be bypassed in top-of-the line models.

Models include: LCR 4000, 3000 (deep-water version), 2000, and 1000.

The CVR 200 and CVR 50 are new color video recorders. These CRT display units feature 8-color, high-resolution displays indicating bottom texture, size of fish through color intensity. Depths are in 10-foot increments to 1000 feet for the 200, up to 2000 feet on the 50 model.

The CH Thirty II chart recorder and Humminbird flashers have improved sensitivity as the result of a new redesigned transducer in new high strength ABS with super-polished bottom to prevent accumulation of air bubbles and result in instant wetting.

The Super three-Sixty and In-Dash units will feature increased power for '85. Both now boast 300 watts, making them as powerful as all others in the Humminbird line.

Techsonic Industries, Inc., 1 Humminbird Lane, Eufaula, AL 36027.

Vexilar has two new units, the 480 and 482. These, too, are computer-driven liquid crystal display sonars. Micro circuits permit thin, compact housing. The 480 has depth-scale entry from 0 to

The Vexilar 482 video-sonar offers important features.

999 feet with zoom expansion feature. There's a display for surface temperature, white-line control for bottom target separation, 38-degree cone angle coverage, and 1000-watt power. The 482 has all of the above features plus ranges down to 2400 feet, trolling-speed display, dual-frequency transducer for 50 kHz or 200 kHz, programmable alarms, and 2000 watts of transmitted power.

Vexilar, PO Box 2208, Hollywood, FL 33022.

Troubleshoot Those Little Outboards—On The Spot

E.F. Lindsley

I've got nothing against big, powerful outboards. They're great for offshore salt water, the Great Lakes, or hot bass boats. But, within thirty minutes of my home there are more small and medium lakes than I can fish in a lifetime, and I don't need big power for those. Anyway, a big, heavy engine anchored to the transom and nurtured by a maze of wires and cables makes launching from an unimproved site tough. Besides, few of today's family cars are really made to yank a heavy boat, engine, and trailer up a muddy ramp.

All of those problems are cut down to size with small (from 2 hp to 15 hp) fishing outboards. The truly lightweight 2 hp Yamahas and Suzukis tip the scales at only 22 pounds. Evinrude and Johnson models weigh in at just 24 pounds. They won't shatter the transom on takeoff, but they're a cinch to snatch out of a hatchback and drop onto a boat. Also, they're whisper quiet for easing into a backwater pool for a little flyfishing or baitcasting.

Move up to 4.5 hp, such as Merc's handsome 56-pound model, still easy to mount with a one-hand grip, and you get forward, neutral, and reverse shifting. Johnson and Evinrude have forward and neutral on their 4 hps, and full three-position shifts from 6 hp on up.

If bare-bones, manual-start motors aren't for you, move up to a 7.5-hp Mercury and you get electric starting. Evinrude and Johnson offer electric start at 9.9 hp but they also offer an alternator to keep your trolling motor and lighting battery nourished even on their 8- and 6-p models. The more you look them over, the more you see that you might not expect to find on these small, gemlike engines.

But, there's another big point in favor of small motors that I haven't mentioned and you can be sure the outboard makers won't mention it in their advertising. What you don't have, you don't have trouble with; and lacking multiple carburetors, tangles of wires and tubes, remote throttle and starting, and a full boat of cams, rods, and levers, the small outboard is simpler for the owner to troubleshoot and fix on the spot. It can be argued, however, that in real life there's a much bigger chance of having starting and operating problems with a small motor than with a big V-4 or V-6. The reason has nothing to do with the quality of the motors. Most small engine problems are caused by the owner himself. Here are some of the reasons. Ask yourself if they apply to you.

- Big motors look, and are, complex so you're more likely to seek regular dealer service. With a small motor you're likely to try to do your own tinkering.
- Small motors are often casually stored in a basement or garage without any real storage preparation.
- Small motors are more commonly stored or hauled while flat on their side.
- Many owners lug small motors around in their car trunks for days, weeks, and months and plan to use them for a spur-of-the-moment fishing session.
- Small motors are more commonly manual start.

The typical scenario starts with an evening phone call from a fishing buddy who has just heard of hot action upstate; can you make a pre-dawn start? You can and do. By sunup you have the boat in the water, rods and gear loaded, and you clamp on the motor that's been in the car trunk all summer. After a few confident pulls on the starter it dawns painfully that something's wrong. Your motor won't start, or, it starts and dies 500 feet from the launch ramp and won't restart.

It's time for some troubleshooting. It's also time to gulp back your frustration and put your mind into thinking mode before you even snap the cover off the motor. Keep in mind the old physician's code, "I will do no harm . . .," which means, here, stay away from heavy-handed attempts at a quick fix.

Even if you consider yourself a pretty fair engine mechanic, get your mind back to ground zero. What does my motor need to start and run properly? Makes and models differ in detail, but all need the following:

- Compression, in both combustion chamber and crankcase.
- Ignition
- Fresh fuel and lubrication

All troubleshooting starts with these basics.

COMPRESSION PROBLEMS

Compression is first and vital. If the piston rings are gummed and stuck, the cylinders worn or distorted from overheating, or if both are scored with rust, you're probably not going to get started. It's time to figure out what you did wrong and resolve to improve your habits in the future.

Think back. Did you try to run on automobile oil rather than approved TCW (Two-Cycle, Water-Cooled) oil? Did you get careless in your fuel/oil mix proportions or try to run on old, rancid fuel? Did you dump your engine into your car trunk with water still in the lower end, from where it could run back into the combustion chamber through the exhaust ports and cause rust, or maybe introduce sand and silt? There are times when it's hard to hold a flashlight and carefully stow a motor with the mosquitos singing in your ears. But, even if you allow a little drainage time, it's bad practice to store or carry your motor with the powerhead lower than the powerleg and lower unit. For now, it has to be said that you're not going to cure a cylinder compression problem with a screwdriver and pliers while sitting in the back end of a boat.

You might, however, cure bad crankcase compression if you have a small wrench to remove the carburetor and reed-valve plate, if your engine has reed valves (most do). Naturally, you'll check for good spark and fuel delivery before pulling the carburetor. If pulling the manual starter seems to indicate good compression in the cylinders, it can be that a small fragment of dirt, or maybe a loose scrap of motor-housing gasket, is holding open a reed valve. Most outboards have no air cleaners or screens, and it's a straight shot through the carburetor into the reed valves. The symptoms of reed-valve trouble are hard starting and low power. Sometimes you can see the offending debris just by removing the carburetor and inspecting the reed valves closely with a flashlight. Sometimes, if you've left old, gummy gas in the engine a collection of it in the crankcase may have actually glued the reeds shut. Remember, reeds are delicate. If you must poke at them, do it gently with a toothpick or the

like. The trick is to unstick them if they're stuck or remove any bit of dirt that's holding them open. The other probable source of lost crankcase compression is worn crankshaft seals. Replacing them is not a dockside repair.

If the big "C," compression, is in good shape, there may well be relatively easy fixes for ignition and fuel problems. Since most small motors are electrically self-contained and lack remote start and choke controls, you don't have to fret about poking around for electrical shorts and loose connections up around the throttle quadrant or in a big electrical cable and plug-in connecter as you might on a big engine.

IGNITION PROBLEMS

Most fishermen faced with a won't-start condition probably will remove a sparkplug, ground it against the motor, and pull the starter rope to check for a visible spark. Properly done, this is a sensible act, but do it wrong and you're headed for trouble. Modern ignition wires are not really wire but a sort of stranded fiber impregnated with a conductive powder to reduce radio interference. If you tug too hard on the wire to get that stubborn little rubber boot off the plug, you'll pull the fibers apart inside the outer insulating material. Once the break is started the engine may run for a while, but inside the wire an arc will be burning the break gap wider. As long as the engine is running, power may get to the plug, but next time you try to start there's no spark. To avoid this always carry a little inexpensive boot remover. They sell them in a bubble pack at automotive supply houses.

Assuming that you've pulled the plug, you can still be fooled if you look for a visible spark while cranking.If you've used automobile oil, or perhaps loaned your motor to someone who did, it's possible for a tiny, almost hair-sized fragment of carbonlike material to be lodged across the plug electrodes and

Starting your troubleshooting with a sparkplug check is good procedure, but don't tug on the ignition wire. Use a little boot remover to free wire and boot.

Use any metal conductor, even a fishhook, to see if power is actually getting to the plug or if the problem is in the ignition system.

shorting them out. To see such particles you almost have to hold the plug to the light or against a light surface. To be sure you've got it, run a matchbook cover between the electrodes. The offending material comes from the additives needed in four-stroke car engines but not two-stroke outboards.

You'll also want to examine the plug tip for signs that you're actually getting fuel to the combustion chamber. If the plug looks wet, be sure it's really fuel you're looking at. Under some cool, moist conditions enough water can condense in the crankcase and cylinder to throw a drop or two onto the plug when you try to start. If the plug looks oily it's possible some residual oil from the crankcase was thrown onto it, or you may not have agitated the fuel and oil enough when mixing.

Obviously, the ideal solution is to install a new sparkplug, which you may or may not have. Lacking a fresh plug, you can try to clean up the old one. If you have a lighter and lighter fluid, a drop or two of fluid on the electrodes and a little flame and heat can work wonders. Don't do this around the gas tank or if there's gas floating on water in the bottom of the boat. Go clear to the bow of the boat to keep away from gas fumes. Another possible cleaning agent might be alcohol if you carry some for medical repairs of nicks and hook punctures. Even just the heat from a match can sometimes help a wet plug.

To check whether power is getting to the plug at all, try running anything metal, a piece of wire, nail, or even a fishhook up into contact with the sparkplug contact spring in the boot. Hold the wire close to the engine and pull the starter. If you can get a spark from this the plug is at fault.

If the situation is desperate, you might want to try one more trick. Push the point of a small, sharp fishhook through the wire insulation just enough to contact the inner conductor and well back from the boot. This may tell you if you've been guilty of tugging the wire off roughly. If you get a spark from

the hook, you know the wire is defective down by the boot. If you want to gamble and there's enough extra wire, you could trim the wire back to the break and wiggle the contact spring and boot back on. This can be difficult and on most modern electronic systems the wire is too short.

There's nothing you can do inside a modern, encapsulated, solid-state ignition system, but before giving up, follow out all of the low-tension leads. These are the thin, light wires that connect the coils, switches, etc. It may be that a loose or corroded connection at the stop switch is at fault, or a primary lead to the switch or to a coil may have rubbed bare and be grounding out the system. The basic reliability of the solid-state system makes it a better than even chance that you'll locate a minor bad connection or wire and be able to fix it.

If your engine is a bit older and has regular flywheel magneto ignition, try disconnecting the primary wire from the stop switch and leave it hanging in the air. Unlike battery ignition on cars, magneto switches are open to run and closed to stop. A cor-

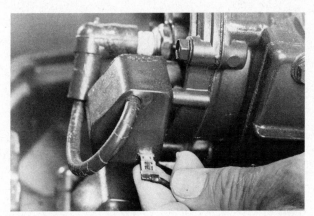

It's easy to accidentally knock a terminal fitting loose. Check all low-tension leads, such as this one to the coil, for sound connection.

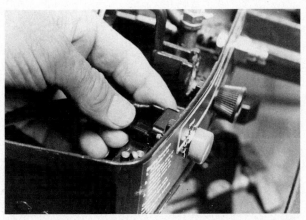

Stop switches or other connections can cause trouble. The switch may corrode, stick internally, or prevent starting.

roded or sticking stop switch can ground out the magneto. If you get a spark now, tape the end of the wire and go fishing; you can always shut off the engine with the choke.

Of course, while checking compression and ignition you'd probably notice if there was any fuel visible at the carburetor inlet, that a choke or throttle link was disconnected, or that the fuel smelled stale and rancid. Since you were probably using the choke, you will usually see liquid fuel in the carburetor throat if the fuel is getting through. It may, in fact, be dribbling, an indication of probable flooding. This is not so easily seen on those engines with intake air silencers, and you may have to remove these boxlike covers for a good check of fuel to the carburetor.

The standard remedy for flooding is to pull the starter repeatedly with the choke open. Often this results in short, sluggish runs until the excess fuel clears out. It doesn't hurt to remove the plugs and ground them near their threaded holes while doing this. If the spark ignites the expelled gases with a poof it's good evidence you were flooded.

Once you've cleared the flooded condition, the engine should start and run normally, but if it doesn't there must be a reason. On engines with an integral tank and gravity feed to the carburetor the carburetor float needle may be sticking open or be held open by a piece of debris. If you can look into the carburetor throat with a flashlight, you may see fuel slowly leaking from the jet. Try tapping the float bowl sharply with a screwdriver handle or the like. This Model-T remedy still works at times.

Any further digging into the carburetor is elective. If you have the tools and the confidence, it's not too hard to drop the float bowl and have a look. There are three potential pitfalls. First, you must be able to shut off the gas flow to prevent a fire hazard. Second, you're gambling that you won't destroy the float bowl gasket so it won't reseal. And, third, there is always a chance of dropping or losing a float needle or other small part. Rig a towel or cloth below the carburetor to catch anything you drop. I'm not necessarily recommending carburetor repairs in the field, but if you want to try to save a fishing trip by cleaning up a stuck float and needle you may come up a winner.

FUEL PROBLEMS

The other likely cause of not starting or lean running is failure to deliver fuel from the tank, either remote or integral. You can make a quick check of the remote tank and primer by squeezing the primer and using a small tool, perhaps a ball-point pen, to push back the little spring-loaded ball or valve in the engine end of the hose. If fuel exits freely, the hose and primer are probably okay.

Any further blockage would be between the hose-connection fitting and the carburetor. Try disconnecting the fuel line at the carburetor to see if fuel comes through when you squeeze the primer. If so, your problem is probably gum or dirt in the carburetor. Many engines have a fuel pump between the fuel inlet and the carburetor. With the line still disconnected at the carburetor, a few pulls on the starter rope should show if the pump is delivering fuel. I wouldn't recommend disassembling such a pump without some knowledge and spare parts. On Evinrude and Johnson, however, there is a small cover marked "Filter" on the pump, and here you can check the filter for plugging. Look for gum. Also, if there is a vacuum-pulse hose between the pump and the crankcase make sure it is intact and secure. The crankcase pulsations power the pump. Other carburetors have a small, built-in, rubber pulse pump which is not visible without removing the carburetor. They require knowledge to install properly, so unless you know exactly what you're doing it's time to back away.

One other fuel delivery problem centers at the remote tank connection to the engine. Typically, you prime the engine and it starts and runs, maybe long enough to get your boat moving, but then it dies. You may do this repeatedly because you're running on the fuel forced into the carburetor by the primer. The cause may be an air leak at the connection because dirt or sand has damaged rubber seals, usually small "O" rings. It's easy to drag the hose end in the dirt and pick up a little grit. It doesn't hurt to have a few spare seals in your tool box.

Before giving up, if you are sure fuel is getting to the carburetor, and if your engine has idle and main-jet mixture-adjustment screws, you might want to

Is fuel getting to the carburetor? Is the engine flooding? Liquid fuel at the carburetor inlet gives you a hint. On some engines, you'll have to remove the air silencer to view the carburetor inlet.

Usually you can pull a carburetor for cleaning by removing two flange nuts with a wrench that fits tight spots. You might wind up needing a new gasket at the flange and for the float bowl if you remove it.

Hose clamps come in many varieties. Be sure your tool kit contains pliers or some other tool to remove yours easily.

Fuel-hose connections tend to get dragged in dirt, which then damages rubber seal rings so fuel pump sucks air. Close inspection and cleanliness is the rule, but sometimes a spare seal will save your fishing day.

try cleaning them. First, determine the original settings by turning the screw down gently and slowly while counting the turns until it just seats. Now back out and remove the needle. Watch for small seal washers, "O" rings, and the antivibration spring so you don't lose them. If the tip of the needle is discolored and gummy, you've probably found your trouble. Try to wipe it as clean as you can without damage. If the needle is hollow and has tiny holes along it, try to clear these holes. The point of a small fish hook may do it. Replace the needle until it seats and then back it out to the original setting. This trick may get you going unless the jet down in the carburetor is so gummed the fuel can't get through.

RIG A TEST STAND

One of the best ways to avoid troubleshooting in the back of a boat is to rig a test stand and a water tank at home. A big, plastic garbage can makes a fine tank for small engines. At the beginning of the season you can check for the conditions I've described and perhaps try some of the techniques so you'll be familiar with them. Even if you don't have to touch a thing, now is the time to work out a tool kit that matches *your* motor. The best place to start is with an exploded-view parts book of your engine, although you may have to study it at your dealer. The object is to spot filters, "O" rings, gaskets, and carburetor and fuel-pump gaskets and diaphragms which are likely sources of trouble and require tools to access them. This is the time to find out that your old, faithful 10-inch adjustable wrench just can't be

applied to the float-bowl nut or maybe can't open far enough to fit the propeller nut.

STARTING TOOL KIT

My suggestions for a good starting tool kit:
- Prop-nut wrench and spare shear pins if your motor uses them.
- Sparkplug boot puller and plug wrench. Be sure it fits the plug.
- ¼-inch-drive socket set. Check engine for metric fasteners.
- 10-inch standard and cross-slot screwdrivers.
- 10-inch adjustable wrench.
- 4-inch adjustable wrench.
- Small (about 4-inch) screwdrivers
- Small needlenose pliers and wire-cutting pliers
- Jackknife
- Special needs: Allen wrenches (metric?), shorty screwdriver, hose-clamp pliers, wire-terminal crimping tool.
- Little parts you might need: hose clamps, "O" rings for fuel line connections, sparkplugs, spare low-tension wire and terminals, fuel filter elements, carburetor bowl gasket, a tube of gasket paste, electrician's tape, and a length of rope for pull starting if your recoil or electric starter fails. My check of some of the foreign-made engines showed a large number of small, plug-in, low-tension wire connectors that may need a special tool to remove them. Check if this applies to your engine.

OFF-SEASON STORAGE

Since so many of the problems you might encounter relate to storage, here's my general procedure for off-season protection:
- Follow the owner's manual for lubes and protective agents.
- Flush out and wipe and wash down if motor was used in salt water.
- Run carburetor dry using fuel preservative mixed with fuel.
- Fog carburetor inlet with internal preservative during final run.
- In lieu of fogging, remove plugs and squirt in lube oil. Crank engine over with plugs out to distribute and clear excess oil. If you have too much and crank engine over with plugs in, you could lock engine and bend a connecting rod.
- Lube all grease fittings and linkages.
- Drain and refill lower unit with specified lube. This is vital in freezing weather since old lube may contain water and burst lower unit housing.
- Wipe down all surfaces with protective oil.
- Remove prop for service if necessary.
- Examine propshaft and seal for fishline or sand damage. You may need a shop repair before next season.
- Store engine in an upright position. Horizontal storage may allow residual water or exhaust products to run into cylinders.

PART 2

BASS FISHING

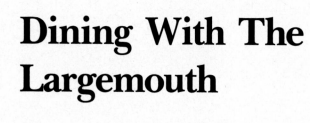

Dining With The Largemouth

Duke Cullimore

Nothing is so unnerving as a dozen ravenous fish rushing at your stomach while you float facedown in two feet of water. They were only largemouth black bass, a species not noted for its ferocity, but I was startled! Fortunately, the attack began and ended in the blink of an eye, and I didn't have time for a real panic.

I had joined a friend, Bill Roston, for an unusual day of photographing black bass in Bull Shoals Lake on the Arkansas/Missouri border. Wearing face masks and snorkel tubes, we were working in shallow water. We kept several bass within camera range by feeding them minnows from a bucket I was holding. After an hour in the water, Bill told me that it was necessary to reload the camera. Would I please continue feeding the fish, holding a minnow out to them and releasing it when one came up to eat, while he went ashore for more film?

It was a new experience for me to lie in the water face-to-face with those fish. I reached into the bucket and trapped one of the minnows between my fingers. Holding it at arm's length, I jiggled it to entice the nearest fish, which was about four feet away. It didn't work. All the bass seemed reluctant to accept the offering, so I turned the minnow loose.

The savvy shiner, knowing that those bass were only a foot or so away, darted for the nearest cover, which happened to be me. The little fish fled past my down-turned mask to hide under me, and out of the corner of my eye I caught another movement. All the bass, some of them weighing seven or eight pounds, were burning rubber to charge the hapless minnow. In a split second, the water beneath me frothed with a mass of wheeling, churning fish. Debris was churned off the bottom like dust in a Kansas windstorm. When the fury subsided, almost as soon as it began, I looked around to see that the bass had again formed a semicircle ahead of me and were

With a Bull Shoals dock dimly visible in background, I'm observing a feeding largemouth with some astonishment.

Photos by the author.

waiting patiently for me to play the game again.

I learned from Roston that such behavior is not unusual. He had experienced similar rushes by these same bass during the five weeks he had been working with them. Bill is a scuba diver, an accomplished underwater photographer, and an avid fisherman. He figured he could combine his various interests and learn more about the fish he loves to catch. Being a physician and a former high-school science teacher, he has a solid basis for his attempts to understand fish.

What he has learned by working with the Bull Shoals bass and with smallmouth bass, walleyes, crappies, and sunfish provides him with interesting beliefs about the behavior of gamefish, particularly black bass, and raised questions about some ideas fishermen have long cherished.

Bill's first concern was to find the right fish. He didn't want to work with aquarium-held fish, because he felt they would be too conditioned to their artificial surroundings and unable to react naturally. The thought occurred that perhaps the fish that stay under commercial docks would be suitable. It's common practice for dock operators to feed fish for the entertainment of visitors. This led him to Bull Shoals Dock on the south side of the lake where owner John Eastwold reported twelve to fifteen black bass of various ages and sizes that lived under the boat stalls.

John occasionally feeds minnows to these fish, alerting the bass to the upcoming feast by tapping on the float with the end of a broom handle.

During his first encounter with these fish, Bill began to sense that they were not afraid of him. As the weeks passed; he became a familiar figure among them. Their trust in him grew to the point where all he had to do was enter the water wearing a snorkel mask and holding a camera and a minnow bucket. The fish came out from under the dock to meet him. This recognition grew so strong over a nine-week period that when winter cold finally forced the bass into deeper, warmer water, Bill was able to find them by swimming (using scuba gear) out into the cove. There the fish recognized him, and almost all of them followed him back to shallow water where they were fed minnows.

The implications of this are staggering. Bill was totally alien to their world—a human dressed in scuba gear swimming out to a place where he had never been before. These dozen fish were scattered; Bill only saw two when he reached the middle of the cove, but even the fish he couldn't see recognized him and followed him to shallow water. This was two months after he had last fed them! Those bass have long memories.

Did they recognize Bill, or would these fish have followed anybody?

Bass can tell one human from another, Roston believes. To illustrate this he tells about the time when a 25-year-old nephew went with him to photograph smallmouth bass in a nearby stream. They both entered the stream but the bass were uncooperative. They wouldn't come near enough to be photographed, though they had done so often in the past. They did not respond to minnows offered to them, although Bill had been feeding them several times a week for the previous three weeks, and they seemed afraid of the two men. Experimenting, Bill and his nephew got out the water and waited several minutes. Only Bill returned, and the fish came to him immediately. He fed them, and then went ashore again. Then the nephew took the bucket and returned to the water. The bass fled. Repeated experiments proved that the fish would come only to Roston.

If bass can recognize and remember individual humans, can they also identify and remember fishing lures? Using lures without hooks, Roston found that they would hit the same plug a few times and then ignore it. However, the following week the same fish would again strike at the same hookless lure once or twice before quitting. Since he didn't want to risk injuring the fish or drive them away, Bill did not use hooks in any of the lure experiments. Conclusions about lure recognition remain guesswork because it is not known what the reaction would have been if the fish had been hooked and then released. It's also true that the bass may have decided that the hookless lures were inedible after one or two tries and therefore refrained from hitting them for a while.

A point to remember, is that big bass get that way because they're smarter than their brothers. Obviously, these fish must remember something, and

Photos by William Roston

Bass in top photo nudges minnow before opening its mouth to cause suction that takes the baitfish deep into his maw (shown in the photo at bottom).

After having just lost a minnow to a rival, the bass at left nestles up against the victor's gill cover, hoping that the minnow will escape through the gills. Minnows often do just that.

lure recognition is not beyond the realm of possibility.

Despite firmly held opinions among some fishermen, there are times when bass will not take anything. For instance, Roston once experimented with a female largemouth. The fish weighed about 12 pounds and had staked out a nesting site under a submerged cedar tree. For five days, Roston offered this bass all manner of artifical lures plus minnows, night crawlers, and everything else that he could think of. Every day, after failing to get so much as a nibble from the fish, Bill donned his scuba gear and visited the nest site. There was the bass, contentedly eyeing him through the branches of the tree. Eventually, a nearby male fertilized the eggs in the nest and took over from the female, which disappeared. Bill then tried to hook the male, but never succeeded. He has had similar experiences with walleyes during spawning.

One of the more interesting results to come from Bill's work with the Bull Shoals Dock fish is documentation on film of the striking technique bass employ when taking a minnow. Variations of the same striking technique were observed with artificial lures.

The first thing to understand is that a bass doesn't rush at a minnow or fishing lure with its mouth wide open as depicted in so many paintings and drawings. It makes sense for a fish to keep its mouth closed until the last possible moment during a strike because an open mouth is a tremendous impediment to speed.

When taking one of Roston's minnows, a bass invariably approached the little fish with its mouth closed or only slightly open. It nudged the minnow with its lips and then opened its mouth wide, taking the minnow into its mouth with the inrush of water. Then it flared its gills, presumably to let much of the great volume of water inside escape, and closed its mouth into a flattened, rubbery-looking line. With the minnow deep inside the mouth and entering the throat, the bass closed its gills and then flared them again. The whole process brings the minnow into the mouth and throat with water and then expels most of the water through the gills. The force of the suction that puts the food in the bass's mouth is demonstrated by photos that show the minnow tumbling about inside the gaping jaws like a sock whirling in a rapidly spinning clothes dryer. Scales ripped off the minnow on its inward plunge are pushed out in the stream of water through the bass's gills and show up as pinpoints of silver light in some of the pictures.

This same high-pressure suction sometimes forces the minnow out through the gills, depriving the bass of its anticipated meal. An interesting observation here is that occasionally another bass expects just that and lies in wait at the gill cover to take advantage of the event. One of Roston's photographs actually shows the second fish with the expelled minnow in its mouth.

When I worked with the dock bass I had to introduce myself slowly to get the bass used to me. Bill warned me that I probably would not be able to see the action when the fish took a minnow. Sure enough, try as I might, I never did see the open-mouth, flared-gill sequence, and I viewed feeding bass from all possible angles. We fed dozens of minnows to those fish, and if I hadn't seen the photographs later, I would have sworn that nothing was happening except the disappearance of the minnows.

This same super-fast feeding action was observed with plastic worms. At first it appeared that the bass would never take the worm into its mouth, but after studying his photographs, Bill found that the fish were inhaling the worm, deciding that they didn't want it, and exhaling it so fast that all the movements went unseen! Think about that the next time you go fishing for bass with plastic worms.

Other inferences about striking techniques can be gleaned from the photos and from Roston's hours underwater with the fish. For one thing, bass don't have any definite stalking pattern. If a bass sees a minnow or plug, it strikes from any angle. Quite often, bass hit Roston's plug from the side and swam away with the ends of the lure hanging out both sides of the jaws. And the age-old belief that bass like to swallow crayfish tailfirst is not necessarily correct, either. Bill has watched and photographed them taking crayfish headfirst and swallowing them without so much as a blink of an eye at the pincers.

Surface-feeding photographs taken from underneath the fish support the closed-mouth strike theory. These show the bass almost touching the lure before opening its mouth even slightly. Then, as the fish takes and explodes through the surface, the gills are flared. Roston has noticed that when a bass hits a surface lure, it seems to be much more excited than it is when feeding on subsurface lures or bait. The fish's dorsal fin is erect, its pectoral and anal fins are open, and there seems to be a fierce attitude toward the lure.

These bass are feeding on crayfish. Largemouths swallow the crayfish alive, unafraid of the claws.

Also noticeable is the action of the tail. It whips back and forth, often driving the fish upward and out of the water. The possibility exists that this explains the thrashing, head-shaking actions of a bass when it takes a surface lure and jumps. Rather than an effort to throw the lure, as commonly believed, the fish's body is perhaps just continuing the thrashing movement begun under the surface—the side-to-side muscular movements of the tail that propel the fish through the surface and into the air. Would a large fish know that by jumping and thrashing its head and body it could shake a lure loose and throw it or fall upon a line and break it? The elements of escape or anger may seem reasonable for such behavior, but the ability to reason is questionable.

On the other hand, Roston does feel that fish are able to reason to some extent.

Webster's International Dictionary defines the ability to reason as, "the power of comprehending, inferring, or thinking in an orderly, sensible, rational way." If you consider the action of the minnows Roston feeds to the bass, there is some justification for believing fish do sometimes reason.

The minnows are the standard commercial variety, available nearly everywhere in the Midwest. The minnows Roston uses are reared in captivity and have never come in contact with a predator fish. They have never even been in the same water as a bass. Yet these minnows, when taken to the lake in a minnow bucket and placed near bass being fed, will not leave the bucket when the top is left open. They will swim to the top and even venture out a little way, but then they dive back down into the bucket. I've seen them do it time after time. They seem to know that there are bass out there that will gobble them up if they venture out into the open.

Conversely, Roston has watched small bass, 10 to 12 inches long, stalking the minnow bucket and has seen them swim into it to get at the minnows.

The behavior of the bass and the minnows indicates that fish do have some ability to reason.

Working with the bass at Bull Shoals Dock provided many observations that indicate bass do know what is happening around them. The indications are that bass have an acute awareness of many things that occur out of the water. For example, whenever someone would step on the dock ramp, the bass would scatter. Roston was working very near the ramp, and he saw that the fish could always sense the presence of a newcomer before he could do so himself. Birds also spooked the bass. Mallard ducks living near the dock often flew over, and the fish fled when the birds' shadows passed. Roston has observed this same fear of bird shadows in other locations.

Herons, ospreys, eagles, and kingfishers all prey on fish in Bull Shoals Lake, creating an obvious need for the fish to be aware of the danger. But the question raised in Roston's mind is how fish learn to be afraid of birds. Is it really a learned fear or is it an instinctive reaction? Either way, if fish grow from immature fry to adults with a fear of moving shadows, don't they also have the same reaction to certain stimuli on or in the water—things such as fishing lures?

Knowing that a particular kind of action or shape in the water is to be feared (even though they may never have been subjected to injury caused by a lure, just as they've never been injured by a predatory bird), isn't it possible that fish often recognize and shun such lures? Roston realizes that this is conjecture, but the idea has enough merit to cause anglers to carefully reconsider the kinds of lures that will be most effective.

Because they live in water, fish are very aware of what happens in their liquid element, but Bill has found that the degree of sensitivity is surprising. While photographing a large bass in about 15 feet of water after working with the fish for some time in which it demonstrated no fear, the bass suddenly sped away to hide among some nearby rocks. Roston looked around and could see nothing that would have spooked the fish. Then he began to hear a faint noise in the water. Almost directly overhead, he saw the bottom of a fishing boat with an electric motor operating at the bow. The sound of the propeller of the electric motor was what he had heard, but the bass had recognized and reacted to that same sound nearly 15 seconds earlier. Perhaps that fish had been caught and released previously or had managed to escape after being hooked. Whatever the reason, it feared the sound of an electric fishing motor.

This was the only instance in which Bill has observed fear of a boat or motor. He feels that most fish are probably conditioned to ignore motor noise in general. An outboard motor can be heard for some distance underwater, and when the weather or water conditions are right for fishing and recreational boating, many fish are probably never out of hearing range of such noise.

Whether you agree or disagree with Bill Roston's theories about fish behavior, it's hard to disregard the scenes portrayed by his photographs, or to discount his observations. His ideas run against the current of some popular thinking, but they are certainly worth considering if you want to know more about the fish you want to catch.

Has his recently acquired knowledge helped Roston's fishing success? That remains to be seen. He started out with that in mind, but the challenge of photographing and studying fish in their natural surroundings has proved so interesting and so time consuming, that his fishing has suffered. Maybe one of these days he'll give up researching and go fishing again. In the meantime, he's willing to share his observations and knowledge with others in the hope that they'll benefit from it.

Bass Myths Debunked

Morris Gresham

"Missed him," I said and groaned as I reeled in a slack line. Setting the hook after I had felt a gentle tap had produced nothing but a mangled plastic worm.

"Rerig and toss it back in there," Ralph Manns directed me. "Another one might hit it."

Manns was right. The next time I set the hook I was rewarded with a pleasantly bowed rod. After a short fight, a five-pound largemouth bass thrashed in the landing net.

"Now, you get one," I said and grinned as my bass splashed in the live well.

Manns complied with a cast that dropped his worm beside the same rotted stump. The line twitched, the rod arched, and he quickly landed a twin to the first bass. Not a bad start for our first look at Texas's Lake Livingston—especially after my traumatic and almost sleepless night.

It had begun innocently enough with my arrival at Livingston's Penwaugh Marina the previous evening for a meeting of the Texas Outdoor Writers Association. Luck of the draw had placed me in the same room with fisheries biologist Ralph Manns, a pleasant mild-mannered gentleman I was meeting for the first time. I had no idea that our meeting would alter the course of my fishing life.

An insatiable appetite for more facts about bass behavior had prompted Manns to become a full-time student at Southwest Texas State University after retiring from active duty in the Air Force where he had spent twenty years as an intelligence officer and a political scientist. At the time of his retirement he was a lieutenant colonel.

En route to a masters of science degree in aquatic biology, which he earned in 1981, Manns conducted a study of black bass in Lake Travis in 1977 and 1978. The study team used electronic transmitter tags and receivers to track fourteen bass while divers recorded the behavior of another 935 bass. Manns's team also used angling techniques to obtain detailed reports on an additional 289 bass. Data on more than twenty different types of behavior and the environmental conditions that might influence the fish were fed into a computer to compile and analyze the results.

Manns's exhaustive studies of scientific literature on bass and his extensive two-year study have led to rather innovative and sometimes controversial conclusions. During my first few hours with him, he crumbled the foundation of my bass fishing knowledge with solid scientific evidence that contradicted many generally accepted fishing theories.

Those first two bass we caught from Lake Livingston, for example, were taken from classic bass structure—a stump on the upper edge of a submerged creek bed. The bass probably had not migrated from the depths, however, to feed in the shallower water as a popular myth would have us believe.

The hypothesis that bass live in deep water, migrate to shallow water on a daily basis to feed, and then return to deep water along established migration routes is generally credited to Buck Perry, the gentleman rightfully recognized as the father of structure fishing. His methods of catching bass have been so successful that other anglers and writers have perpetuated his migration theories.

Ralph Manns agreed that such structures are good places in which to fish but the analytically minded biologist could find no scientific literature to substantiate a deep-water migration theory.

Manns wanted a better explanation for the appearance of bass at certain underwater structure.

"Sure enough," Manns related, "our tracking studies verified data available in at least fifteen other studies that showed the predominant movements of black bass are parallel to the shorelines and contour lines and not perpendicular to them. The movement,

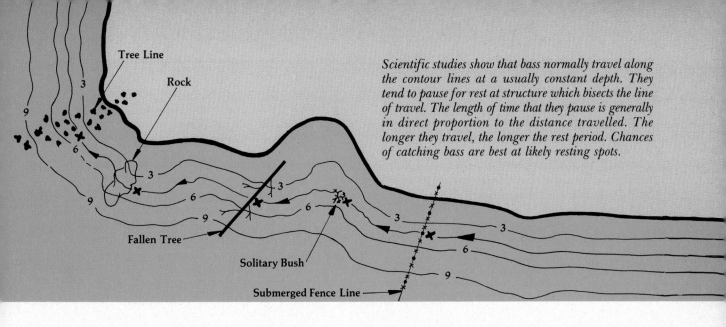

Tree Line
Rock
3
9
6
3
9
6
9
3
6
9
3
6
9
Fallen Tree
Solitary Bush
Submerged Fence Line

Scientific studies show that bass normally travel along the contour lines at a usually constant depth. They tend to pause for rest at structure which bisects the line of travel. The length of time that they pause is generally in direct proportion to the distance travelled. The longer they travel, the longer the rest period. Chances of catching bass are best at likely resting spots.

Erwin A. Bauer

moreover, usually is at a nearly constant depth."

A national magazine published a while back a story entitled "When the Sun Is High, the Bass Go Deep." The author surmised that because more bass are caught in deep water during midday hours, bass obviously migrate from shallow to deep water as the sun brightens. And that's how myths get started.

Manns's study of Lake Travis bass showed no such tendency.

"Our research showed some bass at shallow depths, some at medium depths, and some in deep water at all times," he revealed. "And they tended to remain at that particular depth whether active or inactive. Bass do move vertically but not routinely. A deep fish might pop to the surface to run through a school of shad, but it will grab two or three and almost immediately dive to its original depth because that's where it has established its equilibrium and can suspend without effort."

A bass can hover effortlessly at a particular depth because its air bladder is balanced at that depth and it gets out of balance if it varies much from that point. According to Manns, it takes hours for the air bladder to adjust to a major depth change. The more out of balance a bass gets, the harder it has to swim to maintain its stability.

Manns noted that black bass usually move along contour lines for only short distances and tend to stop at any bisecting lines of structure that obstruct their movement, such as a fence, stump, or rock. By casting to a fence, an angler increases his odds simply because moving bass are likely to pause there.

Most anglers will catch more bass, Manns maintained, if they fish on the better bisecting structures for several minutes during activity periods. Additional schools often stop at the same structure long enough for the anglers to catch more fish.

Some fishermen consider schools of black bass a rarity. Limit catches might be rare but, according to Manns's underwater observations, most bass are in either a school or an aggregation.

"There are almost no loner bass," Manns says. "The few single fish we observed underwater were either very sick, very large, or totally inactive. The sick ones obviously couldn't keep up and the larger

bass were probably unable to find compatible partners in their size range.

"Rule one," he continued, "if you catch a bass, assume it is not alone. As a minimum, it is in a group of two to five fish. Actively striking bass are usually feeding and moving bass. They tighten up their aggregations and move in small schools."

During activity periods, of course, almost anyone can catch bass by tossing an edible-looking lure in the path of a feeding school. It's the inactive periods that separate expert from novice bass fishermen.

"Fishermen should remember that bass are inactive most of the time, even if their stomachs are empty," Manns claimed. "Unlike humans who have a predictable three square meals a day, a bass may be forced to exist for days without eating. That little bit of minnow it ate three days ago must last the bass a long time and it does not waste it!"

The fact that a fish is inactive doesn't mean that it won't eat, Manns admitted. If something passes closely and in front of a bass's mouth, it will usually eat because bass are opportunists. But an inactive bass probably won't move more than a few inches to hit a lure. An angler who is fishing a spot that holds inactive bass may have to cast fifteen or more times before the lure passes through that tiny strike zone in front of an inactive bass.

A fast-moving crankbait offers good odds of getting a lure to an active bass. Because active fish may chase lures for 10 feet or more, each cast effectively covers a wide path on each side of the bait's track. The same lure retrieved past inactive bass, however, may pass by many fish without eliciting a strike.

The success of an angler's technique, then, depends on how active the bass are. Anglers who cast and crank at wide intervals over inactive bass will usually get few strikes. Fishermen who flip worms or jigs to the base of cover objects where inactive bass may hold, however, get close enough to take a few fish. If the same anglers continue to flip slow lures while bass are in an active state, though, they cannot hope to hook as many as those with fast lures. Thus, an angler must match his lure and his technique to the activity level of the bass.

One widely accepted myth claims that bass avoid

sunlight because they have no eyelids. Manns's underwater observations indicate otherwise.

"It was clear to us that bass have no requirement to live in shade," Manns declared. "Moving bass were as likely to stop at a sunny spot as a shaded one. Although bass have no eyelids, their eyes have pigment mechanisms that compensate for excessive light. Water is an excellent light filter, too. Unless a bass is in very shallow, calm, and clear water, the water serves it well as a pair of sunglasses."

Bass that anglers catch from beneath piers, boat houses, and docks are probably there for cover or food rather than for shade. In fact, even slightly colored water refracts sunlight sufficiently to destroy any distinct shade line within a few feet. Even in moderately clear lakes, bass down more than 10 feet experience little or no shading from objects at the surface.

This means that bass a fisherman finds beneath floating structures will probably hold tightly to the bottom of the structure—unless, of course, there are other attractive structural elements on the bottom. Lures retrieved just beneath floating structures, then, will probably be more effective than lures retrieved along the bottom.

Although bass do not need to avoid sunlight, Manns's records indicate that more bass are caught from shaded areas than from sunny ones. He stressed that this statistic is not contradictory because inactive bass may suspend in either shade or in sunny open water. But for an angler to cast his lure near enough to inactive bass to make them strike, he usually must find bass that are suspended close to an identifiable target. While the target creates shade, the shade itself is incidental and not the reason the bass are there.

Another concern of bass anglers is that bass will move when they hear noise coming from above them. Manns's study, however, clearly showed that bass learn to ignore any sounds that don't represent a threat. Bass frequently swam beneath docks where workers were pounding with hammers or sailors were stomping in boots. Bass also ignored outboard motor noises in Lake Travis, which is heavily used by recreational boaters. Surprisingly, however, some of the lake's bass had learned to move away from boats with electric fishing motors and it was difficult to approach such bass unless they were holding tightly against cover objects.

Manns suggests that a great myth of angling literature is that bass seek out preferred temperatures, water clarity, structure, and so on. He stressed that the part of a bass's brain that processes every piece of visual or physical information is about the size of a thumbnail. A bass simply does not have the ability to be intuitive.

"A bass will not run across a lake to an area that has a better temperature level," Manns claimed, "because it doesn't know it's there. Now if a bass is wandering around and finds a more comfortable area, it might think, 'Wow! Isn't this temperature nice?' And if it can stay there without getting hungry, it may hang around long enough for the angler with a temperature meter to catch it."

In Manns's study, bass did not move to deeper water to avoid surface temperatures in the 84- to 88-degree range. In fact, when all other factors were equal, black bass (including smallmouths) preferred the water temperature to be between 78 and 86 degrees—not the 72 degrees that is popularized in most fishing literature. Manns's findings are corroborated by a least twenty other scientific studies published during a forty-year period. Bass found in cooler water are there because of a better food supply or because they are unable to compete with larger predators present in warmer water.

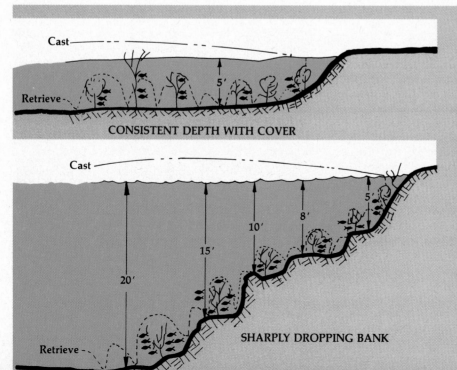

CONSISTENT DEPTH WITH COVER

SHARPLY DROPPING BANK

Although bass hold at many different depths at the same time, the fish are not necessarily active simultaneously. Bass are frequently active at different depths during different time periods. An angler casting only to a consistent depth, such as that pictured in the top drawing, will catch little if bass are not active at that depth. An angler fishing down the dropping bank, as depicted in the bottom drawing, however, can cover several depths with one cast. His odds of finding the depth where they are active are much greater when he can sample more possibilities with the fewest number of casts.

Manns admits that there are optimum chemical environments for bass but in most lakes the fish must be satisfied with less. They merely move into someplace tolerable, adapt to it, and once they've adapted to that condition, any change is a negative change to those fish.

"Most people don't realize that a bass is constantly adapting to its environment," Manns declared. "The chemistry of its body adapts to temperature and water conditions and, if any factors change, the fish is temporarily out of balance. When cold fronts go through, for example, sudden drops in temperature disturb the fish's equilibrium and it becomes slightly sick until it adapts to the new condition. That helps explain why bass normally don't bite as well after a cold front."

A common dream of anglers is catching bass on almost every cast from a "hotspot" where hungry largemouths eagerly await the next cast. The nearest thing I ever found to that fabled hotspot was on Lake Sam Rayburn back in 1968. My partner and I found a timbered flat near a river channel where every cast with our crankbaits hooked a chunky bass. We tied the boat line to a limb and promptly caught sixty largemouth bass from an area no larger than the average living room. In that era of fifteen-bass limits it was the first chance I had to cull bass to improve a stringer.

Our hopes for a repeat performance the next day were short-lived. Our first few casts hooked bass, but the action ceased and we never relocated the bass. Nor did any of our friends ever find fish there on many subsequent trips. Manns offered an explanation for the phenomenon.

"They were probably transient bass, which is a major cause of confusion to anglers. Bass are generally thought of as having one type of behavior pattern. Actually, though, there are two types of black bass: transient bass and home-range bass. The concept is an old one that shows up in scientific literature as far back as thirty years ago."

Manns theorized that the fish's health or its ability to catch prey determines whether it is a home-range or transient bass. Healthy fish establish territories and hold them, moving as little as possible. They conserve energy by feeding quickly and remain in the same general location unless there is a major change in water conditions or the food supply.

Large bass populations or shortages of prey create competition for food, however. Those bass that feed less efficiently must feed longer and move often to find forage. A transient is a transient because it is a loser.

There are many transient bass in our better bass lakes and they almost always school. An angler who finds such a concentration can catch great numbers of them at one time but he should not necessarily label the area as a great fishing hole. Such catches can be the result of chance meetings with transients.

Manns says that an angler should not spend much time returning to the site of a big catch unless he has reason to believe, because of repeated success, that the place is a home-range area. An angler can more consistently catch bass by returning to locations where he has taken one or two fish over and over again. Those are probably spots that have enough food to hold home-range fish day after day.

Manns stressed that bass reactions vary according to how hungry they are. A very hungry fish will probably strike at any lure it can get in its mouth. A bass that has been feeding on shad for twenty minutes, however, will probably only take something that is similar to the shad.

Although bass can see colors, anglers should remember that bass do not perceive them as a human would. Manns recalled a day when he and his partner followed a large school of bass feeding heavily on shad. The two cast all of the traditional shad-color lures without a strike. As soon as Manns put on a gold lure, though, he caught fish on almost every cast.

The bass obviously responded to some flash of gold from the shad caused, perhaps, by the angle of sunlight. The bass had enough color discrimination that they triggered to the tiny variation. Manns, therefore, suggests that anglers who are unsuccessful in catching obviously active bass should change lure colors, sizes, and actions until they find one that triggers the fish.

Bass are not ambush predators as are halibut, angler fish, and sculpin; nor are they chase predators such as tuna or striped bass. A black bass is a compromise fish designed to do a lot of things—none of them perfectly but all of them well. The bass is a seeker with a short sprint. It enters cover for protection and to rest, not to ambush prey. Cover actually limits and hinders a bass's ability to strike and that is why prey fish hide in such areas.

The standard hunting pattern of a bass is to move around structure objects to see if anything strays far enough from cover to become vulnerable. It assesses its ability to catch individuals or prey and strikes only at those it thinks can be caught. The bass ignores prey that are likely to dodge and thus escape. A bass will ignore a lure that looks like a healthy bluegill just as it would ignore a real bluegill under the same circumstances.

"Bass fishing is very mathematical, very predictable," Manns claimed. "It is a problem to be solved. Most of the false concepts arise because writers intellectualize about bass. The reaction mechanism of bass is actually very very basic: a reaction to a stimulus and a response, nothing more.

"A bass can't outsmart you. All you have to do is find something that will stimulate it, put it where it will stimulate it, and you will catch a bass. There's really nothing more to fishing than that."

Manns makes it sound simple and it looks simple enough when you watch him in action. He merely works the odds, covering as much favorable water as possible with a wide variety of lures. But he seems to catch many more bass than the average fisherman. The years he spent in their living quarters are paying off.

The Acid Test: pH For Finding Phish

Steve Price

At exactly 3:10 on a sizzling August afternoon at Mississippi's Tunica Lake, Bill Dance set the hook on our twenty-sixth largemouth of the day, a husky 5½-pounder that nailed Bill's plastic worm. I remember checking the time and the surface temperature—94°—because we recorded every bass we caught during the trip. That fish was the three-hundred-sixty-fourth largemouth Bill or someone with him had caught during ten separate trips to Tunica throughout the summer.

Such statistics are really not that unusual coming from an angler of Dance's ability. A former bass tournament pro who has fished throughout the United States while producing the popular *Bill Dance Outdoors* television program, he is on the water virtually every week of the year and is a recognized expert at catching many other species besides bass.

What was unusual about that day, and those that preceded and followed it as well, is how and where he found those bass. Bill used a new technique known as the "pH profile" to pinpoint their location. It's a system that incorporates the basic pH concept of how water acidity affects fish behavior but it includes a brand-new breakthrough. It's easy, fast, and has proven itself on lakes throughout the country for a wide variety of gamefish.

In a nutshell, here's how it works: An angler chooses the area of a lake he wishes to fish, such as a tributary creek, a large cove, a long point, or a sunken ridge. Using the pH meter probe, the angler takes readings of the pH at the surface and at one-foot intervals to the bottom.

At some depth along that profile the pH will change abruptly. The depth of that point of change or "breakline" is where the fish will be.

"This system does not tell you specifically *where in a lake* the fish will be," explains Dr. Loren Hill of Norman, Oklahoma, developer of the pH profile technique, "but it does tell you at *what depth* the fish should be found and that's a major part of forming any fishing pattern."

Even more encouraging about this concept is the fact that an angler no longer needs to be concerned with the so-called "ideal" pH range. He doesn't even have to understand what pH is and why it works. All he has to do is take pH readings from surface to bottom and note where the most significant break occurs.

"When you know the proper depth, you have two basic fishing choices," explains Dance. "Depending on the species, you can move in toward shallow water until you find cover at that depth; or you can go deeper and chart underwater structure where you'll find fish suspended at that depth. Either way, you're well on your way to catching fish within your first five minutes on the water."

Dr. Hill, chairman of the ecology department at the University of Oklahoma and director of the university's biological station on Lake Texoma, has been active in bass research since he received his doctorate in ichthyology from the University of Louisville in 1966. An active fisherman himself, the 42-year-old Dr. Hill has devoted much of his work to studying the effects of water quality on fish behavior. He developed the pH Monitor used by many fishermen in the early 1970s.

Two years ago, while working with a grant from the U.S. Fish and Wildlife Service to study the effects of thermal stress on striped bass, Hill "discovered" the pH profile system. His work took him on a weekly 47-mile run down Texoma, visiting seven separate checkpoints where he simultaneously recorded oxygen, temperature, salinity, and pH levels in the water from top to bottom.

As he began to compile his findings, he found that stripers could continually be located at depths where the pH showed a distinct break. He then tried the theory on largemouth and spotted bass, crappies, walleyes, Chinook salmon, northern pike, brown trout, white bass, and hybrid stripers on lakes across the nation. The results were always the same: Find the pH breakline and you find the fish.

Hill explained the pH profile technique to me in February 1983, and he was with Dance and me that day on Tunica. Despite the scorching heat and the fact he'd never been on the Mississippi River oxbow before, he correctly programmed the entire day of fishing for us.

At 8:30 that morning, he began taking his pH readings. As he called them out, I wrote them down. "Surface, 7.9; one foot, 7.9; two feet, 7.8," he called out. "Three feet, 7.8; four feet, 7.1; five feet, 7; six feet, 6.8." He continued checking until he reached the bottom at 15 feet where the pH measured 6.

The most significant break occurred between three and four feet, so Dance eased the boat in toward the sandy bank where our casts could work that depth. He caught the first bass within five minutes, I hauled in another moments later, and we were off to the races.

By 6 p.m. we had boated a total of forty-one bass, one sauger, and one bluegill. Nearly every fish came from the very same depth range on either side of the lake, some of them miles apart.

We checked the pH almost hourly and nothing changed until we measured an area where several springs flowed into the lake. There the pH break occurred between eight and nine feet, and that's where Dance brought in the 5½-pounder and I

Steve Price

It doesn't matter what the pH is on the surface, or even at the depth where you record a break in the pH progression. What does matter is that you discover the depth at which the break occurs. Here Steve Price is taking pH readings in order to find that break.

caught one weighing more than four.

One day on the water does not prove a theory by any means, but Hill has spent the last two years testing this concept and has recorded some truly dramatic results. Several weeks prior to our trip, he had been with noted angler Ron Lindner of Brainerd, Minnesota, trolling for salmon on Lake Michigan.

Lindner recalls the expedition. "We had been catching big Chinook at 55 feet with regularity but, when Dr. Hill came up, we couldn't buy a fish at that depth. We trolled with downriggers for nine hours without a strike.

"Then he made a pH profile and recorded a significant break between 38 and 41 feet, and he raised his downrigger to that depth. Within 300 yards he hooked a 25-pound Chinook, and the remainder of that day and the next we caught twelve more in the 15- to 20-pound class at that depth."

Before the Lake Michigan experience, on August 1 when the surface water temperature registered 90 degrees, Hill worked his profile technique to perfection on Texoma's striped bass. Most boats on the famous striper impoundment had downriggers set between 25 and 35 feet but none were getting any action. Hill's pH profile showed a break at just six feet—an almost unheard of depth for summer striped bass at Texoma—but he started trolling anyway. By afternoon, he had caught sixteen stripers, weighing up to 16 pounds.

"From my research over the years," says Hill, who caught his first bass thirty years ago after plowing fields for $1 a day for two weeks so he could purchase a Langley reel, "I honestly feel the level of pH in the water is more important in locating fish than water temperature or oxygen content.

"All pH represents is a measurement of the acidity

Photos/Freshwater

or alkalinity of a solution. All liquids have a pH and pH is measured on a scale of zero to 14. Pure water has a neutral reading of seven, with acidic water measuring less than seven and alkaline water more than seven. The absolute ideal pH range for bass, for example, is between 7.5 and 7.9, but they can adapt and survive in a much wider range, from as low as five up to 9.6 or so. The importance of pH for fish is that it determines how well they react to stressful conditions and how effectively they utilize oxygen from the water surrounding them. This, in turn, affects all their other actions."

Dr. Hill did not develop the principle of pH. It has been used for years by farmers who wanted to know if their land was alkaline or acidic so they could fertilize accordingly for maximum crop production. The same measurements apply to water, even to human blood, which has a pH of between 7.35 and 7.45.

In his original testing to verify the importance of pH to fish, Dr. Hill utilized several test tanks in his university lab. One end of the tank contained good oxygen but poor pH, the other end good pH but low oxygen. He did the same tests with both oxygen levels. In each case, the fish chose the end of the tank containing the correct pH.

In his research at Texoma, Hill cannot consistently correlate any distinct breaks in the oxygen or temperature levels at the same depth where the pH break occurred. Often, he finds suitable oxygen and temperatures well below the pH breakline, but the fish always locate where the pH changes. Among fisheries scientists, temperature and oxygen have

long been considered the two most important factors influencing fish behavior.

"The thing to remember about all fish is that they adapt to their surroundings, whether the correct pH level is present or not," emphasizes Dr. Hill. "Bass and other species prefer the ideal 7.5 to 7.9 range but, it if it isn't present, they will locate as close to that range as possible."

In the past, anglers using pH Monitors were taught to take only surface measurements, because it was believed pH remained constant from the top to a depth of about 30 feet. At the same time, however, they were told the pH of the water 60 feet away at the end of their casts could very likely be different from where they measured at the boat.

The new pH profile concept does away with this thinking. It doesn't matter what the pH is on the surface, or even at the depth where you record a break in the pH progression. What does matter is that you discover the depth at which that break occurs, because there will be a break, even though it may be as little as 0.2 percent.

"The pH of water changes because of several factors," Dr. Hill points out. "First, water changes density with depth and becomes heavier. There is usually less circulation. There is more acid due to the natural decay of organic material on the bottom. And there is less light penetration so that little or no photosynthesis occurs. This is true on all lakes, even flow-through reservoirs where the water is exchanged rapidly and results in a lower pH.

"The change in the pH profile may not seem like much but it is significant to a fish. A 0.1 percent change in pH can equal about a four parts per million change in oxygen and as much as a 5 degree change in temperature. The higher the pH, the more oxygen present—thus, the first significant break in the pH level is the one an angler must concentrate on."

To put the correlation between pH and oxygen in perspective, Dance provides this observation of an experience he had at Tunica when he was catching bass in the shallows despite the heat. Trotliners he spoke to reported bringing up only dead catfish, even though their lines were set in 10 feet of water. The fish went down to eat the bait offered, were hooked, but then could not swim back up to the four-foot depths where oxygen was present. Throughout the summer, Dance had not caught any bass on Tunica deeper than about five feet, except for the one area where the springs flowed into the lake.

Many factors can change the pH of a lake and, if an angler stops catching fish along the pH breakline, or if he changes locations or types of water, he should make a new profile. Green vegetation in sunlight, for instance, allows photosynthesis to occur. In several hours, this can raise the pH of the surrounding water significantly. Bass that earlier had been underneath or along the edge of the vegetation have probably moved 10 to 15 feet away or dropped to a deeper depth.

A heavy rain can change the pH faster than photosynthesis can. Normally rainfall registers a pH of about 5.1 but it can alter the pH of a lake drastically if the precipitation is polluted acid rain. The runoff after a rain can cause a pH shift, too, depending on the acidity or alkalinity of the surrounding terrain.

Ron Lindner feels fairly certain that the pH makeup of the particular portion of Lake Michigan that he and Dr. Hill fished changed because of a massive storm that pushed through the area two days prior to Hill's arrival. The upwelling caused by the heavy wind and wave action could certainly have raised the pH breakline 15 feet during that length of time.

Roland Martin who, like Dance, is recognized as one of the nation's top anglers, helped in the initial testing and research of pH Monitors. He feels pH can be one of the most valuable tools available to an angler in his search for fish.

"The key is finding what depth the fish are using," says Martin, "because then you can quickly figure out the most effective lure and presentation to use. I've used pH to locate everything from bass to muskies and it's become an important tool for me.

"Whenever an angler goes to a lake to fish, his first question is usually how deep the fish are. Knowing the depth, he can then find the right area, choose the correct lure, and, normally, catch fish. With pH, a fisherman can find the correct depth in minutes."

Aside from the basic interpretation of pH, another problem early proponents encountered was in the pH metering device itself. The probe featured a very fragile glass nose that was easily broken, and the cord—when used to measure deep water—was unwieldy and frequently knotted. Still another problem was the accuracy of the monitors themselves: Two probes dropped side by side often registered different pH levels.

According to Joe Meirick of Mt. Vernon, Missouri, whose firm, Lakes Illustrated, manufactures the pH Monitor, these problems have been solved. Probes are now encased in a steel tube and are described as virtually breakproof.

New pH Monitors are available from Lakes Illustrated, Route 3, Box 233-M, Mt. Vernon, MO 65712; or call (417) 466-7136 or toll-free (800) 641-4371. The people at Lakes Illustrated will recondition and upgrade any existing pH Monitor, regardless of the unit's age or condition. Anglers simply need to send in their old units along with payment.

Research is still continuing on this new pH profile concept as Dr. Hill, Dance, Lindner, Martin, and others try to refine the system even more. For the moment, however, the pH profile technique represents a new exciting and accurate way to locate fish.

Are These Bass Baits Too Good?

Jerry Gibbs

I'd rather fish with lures—call them artificial baits if you prefer. There's no fuss, no messing about with slimy gunk and things that could nip you. Besides, with artificials I just feel I'm doing more *myself*, rather than having some other critter wiggling up the bass for me. Still, in the back of my mind there's always this nagging thought: If you know what you're doing, live bait will catch more and bigger largemouth bass (probably smallmouths, too) than anything else. You know as well as I do that bass eat all kinds of bait—things like night crawlers or tackle-shop minnows. I even know a guy whose largest bass was sucker-punched by a single salmon egg fished for trout off a dock. But there are baits and then there are superbaits that are sometimes so good that it's almost sinful to use them.

There are no totally secret baits anymore, but in the old days local guides and hotshots could get downright hostile if you pressed them about some gourmet tidbit that had bass almost panting in expectation. The thing that isn't widely known is that some superbaits used in one region usually are available in slightly varied form (perhaps a different species) elsewhere and not used because they aren't traditional. The first angler to experiment with a bait unusual to his bailiwick often reaps a bonanza. It could be you who becomes the hero. Just think of the guy who ate the first raw oyster.

Some superbaits are in such demand that they are imported great distances. The situation is really crazy these days. State laws governing imports vary from strict to liberal, and fear of introducing disease or some critter that runs amok in fragile waters still lurks in the heart of every biologist. Regardless of check measures, bait smuggling goes on. Examples? Before he was apprehended, one enterprising runner grossed $280,000 hauling bait fish from Arkansas to Maine. I know of a guy who lost thousands

Erwin A. Bauer

A golden shiner is an excellent bait for truly big bass.

trying to airlift bait from Florida to California.

Importation of some superbaits is not always illegal, however. Smart bait dealers and anglers stand to glean the rewards when some new irresistible fish fare is made available and proved successful on the local lunkers. All that considered, it's now time to examine the wonder baits of the bass world. I have no doubt that they'd work on largemouths anywhere because artificial imitations of them do. Just remember the names of some favorite lures as you read on.

SALAMANDERS

Salamanders are smooth-skinned amphibians with long tails. They look like lizards but they have no scales or claws. Their skin is moist. Salamanders must stay in or near water.

Some salamanders spend all their lives in water, and others lose their gills and develop lungs. Even those salamanders that develop lungs eventually return to water to spawn, which means they're vulnerable to bass at that time. And, of course, as gilled youngsters they're in the water full time just as true aquatic salamanders are.

Salamanders occur virtually everywhere that bass do, and most (a few emit an undesirable odor) are greedily eaten by largemouths.

It's important to know if you're using a salamander without gills because it must come up for air every so often. The gills on aquatic salamanders are evident as feathery appendages behind the head. Naturally, the gilled critters can stay underwater all the time, though they occasionally come up to gulp air.

A few salamanders have stolen the limelight as bait, but remember that if you can't get the so-called superstars, try others—especially those proven successful on fish other than bass.

Hellbenders—These are squat, ungraceful animals that look something like a hotdog that's been stepped on at both ends. The largest living salamander is the hellbender family. It lives in Japan and grows to a whopping five feet. I fear that casting one might be a chore even on my best two-handed bass rod. Our own hellbenders can grow too large for bass bait, too, but until they reach maximum length (almost 30 inches), largemouths are happy to chew on them. Hellbenders are rascals of American folklore. Fecund ladies luckless enough to gaze upon one of these sluggish things had even chances of delivering a harelipped child—or worse, so the legends went.

There is the common hellbender, often known as a stealer of bait. It has a black-spotted body and throat, and ranges from northern Georgia and Alabama west through central Missouri, and north to southern New England. It is mainly waterbound. Though it does undergo partial metamorphosis, losing its gills, one gill slit may remain open. There also is the Ozark hellbender, whose gill slits usually close as adults. These hellbenders can be gray, black, or dark brown, but they usually are covered with dark-black splotches. They are common in southeastern Missouri and northeastern Arkansas.

Hellbenders have no eyelids, which adds nothing to their physical allure. They usually are found in streams or rivers but frequent ponds as well. They have been unjustly accused of wiping out trout populations. They may be protected in some areas, but where they're not, country boys are fond of turning over flat stones in late summer when hellbender males have dug out nests to lure females for egg laying. Big trout eat small hellbenders and bass eat small and large hellbenders. Even if you take a hellbender from a river and dunk it in a lake where hellbenders don't live, a bass will take it. Hellbenders often are hard to come by, but if you're not squeamish about fooling with them, they'll do you good.

Waterdogs—I'd much rather mess with waterdogs than hellbenders, but the first time I wasn't sure. When somebody invited me to bait up with a waterdog, I thought maybe I was getting into a poacher's picnic. When my new aquaintance said we'd be fishing with waterdogs, I had visions of various retriever breeds I'd seen stalking the shallows to grab any fish that was hooked, and some that weren't. I'd even seen one yellow Lab dive off a bank and do some hunting down about ten feet. He stayed under a long time, too. Imagine my relief when I learned the truth.

Waterdogs are totally aquatic salamanders. They have easily seen plumelike gills. The maximum size for different species ranges from 7¼ inches to more than nine inches. There are Gulf Coast waterdogs, Alabama waterdogs, Neuse River waterdogs, and dwarf waterdogs. They are generally colored brownish to brownish purple to black. Some species have light spots.

Waterdogs became very popular as bass bait in the Western desert lakes. Largemouths love to ambush them when the creatures swim up and then vertically down from the surface. Anglers soon learned to cast them close against steep cliffs and let them drop. You also can work them in slow pumps off the bottom. Just keep them from burrowing into bottom debris. Waterdogs bring high prices during periods when they're hard to get. I've heard of enterprising collectors selling twenty dogs to bass-hungry fishermen in Texas for a neat $100.

In Western bait shops not all salamanders sold as waterdogs, are. Often nongilled salamanders are peddled as the real thing. If you must use an imitation, remember, no gills means you've got to let 'em up sometime. Aquatic salamanders like the waterdog and the allied bait that follows were so named because they were supposed to yip like little dogs. They don't. What they do is give out a little squeak that often turns off first-time fishermen about to impale them on a hook.

Mudpuppies—These aquatic, squeaking salamanders are generally blunter in shape than true waterdogs. Their bodies are flatter. They range from yellowish or reddish brown to dark brown, dark gray, and nearly black. Some have vague, large dark spots. Mudpuppies are generally larger and darker in the North, lighter and smaller in the South.

After mating in autumn, mudpuppies spend most

WATERDOG

of their time on the bottom of a pond or lake, which should give you an idea of how to fish them.

Sirens—The first time I went on a siren hunt was almost my last. Where you catch the eellike creatures with their two nearly useless front legs is in hyacinths. You hunt sirens by wading in these water weeds. As I shuffled along, knowing full well that the weeds were infested with things that could do me harm, the bottom suddenly came alive. Both feet began

SIREN

moving out from under me and I thrashed wildly backward. The piece of bottom that went away could have been only one thing—a snapping turtle. Can you imagine a turtle so big I could stand on it with both feet?

That happened in Georgia. And now when I make a rare siren hunt I wear high wading shoes wtih long trousers tucked into the shoes and nylon straps making sure the pants stay put. I also wear a tight belt around my middle. Where the sirens live in the South, there are also snakes and other squirmy things. You also have to watch for 'gators. Regular siren hunters have a somewhat more cavalier attitude. In the worst story I ever heard concerning these creatures, a siren collector suddenly became aware of something moving around his backside at his waistline. The veteran swamp man stood still and judged from the size of the thing writhing back there that it had to be one thing: a cottonmouth water moccasin. The man simply loosened his belt, letting the snake move up. After determining where its head was from the movement, our dauntless hero reached back under his shirt, grabbed the serpent's tail and threw the creature as far away as he could.

Sometimes a few tackle shops in siren country carry the bait. It's nice to get sirens that way, and get them you should. They are among the very best bass baits. Sirens are different from most other salaman-

ders. They are eellike and are totally aquatic throughout their lives. Sirens have obvious gills and two legs just behind the gills.

True sirens have four fingers while dwarf sirens, which are most commonly used as bait, have only three. There are five races of dwarf sirens, the narrow-striped, Everglades, Gulf Hammock, broad-striped, and slender broad-striped. All grow from six to 8½ inches long. They are found mainly in Florida, Georgia, and South Carolina. Other sirens could be used as bait when they are young, but few anglers have experimented with them. There's the Rio Grande siren in Texas; the Western Lesser in Mississippi, Illinois, and Indiana; the Eastern Lesser found in Mississippi, South Carolina, and Georgia; and the Greater siren, which is located in the coastal plain from Washington, D.C. to southern Alabama south into Florida. All sirens can emit a wretched squeaking sound, and they are much feared by superstitious folk.

The dwarf sirens commonly used for bait are caught with a 2×2-foot-square wood frame that has screening in the bottom. Some fishermen use a partially inflated inner tube strapped to the frame. The collector shoves the screen under the hyacinths and lets it pop up. Trapped clumps of weeds are shaken, so the sirens drop to the screen. The sirens are then placed in a bait container.

They can be trolled, still-fished, cast and worked slowly back. The hardest thing is trying to hold them to hook them. They're more slippery than saltwater eels. I've tried rags, gloves, even a bucket of sand to add grit. You'll see.

CRAYFISH

One of the things that makes all forms of salamanders so effective is that they are instinctive enemies to bass. In spring they devour bass eggs. Largemouths grab salamanders hard to kill them. This antagonism seems to continue throughout the year whenever you present salamanders or sirens to bass. Also, many salamanders and all dwarf sirens tend to burrow in the sand or gravel bottom. During spawning time, bass realize their nests are being torn up by such action. At other times of year I think this frantic digging still triggers strikes.

CRAYFISH

When crayfish are naturally available, bass often choose them to eat over any other forage. The key is availability. Much of the time crayfish are burrowed in the bottom. Studies have shown that largemouths will scorn many other baits if given a crayfish, even when the little crustacean isn't naturally swimming about the fish's territory.

Bass like crayfish for several reasons. They are rich in protein, and when found in the open are easy pickings for largemouths (or smallmouths). Crayfish are just no match in speed for a healthy bass. The end result for the fish is a hearty meal with little effort expended.

The "grass crab" or "paper-shell crab" is the crayfish most favored by bait dealers. As its popular name indicates, this crayfish has a thin shell and is easy for bass to crush. Likewise, recently molted soft-shell crayfish are favored by anglers.

Big bass are suckers for crayfish. Many anglers snip off the pincers of crayfish, but that's unnecessary.

William Roston

Some anglers snip off the pincers to make the crustaceans even more vulnerable to bass, but that doesn't initially make the crayfish weak. My point is that after it has been cast or slow-trolled enough or has been on the hook for some time, the crawdad doesn't have its looking-for-a-place-to-hide action anymore. If unweighted, it won't bother working for the bottom. That's when you must change baits.

Think about how many crankbaits are made to imitate the bottom-puffing flight of a scared crayfish. Think about the fact that the second largest bass on record was caught on a crayfish. Little more needs to be said.

CALEDONIANS

The voice at the other end of the line was that of my old friend Henry LeBlanc. I hadn't heard him so excited since he moved from Vermont to Florida.

"Listen to me," he said. "You want dem bass with the big mouths maybe ten pound? You get over here now."

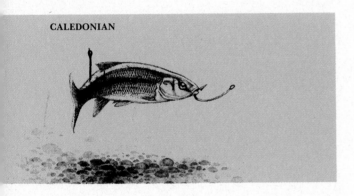

CALEDONIAN

I was in another part of Florida, but had called him to see how things were. Obviously good from the sound of it.

"How are you fishing?" I asked quickly.

"Bait," replied Henry. "I got a bunch of caledonians here and when you come we're goin' to my private lake, eh?"

"You got a bunch of relatives with you then?" I asked, knowing that Henry was from Caledonia County, Vermont, and came from a large French Canadian family.

"Listen," growled Henry. "I don't got so many of them caledonians I can outfit the whole family. You get here and we'll catch the bass on what I got."

I asked him to explain, but still it wasn't clear. He finally told me his bait was also called bullheads so I thought we were going to use those little crayfish. Henry said no. He also said they were sometimes called stoneroller. I figured it had to be the little riffle-loving minnow that's so hardy a bait. Wrong again.

In fact, the caledonian is similar to a stoneroller in shape, but it is not the same thing. Caledonians are native to Florida. They are four- to six-inch-long olive-green minnows with silvery bellies. They are killifish and live in some sand-bottom lakes, and in rivers and swamps. Some anglers seriously feel they ought to be banned as bass bait. The reason, I think, is more the way they are fished in spring rather than the use of the species in general.

Caledonians are seined or caught with tiny No. 18 hooks. Dough balls make good bait for them. In spring spawning season many guides and fishermen in Florida specialize in bed-fishing with the caledonians. Herein lies the controversy.

Nest-guarding largemouths tend to play a cat-and-mouse game with most natural or artificial baits placed near their beds. If a caledonian is tossed in, there's no hesitation. Bass hate caledonians. They'll home in on the little fish and grab them viciously. Too effective, protest some fishermen.

But caledonians are good at other times of year. They're a good secret weapon in the heat of summer when bass are in shallow water, which is most of the time in Florida. I have a feeling they'd do as well elsewhere in summer. Caledonians are tough little critters and can be cast for a long time before requiring replacement. Often they take big bass when not even small largemouths seem to be biting.

GOLDEN SHINERS

Over the years, golden shiners have probably been responsible for more large bass than any other bait. That might not be the case if more of the previously described baits had been used as much as the shiners. Still, the goldens are consistent. Another advantage is that they're available in many areas, though in nowhere near as many places as anglers would like them to be. The minnow ranges from Manitoba and Quebec, over much of the East and down through

SHINER

Florida and Mexico. It has been introduced to the West.

Native shiners often are available at bait shops but true shiner fishing fanatics aren't satisfied unless they catch their own. There are two reasons for that. First, when held in a tank, shiners seem to lose their golden hue. Some fishermen blame the change on the tanks, others on fungicides that commercial operators often put in their tanks. Second is that catching your own usually is the only way to obtain the biggest ones. How big? Lunker specialists in Florida like them from 10 to 12 inches long.

Catching shiners is not hard to do with tiny hooks, cane poles, and dough balls. Many fishermen chum first. Some fishermen make a sport of catching shiners and use small flies. Pound-size shiners are even eaten by some fishermen. You need a two-handed rod to cast shiners and sink the hook and handle

the kind of fish you can expect when using these big minnows.

Big golden shiners can be trolled with or without floats, cast, still-fished with bobbers, and sometimes forced (without bobbers) up under big weed beds. Whatever way you fish, be patient. Bass usually hold and run with these baits, so you must free-spool until your line stops making headway. Then take up all slack. Make sure you're within 45 feet of the bait to avoid too much line stretch, and come on back with everything you've got. Who knows? It could be Big Mamma Mossback on your hook.

The superbaits are no joke, though you might think it from the grins some bait dunkers give when asked how the fishing was. If that happens, you can bet that your nagging suspicions were right again. Give your favorite plug a rest, grab the bait pail, and as they say, go for it!

HOW TO RIG THE SUPER BAITS

SALAMANDERS

Salamanders can be hooked through the lips, nostrils or back. With aquatic salamanders, lip hooking is acceptable. Some salamanders must gulp air through their mouths every ten to fifteen minutes. Nostril hooking allows them to open their mouths to do this. When back-hooking salamanders, be careful not to hit the spine. The tail has good action. Don't hook a salamander there.

SIRENS

Sirens are best lip-hooked or back-hooked. Their mouths are small, so if you choose lip hooking you probably will need a thin wire hook. Don't forget that such hooks are easily bent. A lip-hooked siren is easy to cast. A back-hooked siren presents more air resistance but can be lobbed. Again, be careful of the backbone.

CRAYFISH

Most anglers prefer to hook crayfish in the tail. There are two ways. The simplest method involves pushing the hook from the underside of the tail (about the third segment from the end) straight up and out through the back. In the other method you embed the hook bend and most of the shank in the tail. Only the point sticks out. Start at the end of the tail's underside. Insert the hook point and thread the hook on, going toward the head. These methods somewhat restrict the crayfish, keeping it from backing under cover. If you want your crayfish to have more action, hook it through the back edge of the carapace, the shell segment above the legs. Slip the hook point under the carapace and push it up and out.

CALEDONIANS

For casting and slowly retrieving a caledonian (similar to the way you'd use a plastic worm) hook it up through the lips. For still-fishing with a bobber, hook the bait behind the dorsal fin. This position encourages the caledonian to swim downward. Hooking ahead of the dorsal does not. It also sometimes causes the hook point to turn back into the bait on the set (you rehook the bait, not the bass). Finally, for still-fishing caledonians in pockets on the bottom, hook the minnow just ahead of the tail. Rig a fixed weight about 18 inches up your line. The bait will try to swim away from what's tail-holding him. Don't do a lot of retrieving or the caledonian will drown. You can move the bait but do it slowly.

GOLDEN SHINERS

Shiners can be hooked the same way you'd hook a caledonian. Because you're dealing with a larger bait, naturally a bigger hook must be used. I lip-hook shiners when I troll them slowly along weed edges behind a streamlined bobber so they can't swim deep. For still-fishing beneath a bobber, I hook them behind the dorsal. The pocket-fishing hookup for caledonians also works. Hooks must be matched to bait size. Sizes from 2/0 to 8/0 are used by some anglers, who prefer a short-shanked model such as a saltwater tuna-style hook. To keep the hook from turning and rehooking this big bait on the set, shiner specialists frequently use two tiny rubber or hard plastic washers. You can use the washers included with packages of stinger hooks for spoons or spinnerbaits. Slip a washer on the hook, put on the shiner, then slide on the second washer. Use this trick mainly when lip-hooking shiners.

I Love To Fish With Sally

John Weiss

"It's weird, just plain weird," Bill Parker muttered as he raised and lowered his rod tip with a steady, bass-coaxing rhythm. "I've never fished a bait that you could feel scrambling around on the bottom. Sometimes it even seems as if the creature is trying to climb up my line like a monkey on a string."

I almost started to laugh as I reflected upon Bill's comments because they were the same as my own when I first fished salamanders and newts long ago. Suddenly, I was brought out of my daydreams when Bill's face turned serious and his body tensed.

"Something's happening down there!" he said and gulped. "It feels as if a big bass is violently shaking its head back and forth. But I haven't even set the hook yet!"

"Your sally is going to its great reward," I answered while quickly reeling in my own bait. "Just don't be too anxious. Let the fish run with it."

Seconds later, Bill's fluorescent line stopped twanging and very slowly and purposefully began moving away from the boat. He engaged the gears of his free-spool reel, leaned forward a bit, then quickly swept the rod tip back in a wide arc. Almost instantly, the bass came topside and wallowed in a spray of water, then dove back for the bottom. It was a dandy fish—maybe six pounds. As I reached for the net I saw a smile begin to spread across Bill's face.

We were fishing on Gull Lake in central Minnesota and it was a cooperative effort. It was the first time I'd fished in Gull Lake, and it was the first time my partner had fished with salamanders. This provided us with a good opportunity to try to teach each other a little something.

"Nowadays, salamanders and newts are probably the hottest big-bass baits you can use," I explained. "Putting one on your line charges you up. Every little twitch you see and every little bump you feel rivets your attention on the fishing because you know anything capable of grabbing a bait that is seven inches long is definitely *not* a little fish. This eliminates a whole area of doubt and uncertainty and turns the show into adrenaline-pumping excitement."

William Roston

Dozens of salamander species are native to North America. Nearly all of them effectively catch bass.

John Weiss

Depending upon the area, salamanders may bear a number of nicknames. Call them mudpuppies, waterdogs, spring lizards, chameleons, sirens, or "sallies," but, by any name, they are pure dynamite when it comes to fishing for big bass.

One of the many explanations for their effectiveness is that bass maintain a strong, love/hate relationship with salamanders and newts. When bass are hungry and actively feeding they love the creatures: Salamanders and newts are highly nutritious, large in size, and easy to catch and swallow.

On the other hand, when bass aren't hungry, they despise salamanders and newts, viciously attacking and trying to kill them at every opportunity. Bass seem to instinctively know that they are bothersome nuisances and highly detrimental to their own kind. This is particulary true during the spring and summer when two or three sallies can invade a spawning nest and, in a few minutes, wipe out all the bass eggs or newly hatched fry. I've seen spawning sites in shallow, clear water where the perimeters of the fanned-out beds and fry-rearing areas were littered with bits and pieces of mauled salamanders and newts.

These two attributes of the amphibians—being prime food that bass will not hesitate to try to capture when hungry, and being a threat to eggs and fry that bass will try to kill even when they're not hungry—are super, fish-catching features no other lure or live bait can duplicate.

While salamanders and newts can allow any angler to catch far more big bass than ever before, acquiring and storing the baits, and learning to fish them entails many critical considerations.

There are virtually dozens of salamander species native to North America and nearly all of them effectively catch bass—provided the bait is in its aquatic stage of life.

This is crucial because, just as tadpoles eventually develop into frogs, most salamander species also begin life in water and, at a later stage, change into land-roving creatures. Unlike frogs, however, which bass will eat in any stage of development, salamanders going from an aquatic to a terrestrial stage experience a hormonal change. This causes their skin to begin secreting a noxious substance that repels bass. Although the exact cause of this transformation has not been verified, many scientists believe it takes place when water temperatures suddenly begin to warm and that it's nature's way of ensuring the survival of salamanders from overpredation.

To illustate the importance of this aspect of salamander development, let me give you an example. One day last year, a friend came to my house in a real huff. No, make that *steaming mad*. I'd given him a half-dozen sallies, almost guaranteeing that he'd catch a couple of five-pound bass in a nearby lake. As it happened, he didn't get a nibble all day.

Of course, no one can guarantee fish-catching success, but I was surprised he didn't get at least one nice bass. After doing a little sleuthing, I discovered the problem. My pal had stored his sallies in a pail of water, just as I had instructed, but he had neglected to keep the water very cold. In fact, the water was quite warm and, over a period of only a few days, the sallies had begun to develop into their terrestrial stage of life.

So here are two of the most important tips any angler can heed: First, no matter how you acquire your sallies, or where you buy them, inspect them closely to ensure that they are in their aquatic stage of life. You can do this by checking for three sets of gills along the sides and back of the salamander's head. If the gill slits have disappeared, the amphibians are now in their lung-breathing, land-roving stage of development and are useless for bass fishing.

Second, keep your sallies cold. I've stored them for up to nine months in an old refrigerator in my basement, using a foam cooler with two inches of water in the bottom and several rocks for them to climb upon. If you don't have an old refrigerator, store the cooler in a shaded location and, once a day, add a tray of ice cubes to the water. Be sure to use unchlorinated tap water or, if this is not available, use water from a local stream or lake. Feeding the sallies on a regular basis is not necessary but, if you're going to keep them longer than a month, it is wise to occasionally let them have any minnows left over from a fishing outing. Even dead minnows, which can be obtained free at any bait shop, are suitable.

The least expensive way to obtain sallies and newts is to gather them in shallow streams, ponds, and marshes by scooping them up with a small, fine-mesh dip net. Just after ice-out in early spring, the amphibians swarm into shallow water to breed. The best time to collect them is after dark, using a flashlight. You can easily see them suspended in the water's surface film near vegetation and sitting on moss and rocks along the banks. Don't be afraid to handle sallies and newts. They don't bite and none of the North American species are poisonous. Do check your local laws, though, to see if any regulations pertain to gathering them.

Another good place to obtain free salamanders and newts is your state's various hatchery facilities. These creatures often become a serious problem at hatcheries because they like to invade holding tanks and rearing ponds to eat the small fry being raised for stocking. As a result, biologists will invariably let you gather all the sallies and newts you want. Call your state's fish department to find out the phone number of the hatchery nearest you.

Another option is to buy your bait. Check with your local bait shop; if your dealer doesn't customarily stock them, he may be able to order them. There are also bait dealers that specialize in shipping salamanders around the country. The sallies are put into heavy-duty plastic bags partially filled with water and then shipped directly to your door by United Parcel Service. One such bait company is Live Bait Unlimited, Box 2501, Baxter, MN 56425; or call (218) 829-1656.

Salamanders and newts are more expensive than any other live bait. This is due to the time and effort involved in catching and properly storing them. Yet the relatively high cost is offset by the fact that they consistently dredge up bigger bass than you can imagine. Salamanders and newts are quite hardy and it takes a bass a good deal of effort to kill one. This means you can often catch several nice bass on one bait before having to put on a new "dog."

The one instance in which sallies and newts don't last long is when anglers are fishing where there are toothy fish such as muskies, northern pike, and walleyes. These gamefish love sallies, too, but, naturally, when they chomp down upon a sally with their razor-sharp teeth, it's lights out for that bait.

There are other safeguards to preserving your

sally or newt. Never cast them, because repeatedly slapping the baits against the surface of the water will kill them. Instead, pay out line from your reel so the bait gently sinks straight down directly beneath the boat, then drift-fish or troll slowly. Many anglers also make the mistake of hooking a sally or newt through both lips, as they would a live minnow. This greatly impairs the amphibians' ability to work their gills, so hook them through the nostrils, which they use only for smelling, not for breathing.

There is no magic place in a body of water to fish sallies and newts. As with any type of lure or bait, astute anglers should take into consideration the time of year and the weather and water conditions, then make educated guesses as to where the bass should be. There are a few places, nevertheless, that seem to pay off more consistently than others.

One such spot is the outside edge of thick weed beds that blanket the surface, where the depth of the water abruptly drops off. From late spring through the fall, these conditions can be found on almost any lake or reservoir and they are tailor-made to the needs of big bass: The weedline offers countless ambush locations; the overhead shade offers relief from the bright sun; and, if anything spooks the fish, they've got a ready escape into nearby deep water.

Tark Williams and I like to position our boat about five or six feet from the edge of a lengthy weed line, especially where the water depth drops from about eight feet to 20 or more feet deep. Using a sculling paddle or electric motor, we very slowly follow the winding contour of the weed bed, letting our sallies swim as close to the edge of the weeds as possible.

Sallies and newts are relatively heavy baits but more weight must be added to prevent them from swimming to the top. This means rather heavy line, such as 15- to 17-pound test, is required. Rods should be stiff and should have limber, sensitive tips with plenty of backbone to adequately handle big fish.

When working a sally or newt along the bottom, manipulating the rod tip is extremely important. If the bait is given too much slack line and freedom, it will try to hide under rocks, logs, and other bottom debris. Gently raising and lowering the rod tip every ten seconds prevents this and keeps the bait in clear view of any bass that may be lying in wait. The combination of the amphibian's four legs continually going and its strong, whiplike tail, which works just like an alligator's tail, produces a lively enticement big bass just can't refuse.

Tark and I were once exploring the edge of a weed line with our sallies when Tark's line suddenly began vibrating like a banjo string. This is usually the first evidence of a bass trying to kill a sally before attempting to swallow it and it's generally best to give a bit of slack line so the bass doesn't feel resistance and drop the bait. That's exactly what Tark did, and then the line began suddenly cutting a sharp V

through the water, straight in the direction of my sally several yards away.

"Uh-oh," I said and gasped. "I didn't count on this."

Sure enough, seconds later my own line began quivering, but there was no choice but to play the waiting game. An instant later, Tark and I both reared back on our rods and together played the seven-pound bass that was hooked with both sallies in its huge mouth. It was the first and only time I've ever seen a bass take one angler's bait, then rush to take his partner's, as well. All of which shows the lengths that a bass will go to catch and eat sallies.

Another prime place to fish sallies and newts is where there are stumps on the bottom in 10 to 12 feet of water. This is ideal because vertically working any kind of lure or bait directly beneath the boat is the only way to prevent repeated snags. In late summer, and throughout the fall, I also like to work steep, shoreline points that guard the entrances to backwater coves and embayments. Such points, typically, have one side that gently slopes and another that drops off sharply. I've noticed that, during the summer, bass seem to like the gradually tapering side but, as the water turns colder, they immediately switch to the steeper side.

At certain times of year, and in certain areas, salamanders and newts may not be available. Properly caring for sallies and newts when you're fishing away from home also may pose an inconvenience you don't care to endure. When this is the case, I still like to take advantage of these critters' inherent, fish-catching characteristics by using sally look-alikes made from plastic or pork.

Plastic salamanders are made from the same polyvinyl-chloride materials as plastic worms and, at times, they can work as well as real sallies. Rig and fish the imitations exactly as you would worms, by threading a sliding sinker onto your line, tying on a 3/0 or 4/0 hook, then imbedding the hook into the plastic sally Texas-style to make the lure weedless.

Pork lizards are equally effective because they have the feel and texture of real meat. Most anglers prefer to rig these baits in conjunction with some type of leadhead jig.

Pork and plastic sallies and newts are rigged to be weedless, so you can work them in the thickest, most foreboding cover you might chance upon.

One major difference when working pork and plastic look-alikes is that you have to set the hook the very moment you sense that a bass has inhaled it. If you allow a bass to mouth the bait and run, as is customary when fishing live sallies and newts, the fish will quickly discover that it has been duped by a counterfeit and will spit out the lure.

This is bass fishing's newest and most exciting wrinkle. One that's sure to add a dimension to any angling adventure. Catch lunkers with this unique bait and you'll love to fish with sallies, too.

Worming Techniques Of The Pros

Al Ristori

Talk to ten experts about fishing plastic worms and you'll likely get ten different opinions on how to rig them, whether to fish them slow or fast, strike quickly or let 'em run, etc. There are few rights and wrongs. It's basically a matter of what works for you in your area. In this article some of the top bass fishermen in the country will give their ideas on how to use worms. You won't recognize many famous names in the group I've assembled. These anglers aren't national tournament pros. However, they are expert in their own areas and I'm sure, if given the opportunity, would fish with the best of the national pros on any waters. The techniques they use are often divergent but since they all work well under the conditions the expert is fishing in they deserve your consideration. Try them all and see if you don't come up with something that just might turn your season around!

STANDARD WORMING

Will Whitehead of Hagerstown, Maryland, one of that state's finest bass anglers, summarizes the usual methods and touches on some variations that may make the difference on any given day.

"I imagine there are as many ways to fish a plastic worm as there are worms, but I have settled on the methods that have produced best for me. Under certain conditions, different methods produce best and I am constantly changing to find out what bass want on a particular day.

"The most important item in plastic-worm fishing is tackle. While a plastic worm may be fished on just about any type of rod-and-reel combination, the efficiency and success of fishing them will be greatly multiplied by the right outfit. First, you need a good stiff worm rod from 5½ to 6½ feet in length. The stiff rod will allow you to feel the worm over the bottom and transmit the slightest tap to your senses. It will also allow you to drive the point of the hook home and enable you to haul that lunker out of cover in a hurry. Level-wind bait-casting reels are by far the best for worming. For line you want a good monofilament with little stretch and memory characteristics. I use 15- to 20-pound line, 25-pound test at times. Admittedly, this is heavy line, but when you are wormin', your lure is right down there in 'Hawg Haven.' That means you'll be fishing in, over and around logs, brush, rocks, and weeds. To be successful you'll have to haul that eight-pounder out of there in a hurry, before he has your line tangled around something. If you think my tackle is too heavy and unsportsmanlike—so be it. Personally I'd rather be unsporting, and land a nice bass for release than have it swim around with a hook lodged in its throat because my tackle was too light!

"After deciding upon color I always start off with a large worm eight to nine inches long. A worm this size calls for a 4/0 or 5/0 worm hook and a three-eighth-ounce slip-sinker. The slip-sinker is placed on the line, pointed end toward the rod. The hook is then tied on using a Palomar or improved clinch knot. Next the point of the hook is inserted in the head of the worm and brought out about one-half inch back. The hook is pulled into the worm until the eye and knot are inside the worm head. Turn the hook over and insert the point and barb back into the body of the worm. You now have a weedless and snagless Texas rig. At times when the bottom is thickly tangled with logs and brush I will lock the sinker against the worm head by placing a bit of toothpick in the sinker hole. Your worm is now ready for action.

This article originally appeared in *Secrets of the Pros* (published by Athletic Activities Publishing Co., Paterson, NJ), and was updated for *Fishing World* magazine.

Photo by William Roston

Regardless of the specific technique used, all the anglers interviewed for this article agree that the plastic worm is very attractive to bass, which come right in to take the bait.

"I normally use a slow, steady retrieve, inching the worm along bottom, actually feeling my way along as the sinker slides over rocks, logs, and brush. With a little practice you'll be able to tell just what the worm is doing down there. I cast out to likely looking spots such as overhanging limbs, brush, or bottom structure, letting my lure fall to bottom on a slack line. When it has settled to bottom (if it makes it that far), I take up slack, hold my rod vertically in front of my nose, and s-l-o-w-l-y turn the reel handle to crawl the worm over bottom. When a bass spots that plastic worm inching along the bottom he just has to take it. You might feel a hard rap or a gentle tap-tap or your line may just stop. I quickly lower my rod tip, pointing it at the bass, and stretch my arms out as far as I can reach. This action will give the bass about six to eight feet of slack line and he should move off with the worm in his mouth. When he reaches the end of the slack that's all he gets! I rear back, raising the rod tip, and sock that hook through

the worm and into his bony jaw. Unfortunately, there are those days when this method won't produce. The worm may be too large, the line too heavy or the fish are just mouthing the lure and not inhaling the worm. It's time for a change in tactics.

"If the bass are feeding near the surface, I will rig my worm the same as before but without any sinker. This will allow me to cast out and swim the worm along the surface like a snake or lizard.

"Other times the bass will seem to pick up the worm and just play with it or follow it to the boat and not hit. Now is the time to switch to a four-or six-inch worm. I work this smaller worm on lighter tackle (eight- to 10-pound line) and make up for the relative lack of hook-setting ability by changing the worm rigging. Rather than a large hook buried in the worm, I use a No. 1 or No. 2 hook with a wire weedguard. The small hook is rigged as previously described but the hook point is left exposed (protected by the weedguard). A split shot just sufficient to sink the worm is placed about six inches above the hook and the rig is fished on bottom exactly the same as the larger worm.

"Another retrieve method is to let your worm settle on bottom, lower the rod tip, take up slack line, and raise the rod tip slowly, jigging the worm off bottom. Lower the rod tip, allowing the worm to fall back to bottom, then repeat the process all the way back to the boat. When a pick-up is felt, give him a little running slack and then bust him. I may get some argument on my methods from other wormin' men but that is what works best for me. Some say to strike as soon as a pick-up is felt, others prefer to let a bass run with the worm and count to ten. These methods may be all right and I'm not saying they're not, however I've never met a worm fisherman who connected with 100 percent of his pick-ups—and I don't either. Then again, I don't miss any more than the next guy.

"Another trick I use at times is to slide a rubber skirt on the line before I tie my hook on. After the worm is rigged, the sinker will hold the skirt against the worm head and it will add a good bit of action and attraction.

"Plastic worms may be double rigged by tying a short length of mono to the eye of the hook in the head and tying the other end to another hook. That second hook is embedded Texas style into the tail section of the worm. Obviously this rigging will interfere with the worm's action but often it's the only way to deal with short strikers."

"SPEED" WORMING

Most experts like to fish plastic worms slowly. However, just as there is more than one way to skin a cat, there are many ways to work a worm. If you never vary your method, you just may be passing up something that will make all the difference on any given day.

Butch Hudkins was a top guide in the Broken Bow, Oklahoma, area before becoming a manufacturer's representative. His opinion of the "slow retrieve and let 'em run" school is low.

"I fish a worm fast! By fast I mean using the lightest weight I can to get the worm to bottom and then skipping it back with a medium retrieve, taking in a long sweep of line by raising the rod tip straight up and shaking the devil out of it all the time. I then quickly lower my rod and take out all the slack, then repeat the process. I usually only stop the worm for just a second, one or two times on each retrieve, to make sure I'm still close to bottom. The bass are normally not right on bottom but suspended beside or above the deep brush close to the bottom. I try to keep my rod tip high at all times in order to see the line better and detect the slightest tap. The tip only goes down when I'm taking in slack. I hit my bass as soon as I feel that telltale tap by very quickly reeling my uplifted rod to the horizontal. The bass usually inhales the entire worm at once. If you wait on him, he is either going to spit it out or tie it to a

snag. So on the first tap I rapidly reel down to him and cross his eyes.

"Always keep that worm hopping, skipping, or jumping along. Make it look alive, not like a half-dead snail. There is very little fish appeal in a slow-working worm that is merely sliding along bottom. Another mistake many 'experts' make is to use very heavy line. You can't feel a tap as well with heavy line and the increased drag means you either have to use a heavier sinker or waste valuable fishing time while the light sinker works its way to bottom. In my opinion a 15- to 17-pound line will get more strikes in the clear lakes of Oklahoma, Arkansas, and Texas."

To prove his point, Butch just missed the Oklahoma state record in 1973 when he hooked an 11-pound two-ounce bass on a six-inch worm and boated it on ten-pound mono!

WORMING DEEP WATER

Butch Harris of Charlotte, North Carolina, is a member of The International Fishing Hall of Fame and a very well-known bass angler in the mid-South. While it's easier to find bass-holding structure in shallow water, Butch advises that the surest way to consistent stringers is to work the depths. Here's how the old master does it.

"In all my fishing years the best method I've come up with is the jig with pork-rind tail or plastic worm. The worm is by far the cheaper and will work as well as the pork rind. I have found that bass spend just about all of their lives in very deep water, even up to 70 feet deep, and have caught a lot of bass at the hottest time of year in such depths.

"The way I jig fish is to find the river channels or creek channels with a depth sounder and then fish just along the drop-offs, cast the jig, let it go to bottom, and then give it a few jumps. By this I mean raise it off bottom a few feet and then let it settle to the bottom again. The strikes will come as the jig is going back down to the bottom. Colors aren't critical. Indeed, I've caught bass with all colors on the very same day. If you've mastered the technique of using the jig and worm, any color will do the job. The only exception may be under drastically different water conditions.

"Once you find where the bass are schooled in the deep holes, you may be able to put several on the stringer before the rest spook. Get your hooked bass off bottom quickly and you may be able to fill a limit without moving. Be sure to take ranges on holes that produce and fish them every time you try the lake. You may not find bass there every time but sooner or later they will return.

"Bass will often hit a jig and worm with enthusiasm in the middle of the day. I don't know why but I have caught some of my largest bass in July when the sun was high. One big change in this fishing I've noted in recent years has been the tendency of bass to strike better on small worms. I've switched from using six-, seven-, and eight-inch worms to the four-inch size."

WEIGHTLESS WORMING

Another common assumption about plastic worms is that they are strictly a bottom bait. "It ain't necessarily so!" Bass are often suspended at mid-water depths in lakes, while in the shallows they're looking up for their food rather than down.

Mike Murphree of Macon, Georgia, points out the advantage of using a small slip-sinker so the worm may sink slowly. Shake the worm as it descends and pay close attention to your line for any sign of movement. If the line twitches, reel in the slack and set the hook immediately. This is especially deadly in lakes if you spot schooling bass on your depth sounder or graph recorder.

Maurice Fitzgerald of Metaire, Louisiana, has a real problem in his home water. During the mid-summer period vegetation gets so thick that it virtually closes off productive waters. In order to get into such areas local anglers use flat-bottom boats (powered by air-cooled inboard engines) which will skim right over the grass. Next problem is to catch the bass that lurk in the shade of lily pads. Even most weedless lures get ensnarled on every cast into this jungle. Therefore Maurice uses a spinning reel to cast a weightless plastic worm rigged Texas style directly on top of a pad. He then eases the worm off the pad. If Mr. Bass is there he's not likely to hesitate! For this fishing you need stout line to get the bass away from the lily-pad roots and yet must be able to make accurate casts with a virtually weightless lure. That dictates the need for spinning tackle.

The use of weightless worms is common in Florida. Try it in the pepper-grass beds of Lake Okeechobee when the bass are just swirling at your plugs or spoons. When boating conditions aren't right in the Everglades, Ray Borlie of Fort Lauderdale eases into water less than five feet deep and starts wading. Shorts and tennis shoes will do the job in this warm water and Ray has found that the alligators and water moccasins are just as afraid of him as he is of them! Ray describes his method as follows.

"When the fish aren't biting or it's too windy to use the electric trolling motor, or the temperature is dropping, or a front is passing through—don't quit fishing and go home. First check the depth of the water. If less than five feet deep, tie up the boat and start wading. I carry extra worms and hooks in my hat and hook a stringer to my shorts. The tackle consists of a six-foot worm rod, heavy-duty bait-casting reel, and 20-pound line. I use a 9¼-inch worm rigged weedless and without a sinker. This method is good when fishing in weeds, lily pads, or any heavy cover. Cast the worm to a likely looking spot and reel the worm back on top of the water. Don't reel too fast but fast enough so the worm won't *sink*. The worm wiggles back and forth like a snake. Set the hook as soon as the fish hits. Work him hard so he doesn't get to the bottom but if he does, simply walk

over and get him out. Once the fish is tired bring him alongside you. Put your hand under his belly and you can hold the fish until you get him on the stringer. He won't flop around when you hold him in that fashion. This method is fast and you can cover a lot of water wading. The worm is always in the water. I have caught hundreds of bass using this method both wading and out of a boat, but wading produces better results."

Gene Hulcher of Jacksonville is another advocate of surface worming. Following are his three favorite techniques.

"On that dream trip to Florida remember that much of the water is shallow by other state-reservoir standards. Try using a one-sixteenth-ounce weight about six inches in front of your weedless worm. Secure it with a toothpick and trim off the excess. Fish the worm over grass beds and at the eges of lily pads in jerks just as you would fish a floating minnow plug. The jerks against the weight cause the worm to whiplash back and forth. The light weight will not sink the worm into the grass rapidly and bass love the little eellike movements. This works best with 7¼-inch worms but is also used on worms up to 10 inches. It is best to use at least 20-pound line."

Another favorite trick of the Florida boys is to use a six- to eight-inch floating worm with a 3/0 Aberdeen hook threaded into the worm until it exits at the egg sac. When fished without a weight on about 12-pound line, this floater will slay fish in five to six feet of water.

Still another Florida trick is the spinning or swimming worm. Attach a barrel swivel to your line and about five to 18 inches of leader to the other end of the swivel. Tie on a No. 4 or No. 2 bait-holder hook. Then thread on a six-inch worm so that the head is about 1½ to two inches up the line above the hook eye and the point exits the worm with the worm following the bend of the hook. Cast and reel in so it spins, and hang on!

Owen Chaney of Orange Park also likes to work a weightless worm far back into the grass and pads. However, Owen also points out another facet of worm fishing that's often overlooked: "It's a great lure for slow trolling!"

SPECIAL CONDITIONS

An entire article could be written about how to fish worms under particular circumstances. Here are just a few examples.

Ever try to fish a cove completely covered with vegetation, particulary the gooey type that fouls up the most weedless of lures? Bob Mareno of West Mifflin, Pennsylvania, has to fish under those conditions every summer but manages to take some nice fish by using a special technique. The rigging is a Texas-rigged six- to seven-inch worm with a toothpick in the bullet sinker to prevent it from moving. The sinker is either ⅜ or ½ ounce and if cast into that mess in ordinary fashion will just lie on top of the weeds, algae, etc. The trick is to rifle the rig into that cover so it breaks through the surface slop. A jigging motion then will often result in a smashing strike from a lunker bass. Of course, heavy tackle is a must in this fishing.

Terry Barnes of Davidson, North Carolina, is an expert at working brush piles. He should be—he makes his own! Terry plants Christmas trees underwater every season, though he concedes that field pines are really better. He makes his sets in water both shallow (10 to 12 feet) and deep (20 to 30 feet). When the dog days of summer come around Terry always has some honey holes that never fail. Best lure for working these brush piles is a worm rigged Texas style with a ¼-ounce bullet sinker. Terry casts beyond the pile and then lifting the rod tip only about a foot at a time brings the worm to the pile. He slowly works the worm over the pile with the rod, not winding in. If the fish is in the one-to-three-pound class he will *tap* it. Terry drops his rod tip, reels up the slack, and hits him within two seconds. Bass over three pounds usually don't tap—watch your line where it meets the water for a slight *ping* or movement to one side or twitch. If that happens drop your rod tip, reel up the slack, and hit that lunker hard!

If weed is thick on the bottom and your worm is obviously getting lost in the mess, try the method used by Donnie Vestal of Kirksville, Missouri. Donnie wedges the sinker to the line about 12 to 14 inches above the hook with a tiny split shot. This permits the floating worm to work above the weeds in view of any bass.

Ron Yurko of Conneaut, Ohio, not only catches over 2,000 bass a year in his area, but has also established an enviable record in local tournaments: first or second in sixteen out of twenty-two fished in the space of three years. Ron has lots of suggestions about fishing worms, but the most interesting is something that should be obvious. It is simply to fish in the opposite direction from everyone else. On lakes that are fished primarily from boats, the "survivors" may be wise to a worm being worked from shore back to the boat as most anglers do. If the standard procedure isn't working, try moving the boat in close to shore and casting out.

WORM PERFUME

There has been much discussion in recent years about the effect of human odors on lures. Some feel that such smells can ruin the effectiveness of a lure and a number of preparations have been devised to overcome this problem. Beyond that, certain odors are reputed to be so attractive to bass that they just can't turn down anything reeking of that particular oil. I'm sure the debate about odors will go on forever but let's look into a couple of tricks you might want to try.

Clyde Payne of Wichita, Kansas, has a unique home remedy for human odor on worms that applies a little scent at the same time.

"Keep a baby-food jar of toothpicks and cotton in your tackle box soaked in anise oil and anise extract with a small hole punched in the lid. This will let the anise odor permeate the tackle box and overcome human odor on everything in the box. The toothpicks, of course, are for worm fishing. Push them through the hook eye and worm to hold the worm on the hook better and clip off excess or use them to wedge a bullet head to worm head by inserting toothpick point in the hole of the weight, thereby wedging line to weight. The toothpick pieces serve to overcome any human odor on the worm. The best formula I have found for this is two ounces of anise extract and one ounce of anise oil. The extract is available in grocery-store flavoring departments and the anise oil in drug stores. The reason for mixing them is that anise oil will congeal badly in cold weather. However, the extract has an alcohol base and prevents this from occurring. Anise oil has a softening effect on many plastic items. Keep it in a sealed glass jar so it won't leak out. A baby food jar will hold a box of round toothpicks stood on end and some cotton. Pour in three ounces of anise mix and in a few days the toothpicks and cotton will absorb it all. Then you can punch a small hole in the lid, put it in the box, and it won't spill. It works just like *Airwick* and if it dries out too much just add some more mix."

Will Whitehead is also a believer in anise oil. Will's procedure is as follows:

"I remove newly puchased worms from their package and wash them in a solution of warm water and a mild liquid detergent, removing the foreign and human odor. These worms are then laid on paper toweling to dry and placed in a container of anise oil overnight. Upon removing them from this container they are placed in my tackle box trays still dripping with the anise. Keep each color and length separate. Bass, I feel, have a keen sense of smell and I have found that there is a marked difference in the way they will take a worm that has been prepared this way as compared to one straight from the package. I smoke and therefore rub anise oil on my hands periodically while fishing to kill the tobacco odor as well as my human odor."

CONCLUSION

Perhaps the main point to be learned from all this is that the artificial worm may be worked in many different ways and will still produce big stringers of bass. The real secret appears to be the skill, time, and patience devoted to the method. One recurring theme has been the proper-size worm for various conditions but few of the local experts I talked to were much stuck on color. We didn't even get into the many new variations on the basic worm as, once again, the experts felt it was skill not a new type of worm that was the key to success. Give some of these techniques a try this year and see if there isn't one there that will work for you. If it does, let me know about it; I'm always anxious to learn more about bass fishing from new experts as well as veterans!

Mr. Spinnerbait's Secrets

Jack T. Lewis

It's been twenty-three years since I used my first spinnerbait, but that experience was so profitable I'll never forget it. The bait was a purple Tarantula that weighed a full half-ounce, had a shiny nickel blade, a round head, and a skirt made of individually hand-tied rubber bands. In just one day of fishing the Tarantula in a small lake near my home in San Antonio, Texas, I caught five large-mouth bass, and the smallest weighed more than six pounds.

Until then I'd fished almost entirely with plastic worms in deep water. I'd even come to think that big bass rarely entered shallow water. But after that first experience with a spinnerbait, I got serious about using the odd-looking lures. Soon I learned that big bass in my part of the country can be found year-round in very shallow water—about three feet deep—except when it's extremely cold. The spinnerbait has become the main ammunition in my bass-

fishing arsenal, and the lure has treated me well in tournament fishing as well as in fishing for fun. I began to use spinnerbaits so often and to catch so many bass on them that my peers began calling me Mr. Spinnerbait.

My love affair with spinnerbaits led me to a detailed study of them. I think that much of what I've learned could help you catch more bass.

Nobody knows how the first spinnerbait was invented, but many fishermen suspect that the first one was made from a safety pin. Hence, the name safety-pin lure or safety-pin spinner. Now spinnerbaits are used wherever black bass exist, and many colors, sizes, and designs are made.

One of the main differences in design concerns the loop to which the line is tied. One kind of loop, called the inside loop, looks like the springy end of a safety pin. The outside loop is made by twisting the spinnerbait wire over itself. The wire does not

This collection of spinnerbaits shows the wide variety of colors, sizes, and designs.

cross itself in the open loop. The open loop is the only one of the three designs that you can use without having the fishing line become wedged between sections of wire. You must check the other two kinds of loops occasionally to make sure the line is free. You won't land many big bass if you're using a line that is frayed or pinched.

The leadheads also vary in size and shape. The most popular sizes are ¼, ⅜, and ½ ounce. There are three basic shapes—round, bullet, and pointed. The choice depends on your fishing style.

Novice fishermen can be satisfied with a round or bullet shape because they use the lures only in open water, and the only "feel" they're concerned with is that of a fish grabbing hold. The round head can drive you crazy if you retrieve it over and through brush, logs, or rocks. That's because when a round head hits a rock or log you feel a sudden jolt that is almost impossible to tell from a fish's strike. So when you feel a jolt you naturally set the hook. If the jolt was caused by a fish, the action begins. But sometimes you have a snag, and then you might ask yourself: How am I going to get my $2 spinnerbait out of the old stump?

This isn't to say that round-head spinnerbaits are poorly designed. They're excellent when retrieved around, over, or beside a structure, but never in or through it. The pointed head is better suited for those uses. Its design allows it to cut the air and water cleanly. Because it's perfectly in line with the keel arm, the pointed leadhead virtually slides over structure with hardly a quiver. Get the picture? Now, when that tap comes, you know what's happening.

A bullet head slides over brush more easily than a round head but not as easily as a pointed head. Almost all the best spinnerbaits today have pointed heads.

Experienced anglers know that to be successful in fishing they must fish structure of all types. After many years of spinnerbait experience, I think the ultimate design has been achieved and that this design is the "best."

Spinnerbaits are most often used in water ranging from six inches to six feet deep. Consequently, you can use them year-round, with the possible exceptions of December, January, and February if you live north of the Mason-Dixon line. I believe that the widespread introduction of Florida bass eventually will abolish the theory that in cold weather you should fish deep. The Floridas' shallow-water heritage may cause them to frequent the shallows often, even during winter's coldest periods.

No matter how good shallow-water fishing gets, successful spinnerbait anglers must know how to use the lures and how to modify them for improved performance. I think a spinnerbait's skirt should be trimmed to a quarter of an inch behind the bend of the hook. This helps eliminate short strikes. My ideal spinnerbait features this modification as well as a small willow-leaf blade attached to the hook with steel split rings and a ball-bearing swivel. This "teaser" is kept on the hook by adding a small piece of plastic

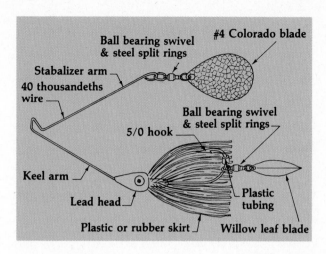

tubing ahead of it. The only other change made is a shortening of the stabilizer arm. That change allows the spinner blade to extend about half an inch beyond the bend of the hook. This is one of my most important modifications. It virtually eliminates roll over on fast retrieves and makes short strikes a rarity.

The single most important component of the spinnerbait is the ball-bearing swivel. Always insist on American-manufactured swivels. These swivels allow the blades to spin from the minute they hit the water until you lift them out again. The rhythmic throbbing beat of the spinner blade is the signal that tells you what's going on beneath the surface.

Once you manage a feel for this beat, you have mastered the major part of spinnerbait fishing. This feel can even tell you when a fish has made a pass at your lure. The current created by a fish moving toward the lure and then turning away will change the beat of the blade. The next cast to the same spot should produce a fish.

Positive anticipation works wonders in bass fishing. One particular strike is called the nothing strike. When retrieving and feeling the rhythmic beat of the blade, you suddenly feel nothing. And, unless you set the hook fast, you will get nothing! This feel is created by the bass taking the entire lure into its mouth while swimming directly toward you at the same speed you're retrieving. Don't get the idea that you have a strike anytime this occurs. Sometimes a piece of grass or moss will tangle in the blade or swivel and stop its revolutions, thus creating the same effect. Set the hook anyway. You could be in for a pleasant surprise. Nothing strikes seem to produce larger bass than ordinary.

There is another strike to watch for during "drop" fishing, which happens when you're allowing the lure to sink. Keep your eye on the line where it enters the water. When the blade helicopters as the lure sinks, a bass may take the spinnerbait and move off. Such fish will swim to the right, to the left, or toward you, but seldom will it move away from you. Since you drop a spinnerbait on a slack line you hardly ever feel a strike, but if your line quivers or twitches, set the hook: Do not hesitate or you'll come up empty. This illustrates why you see the word *concentration* so often in fishing articles. You must think strike on every cast. If you can do that, you'll definitely put more fish in the boat.

Buzzing is one of the most popular ways to fish a spinnerbait during spring and fall. Do it by reeling fast enough to keep the blade just beneath the surface. The spinning blade will make a slight V-shaped wake. It's a very exciting way to fish because you see the strikes. Many times you see bass moving after the lure from as much as five feet away. That kind of action really tests your composure. The half-ounce spinnerbait with a No. 4 Colorado blade and a willow-leaf teaser has proved to be my best combination for buzzing.

My favorite color combination for most of my fishing is a chartreuse skirt and a hammered-gold blade. For a trailer I use a chartreuse twister-tail or a small gold willow leaf. I prefer a hammered blade to a smooth one for two reasons. A hammered blade reflects light much better than a slick blade. But most important is the feel created by the hammered surface spinning against the water.

In the clear water of rocky-bottomed lakes or streams, a chartreuse-and-white skirt and a silver blade produce well.

When smallmouth fishing, try a brown skirt and a copper blade combination for some fast action. Jason Mullins, now retired from the Air Force and living in New York state, says the quarter-ounce spinnerbait with a No. 2 blade really turns the brown bass on.

In sandy-colored waters, try a white skirt and a silver blade. It seems to glow in this kind of water. Use a white curly-tail or small silver willow leaf as a trailing teaser.

During December, January, and February bass hang around heavy, deep structure such as stumps, logs, and rocks. One of my favorite spinnerbaits for this period has a black skirt, a silver blade, and a black pork lizard. Always trim away most of the fat where the lizard is impaled on the hook. This improves the hooking odds on strikes.

Heavily overcast days often present problems in selecting colors that offer high visibility. I've found that a chartreuse skirt, a chartreuse blade, and a chartreuse curly-tail combination seems to fill the bill. It's very effective in the fall when buzzed on the surface early and late in the day.

Often nothing seems to produce. This occurs during two prime fishing periods, spring and fall. Heavy rainfall and the resulting runoff causes the problem. No matter what color combinations are tried you normally strike out. After considerable trial and error, I have come up with a winner. Try a fuchsia-and-yellow skirt with an orange blade. It's tough on the eyes but, believe me, it produces!

Here are a couple of rigging tips. Try replacing the Colorado spinner blade with a willow leaf, which works well when retrieved fast. Have you ever wondered why bass strike these odd-looking creations? Many fishermen say bass think spinnerbaits are crayfish. Or do bass, being the gluttons they are,

simply strike the skirted leadhead to keep that spinning blade just above from eating it first? No one really knows, of course, but one fact is clear—the blade is hardly ever hit.

Many spinnerbaits are made with tandem blades. This is done by adding an extra blade on the stabilizer arm with a small clevis. It's normally a smaller blade. The thinking is that two blades produce more flash and sound than one. Perhaps, but it also kills the rhythmic beat of the main blade, and this beat is much more important than flash or sound. What causes the change in beat? Simple—the smaller blade spinning just ahead of the large blade creates a vortex, causing the large blade to wobble rather than revolve smoothly. To eliminate the problem, just cut the clevis with a pair of wire cutters and remove it and the blade.

Most blades eventually tarnish or become discolored. I've found that polishing them with silver cleaner or chrome polish restores their original brightness. Remember, the brighter the blades the more sunlight they reflect. Spinnerbaits normally are used in one- to six-foot depths, but occasionally you might want to use them in deeper water when fishing dam ripraps or rocky ledges. When using a half-ounce spinnerbait in deep water, I've had success by replacing the No. 4 or 5 standard blade with a smaller No. 2½ blade. The smaller blade allows the lure to sink faster, but most important, keeping the lure deep is easier when the blade is small. Larger blades make a spinnerbait rise too fast.

An important part of a spinnerbait is its skirt. Through the years, we've gone from skirts made of squirrel tail to "living" rubber. Bucktail, nylon, plastic, and rubber are the most popular materials used to make skirts. Bucktail or squirrel tail is good almost anytime, but you can't get vivid colors in them. Nylon and plastic come in almost any color imaginable and are tough and durable. They also have plenty of built-in action except in winter. When water temperatures drop below 60 degrees, synthetic skirts get stiff and lose their pulsating action. This is where the living-rubber skirts excel. The thin bands of colored rubber pulsate continuously, no matter how hot or cold the water. For the best flaring action, all skirts should be put on the leadhead in reverse. Most spinnerbait manufacturers do this, but you might find some that don't.

Here's a suggestion that will keep your skirts fluffy and flared. Many tackle boxes feature spinnerbait hangers that are slotted panels usually made of plastic. They're designed to hold spinnerbaits by the V-shaped wire. A lure's skirt hangs on one side of a panel while the spinner blade hangs on the other side. When stored in this way, the skirt eventually becomes limp and loses its flare. I hang my spinnerbaits by their hooks instead. This allows the skirt to hang limp until I use it. This flaring action of a skirt is vital to good spinnerbait fishing.

Spinnerbaits are year-round lures, and only continued use of them will give you the confidence and success enjoyed by many anglers.

How To Fish Crankbaits, Jigs And Jigging Spoons

John Weiss

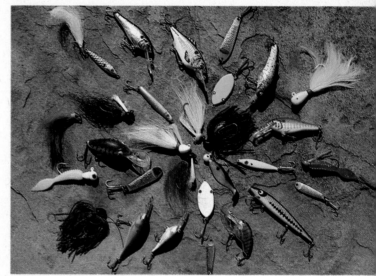

Photos by the author
For those intermediate depths unsuited to plastic worms or spinnerbaits, savvy bass fishermen rely on crankbaits, jigs or jigging spoons.

If plastic worms and spinnerbaits are the first and second choices among savvy bass anglers, then crankbaits, jigs, and jigging spoons undeniably are the third most popular lures.

Although there are exceptions, in a majority of cases plastic worms are intended to be fished in relatively deep water while spinnerbaits are preferred for fishing the shallows. That leaves a wide range of intermediate depths that are precisely suited to the use of crankbaits, jigs, and jigging spoons.

Professional guides and tournament anglers, whose livelihoods depend on consistently catching bass, have long accepted the importance of mastering all three types of lures. If you do the same you'll be able to fill your stringer regularly, whether the fish are in the shallows, in the depths, or somewhere in between.

CRANKBAITS

Crankbaits are a specific breed of plugs made from hollow plastic, balsa, ABS foam and, sometimes, wood. The one thing they all have in common is that they are designed to be retrieved at moderate to very fast speeds and in most instances to represent fleeing baitfish or panfish. Most of these plugs float at rest, dive to certain depths on the retrieve, and then exhibit a tight wiggling action as they quickly track their way back to the boat. Because of these characteristics, crankbaits generally are used when the water temperature is warm (60 degrees or higher) and the bass quite active.

Each crankbait has its own narrow range of depth, which depends primarily on the width, length and slant of the clear plastic bill on the nose of the plug. For example, one crankbait, depending on how fast it is retrieved, may run two to four feet deep; another with a longer or more acutely angled bill may dive to six to ten feet; and still another may reach the 12-

to 15-foot level. I am not aware of any crankbaits designed to run deeper than 20 feet, so in addition to warm-water situations they typically are used for fishing shoreline cover and relatively shallow bottom structures or contours. The depth range of a crankbait is usually stated somewhere on the package in which the lure is sold.

I recommend having on hand at all times an assortment of crankbaits with a variety of depth ranges. Within each particular depth-range category, I also recommend having crankbaits in numerous body designs so you can select one that closely simulates the predominate forage in the lake you're fishing.

For example, if bass in a reservoir customarily feed on panfish such as bluegills, sunfish and crappies, you'll want to rely heavily on short, blocky, "fat-plugs" or "alphabet lures." Cordell's Big-O, Norman's Big-N, Plastic Research Company's Rebel plugs and the B-series of crankbaits made by Bagley Bait Company would all fill the bill.

This article is an excerpt from *Advanced Bass Fishing*, 2nd edition, published by Outdoor Life Books, NY.

On the other hand, if you're working a reservoir where bass are feeding mainly upon threadfin shad, you'll want to use crankbaits slightly more elongated in body shape—for example the Bomber Bait Company's Model-A, Mann's Razor-Back and Pig lures, Bagley's Small Fry series, Bill Lewis Lure Company's Rat-L-Trap and Normark's Shad-Rap.

For working a natural lake where bass may be gorging on bluntnose shiners, emerald shiners, dace, or perch, long and slender crankbaits of the slim-minnow design will undoubtedly fare best. Examples of these are Mann's Hackelback series, Smithwick's Rogues, Normark's Rapalas, Rebel's Minnow series, and Bagley's Bang-O-Lures.

Of course, countless other brands are available as well. But regardless of their makers, remember that lures must have the proper depth and speed capabilities, for the given conditions, as discussed in the previous chapter. Only after these prerequisites are met should lure shape, design, and action be considered.

As for the color of crankbaits, I usually have success with a very few standard hues. Topping the list are shad-gray, mullet-blue, perch, bone, crayfish (brown with orange belly), and chartreuse. Crankbaits are also available in a wide variety of *naturalized* patterns.

Fan-casting is a popular method for eliciting strikes with crankbaits in relatively shallow, warm water, where they are most suited. In this method, an angler saturates the cover with a series of casts in a radial pattern, like the spokes emanating from the hub of a wheel. Once he completes a series of casts, the angler moves his craft and repeats the fan-casting pattern; this allows him to fish the same cover from two or more directions. Only the bass can explain why, but time and again I've seen a fish totally ignore a lure traveling by a stump or other cover at a certain angle, then blast it on the very next cast when the angle of retrieve is changed slightly.

Fan-casting crankbaits in this manner is especially popular with tournament bass anglers who are pressed for time and don't want to risk looking for widely separated schools of bass on deep, midlake structures. So they saturate areas that have shallow cover, machine-gunning crankbaits, searching for stragglers, trying to cover as much water on a given day as possible.

A rather stiff rod with a limber "working" tip is best for crankbait fishing, and watching tournament pros such as Jimmy Houston at work is like observing the inner workings of a well-oiled machine. He casts a fat-plug, for example, several yards past a stump and then retrieves it as close to the cover as possible. When the lure nears the rod tip, toward the end of the retrieve, he yanks it quickly from the water and sends it on its way to the other side of the stump or the next likely looking spot. The motion is often so fluid that it's difficult to ascertain exactly when the retrieve ends and the next cast begins. He hopes that if he retrieves his lure past more potential fish lairs during the day than other competitors, he'll elicit

the greatest number of aggressive responses.

A bass lying in the shade of a felled tree or some other cover will nearly always hear the rattling or vibrating commotion of an approaching crankbait before he actually sees it. This alerts him. Suddenly, it brushes by his nose! There is no opportunity to take a lengthy look at it or to decide whether he's hungry or not. He reacts and strikes.

Aside from this most popular method of presenting crankbaits, a number of refinements can add more fish to the stringer. Some tournament pros find they get more strikes by varying the lure's speed numerous times during each retrieve. After casting the lure, and cranking it down to the depth at which it is designed to run, they may slow the lure speed momentarily, quickly rip it forward several more feet, slow it again, and so on. Other times, they may allow long pauses in between each forward movement of the lure, so the plug begins to float back toward the surface, whereupon they crank it back down again.

When fishing around boulders and especially woody cover such as stumps, logs and standing timber, some pros use another recent innovation, called *banging* or *bumping*. In this technique, an angler casts beyond the cover, begins the retrieve, then suddenly moves the rod tip to one side or another, causing the crankbait to actually ram into the cover and just as quickly glance off. Particularly when bass are in an inactive state of behavior, this technique can be so effective it must be seen to be believed.

Another way of fishing crankbaits is *stacking* the lures and *straining the water*. This is used primarily to find the depth at which bass are holding when they are near weed beds that border very deep water and especially when bass are clinging tightly against steep shorelines where sheer rock walls drop off abruptly into the depths. In this technique, an angler positions his boat close to the weedline or rock bluff and casts parallel to it, first using a crankbait designed to run two to four feet deep. If he has no luck, he ties on another crankbait with a slightly longer bill that is designed to take the lure down six to eight feet deep. Still no bass? He now fishes the same water again, this time with a crankbait that runs

An assortment of crankbaits with a variety of body shapes and depth ranges should be in every bass angler's tacklebox.

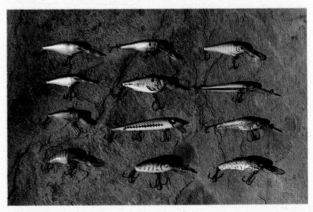

at the 10- to 12-foot level. In other words, he systematically works deeper and deeper, until fish are located, and from then on continues working the same productive depth range.

Fan-casting crankbaits isn't restricted to working visible cover or shoreline features. It's also an ideal technique for quickly checking bottom contours in midlake areas such as stream channel bends, drop-offs, ditches, underwater ridges, timbered points, submerged rock-capped islands, and all manner of other structures. Fishing crankbaits in these areas may lead an angler to an occasional straggler fish or two and on occasion to an entire school of bass.

During a day of serious crankbait fishing, an angler will eventually find his lures are no longer tracking a straight course on the retrieve but are veering off to the right or left. When crankbaits operate in this erratic manner, their depth can no longer be properly controlled, which reduces their effectiveness. This veering behavior is caused by crankbaits repeatedly banging into cover, or digging into the bottom, which alters their running characteristics. In fact, many brand-new lures fail to track a straight line on the first cast, due to the vagaries of mass-production techniques.

These problems can be rectified by tuning your lures. Tuning is accomplished by using a pair of needlenose pliers to bend the wire loop on the nose of the lure to which the line is tied. If the lure consistently angles off to the right on the retrieve, slightly bend the line-tie to the left, or vice-versa if the lure veers off to the left. Be careful not to make radical adjustments; just bend the line-tie a tiny bit, in the direction you want the lure to travel, and you'll correct the problem.

JIGS AND JIGGING SPOONS

"The very hottest big-bass lure of the 1980s may well prove to be the jig 'n pig," Bo Dowden exclaimed as he horsed a four-pounder to the boat and dropped it into the live well. We were on the St. Lawrence River in upstate New York, and the big bass clinched a $41,000 first place award for Bo in a recent BASS Classic. Later, he gave me that very lure as a souvenir.

Although jig 'n pig lures are probably mistaken by bass for crayfish scurrying along the bottom, no one is certain why they are so appealing to very big bass. They just are.

Ideally, the jig should weigh somewhere between ¼ and ½ ounce and it should be of the banana-head design. Further, the jig should be outfitted with some type of fiber weedguard to reduce the possibility of snagging. And instead of bucktail or feathers, a majority of pros prefer a rubber skirt that breathes and pulsates as the lure is being manipulated. Undeniably, all-black is the favored color, with all-brown running a close second.

The "pig" is a size 1 black pork frog slipped onto the hook, although some pro anglers also use black pork chunks or even pork lizards. Whatever, the

Jigs come in various shapes and styles, but all are fished vertically, with an up-and-down motion, off the bottom.

combination results in a heavy lure that casts like a bullet and sinks like a rock—just the ticket for summer, fall and winter bassing when most bass are away from the shorelines and hugging the bottom in deep water.

You can fish the jig 'n pig in either of two ways. One is to work the lure vertically right beneath the boat; Simply pump it up and down and hop it along as you use your depth-sounder to bird-dog the edge of the bottom contour. Or, you can simply cast this super bass-bait as you would any other. Be sure to let it sink all the way to the bottom on a tight line as many bass will grab it on the fall. Once you've felt the distinct thunk of the bait hitting bottom, then begin your retrieve by raising your rod tip, lowering it quickly while reeling in slack line, then raising the rod tip again.

The main difference between fishing a jig 'n pig and other types of jigs is that the jig 'n pig can be worked much faster. Bo Dowden and other pros even perform a bit of surgery on their "pigs" by slicing off part of the thick head of the pork rind to make it wafer in. This gives the bait more of a wavering, swimming appearance in the water and allows relatively fast retrieve speeds to simulate a crayfish routed from its hideout.

Curiously, bass don't blast the dickens out of a jig 'n pig. They usually inhale the lure and swim away with it. Be alert for a "weighty" sensation on the end of your line, as if your lure had picked up a big gob of weeds. Or you may merely see your line begin slowly moving off to the right or left. In any event, don't delay! Strike quickly before the bass discovers he's been duped by a counterfeit.

As effective as jig 'n pigs are, every serious angler's tacklebox should be well stocked with other jigs as well. I especially like Powrr-head jigs, which are shaped like anvils and have their hooks pointing up toward the surface at an acute angle. When dressed with a Reaper-Worm or curly-tail grub, these offerings actually stand up on the bottom, making themselves far more visible than other types of jigs that may lie down on their sides. With the hook point so starkly exposed, they also grab bass flesh more readily than other types of jigs.

Although many bass anglers have been devoutly fishing jigs for generations, most never seem to accept the fact that these lures must be fished close to the bottom on a tight line to be fully effective. Furthermore, developing a feel for strikes is critically important, as most occur when the jig is sinking. If the line is allowed to go slack during this crucial period, a majority of anglers are incapable of detecting the very slight ticks indicating strikes.

Jigging spoons are basically similar to jigs. I'm not referring here to conventional teardrop-shaped spoons made of thin, concave metal, such as the venerable Daredevle or Johnson Silver Minnow. Jigging spoons are a breed apart. Some call them "heavy metal" because that's exactly what they are: elongated, pencil-shaped or oval-shaped chunks of steel or lead, some with painted surfaces and others with hammered finishes, some with bare hooks and others with feathered dressing on the trebles. The most popular are the Hopkins Spoon, Mann-O-Lure, and the Strata-Spoon.

Furthermore, as their name implies, jigging spoons are not meant to be cast in the usual way. They *can* be cast if necessary, for example, when you find schooling bass tearing into surface-swimming schools of baitfish; but in this situation the lure has to be retrieved very fast or it will quickly sink beyond the reach of the rampaging fish.

Typically, however, jigging spoons come into their own when fished vertically beneath your boat, just off the bottom, at depths ranging from 10 to 60 feet.

My own jigging spoon expertise has been gleaned from two artists of the trade, Ricky Green and Stanley Mitchell, both of whom have won many prizes over the years in national bass tournaments. In addition to being among the few lures with which anglers can exercise precise depth and speed control in deep water, jigging spoons are incredibly easy to master.

Ricky Green particularly likes to fish jigging spoons on deltas. These are deep sandbars or ridges found along the edges of river beds on the floors of some reservoirs. Once, I stopped fishing and just sat in total dismay watching Green at work as he boated an unbelievable 35 bass from one delta in only 20 minutes.

Green's technique is simple. First, he presses the free-spool button on his casting reel so line can pay out as the lure sinks to the bottom. Then, engaging the gears and taking up the slack, he begins slowly raising his rod in short jerks until the tip is pointed high overhead. This maneuver serves to lift the spoon about six feet off the bottom. Then he slowly lowers the rod tip until it almost touches the surface of the water, causing the spoon to rock and flutter in a tantalizing manner, like an injured baitfish struggling, as it descends into the depths. Most bites come as a distinct "bump" when the spoon is sinking, and Ricky quickly sets the hook and derricks the fish aboard.

Stan Mitchell, on the other hand, fishes his jigging spoons in a slightly different way. He likes to ply his efforts in only moderately deep water, especially in highland reservoirs, where some type of drowned timber is present. It may consist of stumps on the bottom, toppled shoreline trees, standing timber, or even log jams. In these situations, jigging spoons can be vertically lowered right down through the limbs, branches, and trunks to bass hiding deep within the maze of cover and inaccessible to most other lures.

Mitchell begins at the bottom, working the spoon in place by pumping it up and down. Then he raises the lure several feet and repeats the effort, until he's covered all depth levels. Then, without moving his boat, he drops the spoon right back into some other hole in the cover only scant feet away and tries again. It is mind-boggling how many bass can sometimes be hiding in the thick crown of a single treetop.

Occasionally, a jigging spoon's hooks will hang up deep within the latticework of cover, but this is easily remedied. Just give a bit of slack line and jiggle your rod tip. This will cause the spoon to begin flip-flopping back and forth, and its heavy weight will eventually dislodge the hooks.

There is yet one final category of lures, those intended solely for topwater use. Although only productive at certain times of year, surface plugs continue to capture the hearts of anglers because of the explosive action they generate. In the next article, Jack Lewis describes everything you need to know to cash-in on this unique aspect of bass angling excitement.

Jigging spoons are also designed to be fished vertically beneath a boat, at depths of 10 to 60 feet.

Topwater Temptation

Jack T. Lewis

My first catch on a surface lure will remain in my memory forever. It was a warm July morning and I fished a small stock pond near my home. I was eager to try a frog-colored Jitterbug. After making half-a-dozen casts to get a feel for the paddle-wheel-sounding lure, I spotted a pile of willow brush barely beneath the surface in about five feet of water.

I tried to place the cast so that the lure would be retrieved over the brush pile, but the lure wound up a few feet right of target but beyond the brush pile. Disappointed, I reeled the sputtering Jitterbug past the brush pile, sure that there would be no takers after such a sloppy cast. About two feet this side of the brush pile, there was a terrific swirl that completely engulfed my lure. The subsequent hard pull convinced me that there was one big bass cutting across the pond and straining the 12-pound-test monofilament. Only the smooth drag of the spinning reel made it possible for me to bring the big fish to the grassy bank some two minutes later. Much to my surprise, the big fish turned out to be a 10-pound flathead catfish!

I was hooked myself. If a topwater lure could trigger so much action from a comparatively sluggish flathead, I reasoned that fishing for bass with topwater lures would be a real ball. It is.

Late spring and late fall are usually thought of as the best periods for topwater bass angling throughout the country. But drought and resulting low water can provide excellent surface action all summer long. Usually the flat-country lakes are much more productive for the topwater angler than the deep-water impoundments found in hilly or mountainous areas of the country. There are some exceptions. Two outstanding examples of deep, canyon-type lakes that are tops for surface action are Lake Mead in Nevada and Amistad Reservoir in Texas. Both are very deep and extremely clear.

The so-called "magic hours," the times to fish surface lures, occur early and late in the day. In most areas of the country there are more big bass on the surface in October than in any other month. The last few hours before dark seem to be the very best.

Always cast your lure near a target. Don't waste a cast by throwing to open water. Stumps, rocks, logs, brush, fencerows, and moss beds are all prime targets for the wise surface angler. But schooling bass in open water make a good target, too. By all means, get a cast into breaking fish as quickly as possible.

Surface lures should be fished very slowly on calm water and very fast and noisily on wind-chopped waters. Another factor to remember is that a sloping, sheltered shoreline is most often more productive than a steep bank. But remember that bass will not move in as close to a sheltered shoreline as they would to a windy bank.

To become a good topwater angler requires concentration, coordination, and fast reflexes. Never take your eyes off the lure when it is in the water. How many bass have you missed simply by looking off at a passing boat or some other distraction? A bass can suck your lure under and spit it out in the blink of an eye when you look away. Hooks must be set like a flash when the lure is hit. Don't expect your rod tip to bury the hooks in the fish's tough jaw. Keep your rod tip low and pointed at the lure during the retrieve. By working the lure with short, downward flips of the tip, you'll be set to strike when a hit comes. Just by swinging the rod up or to the side you'll be able to bury the hooks solidly.

Once a bass is hooked on a surface lure, you can bet your tackle box it's going to jump and try to throw the lure by wild head shaking. Most of us get a kick out of these aerial antics, but if it happens to be a big fish, it pays to control the fish quickly. After the hook-up watch the line where it enters the water. When the fish starts rising to jump, your line will also start stretching and rising. When this happens, you can stick your rod under the water and crank like the devil to pull the fish back down. Although some fishermen consider this tactic unsportsmanlike, it works.

Another tactic depends on good timing and a medium, heavy-action rod. When the line starts rising, haul back on the rod and throw the bass off balance just as the head breaks the surface. This stops the fish from shaking its head and tossing the lure back to you. If you are fishing with a light-action rod and hook a good bass, about all you can do is keep light tension on the line with the rod at right angles to the fish and let the limber tip wear the fish down.

In surface fishing, rather short casts provide enhanced accuracy, but short casts are no good on clear-water reservoirs where 60 to 70-foot casts are needed to avoid spooking the bass. Bass have excellent eyesight, and because the vision enables them to constantly monitor the surface, casting motions can be easily seen if your casts on clear water are short. Very long casts, however, create other problems. Positive hook-setting power is diminished considerably by long casts. This is especially true when using monofilament line. The natural stretch of mono plus the flex in your rod makes it difficult to penetrate when you try to set the hook with a lot of line out. It is frustrating to hang a good bass only to see it throw the lure on the first jump.

For many years I used light-action rods and bait-casting reels spooled with mono and lost a lot of fish. Some years ago I bit the bullet and converted to a medium-heavy 5½-foot fiberglass rod and braided Dacron line spooled on a bait-casting reel. This gave me more power while fishing my favorite type of lure, the spinnerbait. My catch ratio shot up rather dramatically after these changes, and they also turned my surface fishing around. You'll lose very few fish with this kind of tackle when surface fishing. Now when that sudden strike comes at the end of a 70-foot cast, a quick snap of the wrist is all that's required to bury the hooks.

Let's discuss a few of the many surface lures to be found at any well-stocked tackle store. Surface lures can be categorized in three groups: *sticks, chuggers,* and *darters.*

Popular stick types include Smithwick's Devil's Horse, Bomber's sticks, and Heddon's Dying Flutter. Most stick lures are shaped like fat pencils. Propellers

are attached to one or both ends. These props create a purring, buzzing sound when the lure is retrieved steadily or twitched with flips of the rod tip. Flipping sticks during the retrieve is most productive around logs, stumps, and rocks. Work these lures as close to this type of cover as possible and keep lures close to the cover as long as you can. It often takes a good while to aggravate a stubborn bass into striking. I believe that short jerks create sounds that often draw vicious strikes. Don't give up after one cast to a good spot. It may take five or six casts to get a lazy old fish to hit. You must be alert and quick to start moving the fish away from the underwater structure to avoid a hangup. This is one reason why a medium/heavy action rod is good for surface angling. After you hook the fish on top you can keep it there if your tackle is adequate.

Chugger types include: Heddon's Chugger Spook and Pico Pop, Whopper-Stopper's Stumper, Bomber's Popper, and Lazy Ike's Chug Ike. These noisy, cup-faced lures are most effective when the water is not clear and when it is choppy. The loud, blooping sound created by the cupped face will get a bass's attention from a good distance. The addition of a bucktail on the rear hook hanger adds an extra bit of attraction. Real bucktails or plastic skirts work equally well. When these chugger types sit at rest on the surface, the extra attraction is the way it waves and pulsates. This often draws strikes without moving the lure with the rod. Use a fast retrieve on choppy water and a very slow, twitching retrieve on calm or slick water.

Make sure the hooks on your surface lures are needle sharp. The head shaking of a bass on the surface can easily dislodge hooks that fail to penetrate.

The most widely accepted surface-lure colors are those that imitate shad. However, when fishing the surface at night or on overcast days, most anglers like darker colors. One of the most deadly surface plugs for night use is the Fred Arbogast Musky Jitterbug. Lure manufacturers are doing marvelous things with lure finishes. The built-in flash is one of the major improvements. This flash finish looks more like a shad in the water than the real McCoy. Those new photo-finishes are so realistic, it's scary.

Surface-lure colors put the rainbow to shame, and anglers have difficulty choosing the proper colors. Here are a few suggestions on color based on my experience. Let the time of the year dictate the colors you choose. In the fall, try to select colors that imitate perch. Green, brown, yellow, and red are excellent choices. In the fall, bass feed heavily on perch in order to put on fat for the hard, cold winter season ahead. Late in the spring after the spawn, the bass are drained of energy and take shad for a quick pick-me-up. With this in mind, select silver finishes or combinations of silver and black or silver and green. As warmer weather comes on, try to match the colors

Make sure the hooks on your surface lures are needle sharp. The head shaking of a bass on the surface can easily dislodge hooks that fail to penetrate.

M. Timothy O'Keefe

of flying insects favored by the bass in your part of the country. For instance, blue matches the small dragonflies that cling to shallow-water stick-ups in most Southern reservoirs. Black or gray imitates the large dragonflies that fly inches above the surface during July and August on most reservoirs. Yellow or white should be selected to imitate the small, migrating moths that begin moving south at the first

hint of cold air. Strive to match these insect colors as close as possible. They are even more effective if the colors are translucent and a bucktail of the same color is added to the lure.

Darters include: Tiny Torpedo, Skip-Jack, Skin-N-Cisco, Rapala, Rouge, Red-fins—the list goes on forever. Many darting types have propellers on one or both ends while others have plastic or metal lips that make them dart, dive, or quiver very realistically. The darters are most effective when fished on calm or slightly rippled surfaces. The lip darters have fantastic action when retrieved with short jerks of the rod tip in downward pulls. This type of rod manipulation allows you the advantage of setting the hooks quickly and positively with an upward sweep of the rod.

Many anglers prefer working the propeller darters rather fast, even on calm water. The sputtering noise made by the props goads bass into frenzied attacks on the noisy lure speeding on the surface. Try stopping this fast retrieve now and then for a count of five and then barely twitch the lure. This is often more than a following bass can take. The fish often busts the lure with reckless abandon and swallows it whole.

One important assist in surface fishing is polarized sunglasses. They make underwater objects more visible. Being able to see these objects before you retrieve your lure gives you the advantage of anticipating the strike. If you can see the structure, you can make educated guesses about where and when a bass will take. Most surface lures have built-in action or noise attraction, but there are additional things you can do yourself that will make them even more effective. First of all, if your surface lures do not have split rings for a terminal tie point, by all means, add them. They can be purchased at most tackle shops. Use only steel ones. They're very inexpensive, and I've never had one fail. These split rings allow surface lures every chance to wiggle and quiver as they are retrieved. Tying your line directly to the fixed eyelet neutralizes much of the lure's built-in action.

To make surface fishing over moss beds or weed patches easier, remove the leading tine of treble hooks. A pair of side-cutting pliers does the job, and the amputation lessens tangles with the vegetation.

One of the best surface lures to use over vegetation is a chugger. A slow, deliberate retrieve works well. Hooks must be set in a flash in order to keep the fish on top of the vegetation while you attempt to force it out to open water. Many fish are lost in this thick cover simply because they were allowed enough slack to get their heads down. Then it's tangle time. If your fish does get down into moss or weeds, don't attempt to pressure or horse it out. Twenty-pound-test line can be snapped by a two-pound fish under these conditions. One successful method is to paddle or pole to them while maintaining light tension on the line. Once over the spot, lean over the side as far as possible and run your hand along the line until you feel the lure or the fish's mouth. Be cautious. Work slowly while reaching for the fish's lip. A sudden move could put a hook in your hand. A bass feels well hidden all wrapped up in vegetation and generally won't move until you take a grip on the jaw or gill plate. If you can't reach the fish from the boat, go overboard and do the job. If it's a wall-hanger, getting wet doesn't matter.

There's a peculiar happening that often occurs during surface fishing that I find most intriguing. Let's say you're working a Tiny Torpedo across a gravel point among scattered brushy stick-ups. You see a sudden strike and your lure flies a couple of feet into the air! What happened? My theory is that the bass spotted the lure zipping along and decided to hit and stun it rather than eat it. The bass may just blow it out of the water with its mouth or slap it with its tail. If your nerve doesn't fail, just let the lure lie still a couple of seconds after the initial hit. Then just barely twitch it. Hang on because the bass may blast the lure.

One of the favored methods of fishing surface lures in Southern reservoirs is wading the windy points during July and August. Bass are very predictable in such places at this time of year. They often drive large schools of shad onto the windward side of the point, and with an assist from the strong wave action, keep them there until they've had plenty to eat. Beach your boat on the lee shore and walk over to the windy side. Tie on a loud lure such as a large chugger or Pico-Pop with a white bucktail and wade out about thigh-deep. Put your cast way out and work it back as noisily as possible. You'll be astounded at how many large bass you can take using this angling method. Just being in the cool water is a treat at this time of the season.

A landing net with a two- or three-foot handle is highly recommended for wade fishing. It's very wise to net the fish well away from your legs. A fast-moving bass with an extra set of trebles hanging outside its mouth can do a lot of damage.

The introduction of buzzbaits a few years back gave us a new dimension in surface fishing. Although they are not really floaters, they should be thought of as surface lures. Harkin's Lunker Lure was the first of the many buzzers. All shapes and sizes are now available. These buzzers are actually easier to use than regular surface lures because they feature a fixed, upturned, protected single hook riding behind a big propeller that really creates a fuss on the surface. It's downright hard to hang up with one of these lures. They can be thrown into almost any type of cover and you will usually get them back. Bass often hit buzzers hard, the same as they do with a slow-moving chugger. But they also like to catch up to the lure, take it, and move off quietly. It pays to keep a sharp eye on buzzers during the retrieve. Easy to cast and easier to retrieve with 5-to-1 ratio reels, buzzbaits are a genuine pleasure to fish. Single or double propellers are available.

It's often said that one good bass taken on the surface is worth more than a limit taken beneath it. I don't go that far, but I know that topwater temptation produces more pure excitement than any other angling method!

Mastermind A Troll For Big Bass

Frank Sargeant

Bill Murphy is a bass trolling addict. With good reason—in the past few years, the Santee, California, angler has caught more trophy bass than most fishermen ever dream of. He's boated in excess of 160 bass that weighed more than eight pounds—including dozens that went more than ten pounds—in the lakes around San Diego, where Florida-strain fish grow to monstrous proportions. Murphy has taken many fish in the 12-pound class, a few near 15 and one behemoth of almost 17 pounds. Most of these fish struck as the dental technician towed a big lure behind his boat.

In one incredible morning, he made six passes over a single underwater ridge and hooked six bass weighing more than ten pounds! On another occasion, his trolling brought him a five-fish string with a certified weight of 49 pounds.

Bill Murphy attributes his success in large part to a system he calls "programmed" trolling, a combination of lure, line, boat speed, and other factors that add up to trophy fish.

Murphy isn't the only angler to have discovered how deadly systemized trolling for largemouths can be. Several decades ago, a grizzled Southerner by the name of Buck Perry invented a metal diving lure that became known as the "Spoonplug." Perry instituted a new school of thought on catching big bass. He developed his own programming system and his methods decimated bass populations for years. The techniques fell out of favor only with the rise of tournament bassing, where trolling is not permitted.

Programmed trolling is still as effective as ever, though, as Bill Murphy and a few other smart anglers around the country have proven.

"Short of hiring a guide," says Murphy, "it's probably the best possible method for finding fish in waters new to you. The lure is constantly in the water and using the right techniques you can reach the fish no matter where they're holding."

In fact, in clear lakes where bass often go as deep as 50 or 60 feet—a common situation in Western reservoirs—trolling is one of the few effective methods of getting to them. Murphy and other Southern California experts have perfected a system of trolling up to 100 yards of leadcore line to send big Magnum Rapalas probing the depths where the lunkers hide in such lakes as San Vicente, Miramar, and Casitas.

Murphy uses from six to 15 feet of monofilament leader, often resorting to clear mono as light as 10-pound test to fool the trophy fish. His plugs, a central part of his programming system, are custom painted to resemble his concept of exactly what a rainbow trout might look like in the dim light of the depths—the rainbows are a prime food of the Southern California largemouths. He carefully tunes each lure to run true and deep and hones each hook under a microscope. His reels are saltwater models, Ambassadeur 7000s, which are necessary to hold the thick leadcore line. The rods are stout 7½-footers with enough backbone to whip a sailfish.

"There's so much sag and stretch when you're trolling 300 feet back that you need the long heavy rod to have much chance of setting the hook," says Bill. "It's tough to handle fish with that much line out, but the farther out and down you troll and the deeper you find bass, the more likely you are to get action—at least in our area lakes."

Bill Murphy's system works because it's programmed to the waters he fishes. Sim-

Frank Sargeant

ilarly, anglers around the country have learned to program systems for their home waters. Even famed tournament anglers such as Roland Martin enjoy a bit of lure towing now and then when they're fishing for fun.

"Trolling is a really effective method of covering the water," says Martin, "and a lot of times you're showing the lure to open-water fish that never see a plug. That can be deadly."

Wherever you fish, programming a trolling system comes down to several basic variables. Put them together in the right combination and you're almost assured of success. Trolling is not a lazy man's game, as was once thought. It takes know-how and experience and lots of persistence but, when the system comes together, it produces.

Getting your lure to the right depth is the single most important aspect of successful trolling. The

depth reached by a trolled lure depends on several variables, the first being lure design. In general, lures with large diving lips go deeper than those with small lips or no lip at all, and lures with a high density— metal or solid plastic—go deeper than buoyant plugs made of wood or hollow plastic. If you're fishing a relatively clear Tennessee reservoir where bass might predictably be as deep as 25 feet, you might want to choose a weighted plug with an oversized lip so you can reach these fish without resorting to heavy sinkers or leadcore line. On the other hand, if you're trolling a shallow Florida lake where bass might suspend over midlake weed beds, you'd be better off choosing a floating lure with a small diving lip, such as one of the smaller Rapalas or Rebels. Trolled unweighted, these plugs rarely run deeper than six feet.

A second factor in programming your trolling is line length. In general, the farther back your lure

is from the boat, the deeper it runs. A plug that reaches only ten feet when trolled 100 feet back may go to 15 feet at 150 feet back and to 20 feet when you let out 200 feet of line. These depths are even more pronounced when leadcore line is used. Because most bass taken by trolling are caught near bottom structure, accurately controlling the depth of your lure by controlling the line length is important.

Determining the amount of line you have out is easy if you use color-coded mono, such as Berkley's Depth-O-Matic, which has a color change every ten feet. Leadcore lines also offer color codes, with the changes usually coming every ten yards. You can count colors to determine exactly how much line you have out and can then return to that

length easily.

Line diameter and density are also factors in lure control. Thinner lines are less buoyant and usually reach a greater depth for a given line length and lure design. Dacron and braided mono are fairly buoyant and are not good choices if you want to troll deep. Thin mono penetrates the water easily, so light-test lines are generally good choices for deep trolling. However, they have the considerable disadvantage of being easily broken when your lure hangs a snag instead of a bass. (Most deep trollers quickly learn that a plug retriever is a necessary part of their arsenal.)

Adding weight to the line is another obvious way of controlling depth. Simple twist-on sinkers or split shot can add several feet to the running depth of many plugs. If you put the weight at least six feet in front of the lure, it will have little effect on the

Programmed trolling grows in popularity as anglers find it really works. Frank Sargeant successfully combined all the elements of the system to catch this bass.

the other hand, if you go too fast your lure loses its "grip" on the water and planes to the surface. Getting just the right speed is a tricky business and it's difficult to be consistent without some technological assistance. Your outboard's tachometer is a good guide on calm days when winds won't affect your speed greatly. For real accuracy, no matter what the weather, you might opt for one of the trolling speedometers now available. They precisely measure speeds from less than one mile per hour up to six miles per hour—about the maximum you can effectively tow most bass lures. Eagle Claw makes one—the Accu-Troll—that is competitively priced.

Once you've selected a system of lines, lures, and weights that seems right for the waters you fish most often, you're ready to get down to brass tacks. You can locate likely trolling areas by checking contour maps of your lake. Look for submerged ridges, old river channels and creek beds, standing timber, and other likely bass attractors. Note the depths indicated by the contour lines and select lures that you think are likely to run at those depths with your tackle "program." This is all by guess and by golly until you get out on the water and actually test some combinations of lure design, line length and test, weights, and boat speed. In general, you can expect large big-lipped crankbaits to go as deep as 20 feet, smaller crankbaits to dive 12 to 15 feet, vibrating lures to run at six to eight feet, and floater/diver surface lures to reach about five feet. If you add weights or lead-core line, all of these lures will run much deeper, of course.

In the hottest parts of summer and the coldest days of winter, most bass are likely to be in deep water. In murky lakes with relatively low oxygen levels, "deep" is likely to be 15 to 20 feet. In clear lakes with lots of deep-water plants to provide oxygen—or with a current to mix oxygenated surface water with deeper water—bass may go as deep as 60 feet.

action. Leadcore lines are also a good way to get a lure deep. The lines are expensive, however, and tend to twist and snarl after a day's trolling. But for reaching maximum depths, they're hard to beat.

Devices such as the Bait-Walker, a weighted wire rig, not only get lures deep but also help them to "walk" over snags and obstructions. They're deadly when used with buoyant lures that float along just above the cover. Also effective is the Bass Rigger, a miniature downrigger with a 1½-pound ball weight. This device can effectively fish down to 75 feet and could be useful in big Western reservoirs, such as Powell, where the fish go extremely deep to escape summer heat.

Another big factor in programming your trolling is boat speed—this affects both lure depth and lure action. Go too slowly and your lure never attains maximum motion or depth. Most diving plugs run deeper as speed increases, and vibrating plugs have almost no action or sound at all at low speeds. On

The trick in locating bass by trolling is to probe the structure at various depths, with various combinations of tackle, until you find action. In general, it doesn't do much good to troll a lure that runs at five feet over bottom structure that's 20 feet deep. The plug has to get down to within a few feet of the cover in order to provoke strikes and that's where the "programming" comes in.

Suppose you find a brushy point extending from a creek mouth down into a submerged river channel. Clearly, this is a likely spot for largemouths. Water ranges from eight feet deep just off the bank to 30 feet deep at the channel. Your depth sounder shows the drop and the cover. With a chart recorder, you may even see fish above the structure.

You might start working the area by selecting two lures of different shape and color but with similar depth capabilities. If you don't mind an occasional tangle, you can even put out a third line with a variation in lure design, size, or color. Select a depth—ten feet, perhaps—and begin trolling. About four miles per hour is a good boat speed for openers. Let out your smallest lure to a distance of about 100 feet, put the reel into gear, and put the rod in a holder angled to the side of the boat at about 45 degrees. Watch the rod tip to see if the lure is working well. If it is, gradually let out more line, braking the spool now and then to make the lure dig in. Continue until you feel the lure touch bottom, then retrieve about five to ten feet of line. Check your depth finder again to make sure you're still at the ten-foot contour. If so, you now have that lure "programmed" for that line length, test, and boat speed. You know that anytime you want to fish water ten feet deep, you can run that particular lure just off bottom with your set program. If you don't use colored mono, you can mark line length by putting a dot on the line with an indelible ink pen, so you can return to that line length again. In fact, you may want to create a length code, putting one dot at 100 feet, two dots at 150 feet, three at 200 feet, and so on.

Follow the same procedure with your other lures, until each of them is wobbling along just off bottom. Lures with bigger lips will reach bottom on a shorter line and those with smaller lips will have to be let out farther. When you've got each of your offerings just off bottom, make a pass over the point and around both edges of it, following the ten-foot contour line by keeping an eye on your depth sounder and the map. If you don't get a strike after two or

This angler is marking the mono with an indelible pen to indicate specified depths.

three passes, working the edge both coming and going, it's time to try slightly deeper water. Move out to the 15-foot contour and drop your lures back until they once again dig into bottom, then retrieve slightly so that they'll work just above the structure. A few passes at this depth and you may want to go even deeper.

In each case, it's necessary to adjust your combination to maintain a close relationship to the bottom. If nothing works but you can see flashes on your depth sounder indicating fish, you might want to try other lure colors or designs, or to vary your trolling speed. Each time, recompute the variables necessary to get the lure down next to the cover. Stick with it and eventually you'll connect.

In my own favorite Florida lake, most of my trolling is done around a large hole that has about 15 feet of water on the edges and more than 20 feet in the center. Because there aren't many times I need to fish other depths to make a decent catch, I've programmed my system to run just off bottom at that depth and have even written on the side of each plug the exact depth that each of my lures runs on 100 feet of 12-pound-test Stren. I have a 17-foot lure for days when the bass are on the deep side of the drop, a 15-foot lure for times when they're right on the edge, and a 13-foot lure for days when they're on the shallower grass beds above the drop. Using this system, I rarely hook weeds and can consistently catch bass year-round, even on the coldest days of winter and the hottest days of summer. Admittedly, my "program" has yet to bring the rewards that Bill Murphy has earned but I've taken a number of seven- to eight-pound bass this way, as well as hundreds of medium-size fish.

There are a number of other small tricks you'll pick up as you go along. For example, if your depth finder shows a shoal passing beneath the boat, you may want to pick up your rods and hold them high in the air so that your plugs will rise over the shoal instead of plowing into it and snagging. If you note a drop-off, you might want to let out more line so that your lures will dive down the incline. If you get a strike but miss the fish, it often pays to pick up the rod and crank the lure forward as fast as you can for about ten feet. The sudden increase in speed will sometimes trigger a violent strike and a hook up. And, of course, when you catch a fish it's always a good idea to drop a buoy marker and make several more passes through that area. Offshore fish usually travel in schools and, where you catch one, you might well catch a limit.

Programmed trolling takes plenty of concentration and, at times, you'll find yourself busier than a one-armed paperhanger as you try to keep your lures out of the snags and in the strike zone. But it's a fascinating and educational way to fish, and it's just as likely to bring you a boatload of fish today as it was twenty years ago.

The Master Bass Detective

John E. Phillips

The legendary detective Sherlock Holmes always caught the culprit because he was a master of deductive reasoning. Following logical thought patterns, Holmes eliminated useless information quickly. He spent most of his time concentrating on the facts that would lead him to the villain and little time on conversation. Holmes also left no stone unturned and no clue uninvestigated. He would then arrange all of the facts to reveal the solution to the crime. Holmes was a mastermind of information gathering and problem solving.

As a master fisherman, 27-year-old Gary Klein of Oroville, California, has adopted the same style as Holmes in solving the riddle of hidden bass. Klein finds fish through deductive reasoning and he has practiced the techniques that make bass bite.

While on the trail of this supersleuth of bass fishing research, I learned that Klein's method of fishing supplies new information that would help all of us who are trying to solve the mystery of where and how to catch bass.

Two hours had passed since the Hungry Fisherman/Lowrance $100,000 tournament had begun.

"You aren't going to win a speaking contest," the tournament angler in the back of the boat said to Gary Klein, who just smiled and continued to fish.

"I don't compete in speaking contests," he told me later. "I compete in bass tournaments. When I'm fishing I'm trying to read the blueprint of the structure that's in the water in front of me. By concentrating on the structure, I try to determine where the fish are on the structure, how deep the bass are, which way the fish are looking, and where I should place my lure to make the bass take the lure.

"There's really no big secret to catching bass. All you have to do is know where the fish are and put a bait in front of them that they will take."

Although this sounds simple, Klein is not kidding. Klein determines where a bass is through information gained before he fishes—from past experience and by trial and error. He learns more about how to fish a lake before he puts his boat in the water than many anglers do after racing up and down it for two or three hours.

"I have always enjoyed analyzing where a bass is and then attempting to figure out how to catch it," Klein said. "Even when I was younger, I always thought that if I could find bass I could catch them.

"When I was fifteen, I worked at a marina after school and on weekends gassing up boats and waiting on customers," Klein recounted. "One weekend there was a bass tournament on the lake. When the contest was over, Dee Thomas of Fremont, California, had won more money for three days of fishing than I earned in three months of working at the marina. Right then and there I decided that being a professional angler was a much better way for me to make a living than working at a marina.

"Dee had caught all of his bass while flipping, so I watched Dee and tried to learn how to flip. Even though I wasn't doing it correctly, I still was catching more and bigger bass than I ever had before. So I started to study how to read water and structure, how to find fish, and how to flip."

One year later, when he was 16, Klein qualified for the Western Bass Tournament of Champions. At twenty-one, Gary was the youngest angler to win a BASS tournament—the Arizona Invitational at

Lake Powell in 1979. In the same year Klein came in second as BASS Angler of the Year. Klein has qualified eight times for the Western Bass Tournament of Champions and two times for the BASS Masters Classic. For a young man, Klein has built up an impressive record in tournament angling. But Gary has earned that record. He fishes, talks with other anglers, and reads. Every time his lure hits the water Klein analyzes why it does or does not catch fish. He also remembers what happened on each cast for future reference.

"Before you can catch fish, however, you must find them," Klein said. "There are certain questions an angler should ask himself before he leaves home—what type of water he will be fishing is one of them. There are basically three types of water: natural lakes, man-made reservoirs, and rivers. Each type of water tells the fisherman something. A natural lake where the water fluctuates very little will have old structure with bass that are very territorial. Lake Okeechobee and the St. Johns River in Florida and the Atchafalaya Basin in Louisiana are excellent examples of natural lakes with resident bass. If you find a bass by an old dock, that bass always will be there. And most of the time the bass in this type of lake are easy to pattern.

"If an angler plans to fish a man-made lake, he should know how old the lake is and when it was first filled," said Klein. "If the lake is ten years old or younger, there should be plenty of structure, such as standing trees, logs, bushes, and treetops in the lake. If the lake is more than ten years old however, the cover may be washed off most of the bank because of erosion and water fluctuation.

"When you're fishing a river, you know that there will be some current and that there may be creeks and flats that could hold bass.

"Next I think of the time of year. In the spring I concentrate my fishing in the upper end of a lake where more food is brought into the lake by feeder streams swollen from spring rains. I usually find the most shallow-water fish in the upper end of the lake.

"I like to fish for shallow-water bass at any time of year," Klein continued. "If I can find bass holding on shallow-water cover, I can make them bite by flipping—especially if the weather changes abruptly as it does when a cold front moves in. Bass usually get lockjaw in this type of weather but, despite that, if I can get ten bites in a day I can put all ten bass in the boat with the flipping technique. I have proven, at least to myself, that flipping is the most successful form of bass fishing."

To consistently catch bass Klein determines what type of structure and water depth the bass prefer on the day he plans to fish. Gary then carries pattern fishing one step farther. Not only does he try to determine what type of structure the bass are holding on but, in many cases, he actually defines where on the structure the bass are likely to be positioned and which way the bass are facing.

"Water temperatures, sunlight, and spawning conditions determine the type of cover where bass will hold," Klein told me. "If a bass is in a pre-spawn condition in the spring, she is looking for warm water and sunlight. After the spawn she will be searching for shade. During hot weather after the spawn, some of the best structure will be around boat houses. On bright days with clear water, the center of the thickest bushes you can find is the top place.

"One of the best ways to find fish on a new lake or river is to take a small section of the water, such as a cove, creek, or slough, fish it, and watch what happens. When you get a bite, notice how deep you're fishing, what type of structure you're fishing on, how far you are from the mouth or back of the creek or slough, what other structure is close by, and where the fish are in relation to the structure.

"For instance," Klein explained, "if you get a bite in the middle of a cove and another hit on the other side of the cove but no hits in the cove's mouth or in back of the cove, then you know the bass are concentrated in the middle. These fish could be pre-spawn bass moving out of deep water toward the bedding areas in the back of the cove. However, the water in the back of the cove may not be warm enough for them to spawn yet. So the bass are holding in this middle water waiting for warmer temperatures. By fishing only in the middle of the cove that day, you should have your bait in the best water most of the time. This is called patterning.

"Once you know the bass are in the middle water of a cove, you try to decide what structure in the cove's middle water is attracting the most fish. Maybe you are catching bass around trees that have fallen into the water or bushes growing in the water. No matter where you get your bites, though, all of the locations should have something in common.

"If you decide that the bass are on fallen trees, the next step is to know where on a particular tree the bass are holding. To do this you must break down a tree. There is the base of the tree, the trunk, the major limbs, the thick branches, and the top. If you are fishing during the pre-spawn or the spawning seasons, the bass will often be in the shallow water close to the stump in the warmest water.

"I flip to the closest part of the cover, then I work deeper into the cover because there may be more than one bass on the structure. I want to try and catch the fish closest to me first so I won't spook the other fish on the cover. After fishing all around the tree, then I go to the center of the tree. Even if you do flip to a bass and either spook it or miss it, the fish will come back. Sometimes it will return in fifteen minutes or you may have to wait 1½ hours, but the bass will be back.

"Once you know where a bass is holding on the structure, the next thing you need to find out is which way it is looking. When you know this you can drop your lure right in front of its nose and make it strike instinctively.

"If the lake is stable the bass may be looking in any direction. If the lake is falling, though, a bass will usually be facing deep water because most of its food will be moving away from the bank as the water falls. If the lake is coming up, the bass either will be facing the bank or will be parallel to it. On a rising lake much of the food, such as minnows, worms, and crayfish, will be on the bank or moving toward it."

Knowing that the bass are in the middle of the slough on fallen trees, that the lake is rising, and that the bass are facing the shoreline, the next obvious question is how do you flip to catch the bass?

"The cast is simple," according to Klein. "I will flip my lure so the bait lands on the bank close to the stump. Next I drag the lure into the water. The quietest lure presentation an angler can make to a bass is for the lure to hit the bank and then quietly be brought into the water. Another advantage to flipping to the bank is that the angler has a chance to settle down and prepare for the strike before he puts the bait in front of the bass."

But how do you flip to the same tree if the water is falling and the bass is looking toward the deep water?

"If you flip to the bank your lure will be behind the bass and possibly spook the fish," Klein explained. "Under falling water conditions bass are much more spooky than when the water is rising. They are not as secure on the structure as the water above them gets more shallow. So you know that the fish will be staying closer to the tree and may be right up against it. The quieter the lure presentation, the better your chances of catching the bass. When the water is falling, I flip right on top of the tree trunk, then drag the lure off the log and let it fall into the water."

If you can't figure out which way the bass is facing, Klein gives one more clue.

"Watch what happens as your lure hits the water. If you see a swirl as the lure enters it, then you know the lure hit behind the bass and the fish had to turn to take the bait. On the next cast try and place the bait so the bass won't have to turn to take it. Visualize the bass and think of which way it is facing."

After seeing Klein flip and noting the large number of national tournaments that are won by flipping, you may wonder why more people don't use this technique. Many anglers believe the technique is beyond their ability because they have heard or read that flipping requires a great amount of skill.

"That's not true," Klein emphasized. "Flipping is one of the easiest forms of fishing. Even if your technique is not perfect, you're still going to catch more fish and bigger bass than you will with casting. Flipping gives you 100 percent accuracy. You can present the bait to the fish quietly—wherever it is.

"I like Fenwick's 7½-foot flipping rod best because it has lots of power in the butt section and a medium-action tip. Hold the rod in your hand and let the line and lure drop down to the end of the rod. This gives you 7½ feet of line. With your other hand, pull off about two feet of line and engage the reel.

"All the action of flipping comes from the wrist.

John E. Phillips

A natural lake where the water fluctuates very little will have old structure with bass that are very territorial. If you find a bass by an old dock, that bass always will be there. And most of the time the bass in this type of lake are easy to pattern. If an angler plans to fish a man-made lake, he should know how old the lake is and when it was first filled. If the lake is ten years old or younger there should be plenty of structure.

First, drop the rod tip. The bait will swing forward. Practice this until you get used to swinging the lure and line without casting. Now drop the rod tip and let the bait swing forward. As the bait begins to move toward the target, feed the line in your other hand to the jig to extend your flip or pull back on the line to shorten your flip. Do not pinch the line, though. When you pinch the line and release, the bait jumps forward and you lose control of your lure and your accuracy. When the bait enters the water, your free hand should be on the foregrip of the rod ready to help set the hook. Don't be caught with line in your hand as the bait enters the water.

"Eighty percent of the bass will hit the lure within the first foot of its entering the water. The first flip must be a vertical drop straight into the structure. Many anglers will retrieve the bait once it hits the bottom to make another flip but I don't. Instead I pull the jig up through the cover and over the first limb. Then I let the lure fall back to the bottom. I want my bait to work over, around, and through every piece of structure."

Klein always sets the hook as soon as he sees or feels a bite.

"You have to set it—not only to make sure you get a good hook set," he said, "but to get the bass out of the cover before it can tangle your line. That's why I use 25-pound-test line and No. 5/0 and No. 6/0 hooks. With this tackle I won't lose a single fish."

To get the bass to bite, Klein uses two types of lures: six- or eight-inch worms and two jigs, the Monoguard and the Weapon, which Klein designed.

"Most flipping baits are designed to attract fishermen. I only use basic colors such as brown and black or brown with some orange. I do like black and brown pork on the back of my jigs. I prefer to use a three-eighths or one half-ounce jig for flipping."

Gary Klein has sorted through the information available on bass and tested his theories like the masterful Sherlock Holmes. Utilizing these methods Klein has found fish and fortune in competitive bass angling.

UNCOVERING HIDDEN BASS

Gary Klein, one of the supersleuths of bass fishing, explains different angling situations and the tactics he uses.

LOGS AND STUMPS

"Logs and stumps are fun to fish because an angler can catch a lot of bass. If a log is lying flat on the surface, the first thing I do is break down the log. I ask myself: How many branches are coming off the log, where do the branches go, what's holding the log up off the bottom? Whatever is holding the log up is the connection from the surface to the bottom and that will be where I cast first.

"If the sun is out, I flip to the shady side of a stump. If there is current in the water, I flip to the downcurrent side of a stump. When there is an overcast sky and no current, I flip to the closest part of the stump and then flip all the way around it."

REEDS

"First I try to find a wall of reeds that offers a lot of shade. I start flipping to the outside of the reeds to catch the aggressive bass on the outer edge of the reeds first. Then I flip behind the reeds to catch the more dormant fish. By taking the outside fish first I pick off the bass and I work into the structure without disturbing the other fish."

BOAT HOUSES

"Floating boat houses offer only shade. There is hardly any way to determine the position of the bass. Stationary boat houses are much easier to figure out. Fish each piece of structure around the boat house. For instance, the boat house has a walkway, the pilings supporting the walkway, the main pilings, the ladders, the submerged cross members, the corners of the boats in the boat house, the motors on the boats, the back and front of the stall, and all the corners of the boat house. Once you recognize the different structures you can start flipping to them. I fish everything on a boat dock that enters the water and I fish from every angle.

"One of the best boat-house patterns is boat-dock ladders. Bass like to have their lateral lines parallel to some type of structure to help camouflage them. Steps of a ladder are just what the fish want. I start by flipping to the outside rungs of the ladder. If I don't catch bass that way, though, I flip between the ladder rungs and put my bait on the back side of the ladder. That's one of the reasons I use 25-pound-test line. Sometimes I've wrestled eight-pound bass from between ladder rungs to get them to the boat.

"The cross members and round pilings of a boat house are the next best areas. When I flip to the pilings I want the bait to fall straight down it."

BUSHES

"Most of the time, the brighter the sun, the closer the bass will be to the center of the bush. I also look for the heaviest limb that comes off the bush while remembering that bass like parallel lines better than vertical ones. For this reason, you may be able to determine that a thick limb coming off a bush is a sure bass spot.

"On a cloudy day the bass will usually be on top of a submerged bush just under the surface or on its outer edge. A fish will generally be a little more aggressive on cloudy days and will be willing to travel farther for its food. On these days I use a large floater-type tail on a small jig and I leave my reel in gear. The larger trailer causes the lure to fall slower. I let the bait fall away from the bush to try to draw the bass out into open water where it is easier to play because the reel is engaged."

ROCKS AND BOULDERS

"Most flippers neglect rocks. I don't because I have caught some very big bass around boulders. There are several things to see when looking at a boulder. Notice which side of the boulder offers the best access to deep water—this is where a bass likes to be positioned in many cases. Rocks are especially good when the water is muddy. I usually flip on top of the rock and drag the lure into the water close to the rock so I don't spook the fish."

GRASS BEDS

"One of the problems with fishing any vegetation is that if you run your trolling motor through the grass, milfoil, lilies, and so on, you will spook the fish. The best way to fish vegetation is to pull both motors up and let the wind blow you across the weeds. The disadvantage to this is that the angler loses control of his boat and his flipping. You'll either have too much or too little line to flip into breaks in the weeds. It is best to look for a break, such as a channel or a hold in which to flip."

The Bass That Thinks It's A Trout

Jerry Gibbs

River smallmouth fishing is as varied as the rivers themselves and the country through which they flow. For you, river smallmouth fishing may consist of dammed, timberland flowage mazes, or bouncy, rock-studded canoe water interspersed with quiet sweeps and pockets the bass love so well. Maybe your river magic is made of big, easy-gliding waters suitable for a johnboat. Or your memory may summon less tranquil images—the high of a white-water canyon rush by inflatable raft to where the gradient gentles and clear water hurries over countless bronzeback hiding caves and boulder-rimmed pools.

I've fished each of these places and like them all equally. As long as the bass are there, I know they'll be toned hard from current—powerful fighters for their size. The skill involved in hooking smallmouths lies in finding them and doing things just right to make them strike. There will be glory days when you can do no wrong and prideful confidence swells without limits. But just wait—the game grows harder as you play. To begin with, these river fish move more than smallmouths do in lakes. The instability of most rivers is responsible.

I like to start my spring bass season as soon as possible. In many rivers I fish, both resident and transient bass populations are available. The full-timers occur in suitable habitat anywhere within the river, but visiting smallmouths are usually content to operate in lower river sections. The last mile or so before a small- or medium-size river enters a large one, or before the river spills into or out of a lake are prime areas. Those transient bass tend to be around in spring to spawn; they then drop back to bigger water as levels in smaller rivers drop, which is usually in late spring. Why, if they're going to spend more time in larger waters, don't these bass spawn there, as well?

I think it's nature's way of protecting stocks—the reason for separate spring, summer, and fall spawning runs of various salmonids in river systems East and West. Additionally, the normally larger, transient bass would probably not find enough forage if they remained as rivers lowered and the number of good holding areas decreased.

River smallmouths behave more like trout than like largemouth bass or even smallmouths in lakes—sometimes. I'd equate their holding preferences with those of wise, old brown trout rather than riffle-loving brookies or rainbows. In other words, some form of cover is important, as well as water depth and slower current. The latter is most important in early spring.

Smaller rivers seem to settle down first. In high and swollen larger rivers, you'll have to probe spots out of the main flow: setbacks, cuts, or just big eddies. If the bottom makeup is right, the smallies could spawn here, but often they're just waiting until the water tames. During severe runoff conditions, other species will use the same places. Just last spring, while hunting smallies, I stood at the head of a favorite eddy and watched big suckers roll near my feet. A big blowdown reached out from shore, its branches groping for bottom. Soon, a nice brown trout swam close to my waders—then another, and still another. At the bottom of the slow-current sector, I later spotted two walleyes. I knew then I'd have no luck with bass. In most rivers, smallmouths will not be ready to spawn until the walleyes are through—whether or not they use the same areas.

When the bass do move into the eddies and you begin to fish them, remember that the current will

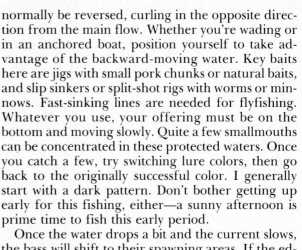

normally be reversed, curling in the opposite direction from the main flow. Whether you're wading or in an anchored boat, position yourself to take advantage of the backward-moving water. Key baits here are jigs with small pork chunks or natural baits, and slip sinkers or split-shot rigs with worms or minnows. Fast-sinking lines are needed for flyfishing. Whatever you use, your offering must be on the bottom and moving slowly. Quite a few smallmouths can be concentrated in these protected waters. Once you catch a few, try switching lure colors, then go back to the originally successful color. I generally start with a dark pattern. Don't bother getting up early for this fishing, either—a sunny afternoon is prime time to fish this early period.

Once the water drops a bit and the current slows, the bass will shift to their spawning areas. If the eddies or setbacks aren't being used, try the downcurrent sides of points or bars near or off the setbacks. Then look for deep, outside river bends that may have better bottom makeup for spawning. If the inside bends have sand or gravel flats and the current has lessened enough, the bass may be there. If a small tributary mouth is nearby, so much the better. If good gravel is on the bottom, man-made riprap or naturally rocky shorelines can be productive now. In some rivers, the bass must use channels or cut fingers in limestone ledges, and they'll pick those that have some current-breaking protection at the upstream ends.

With the water warming and the currents easing, this spawn period is the time to try fishing with small, deep-diving plugs, in-line spinners, and little spinnerbaits. Jigs continue to work, as well. For fly-fishermen, head-heavy streamers, jig flies, and fly-and-spinner combos work very well.

I tend to start with lighter colors during this period. As with river smallmouth fishing in any season, keep moving until you find fish. An area might look perfect but, if you don't hit bass in a certain area during this time of year, something is wrong with the spot. Keep hunting.

With early spring's flush of activity behind, days lengthen and the weather warms. Rivers stabilize, at least for a time, and smallmouths take up station in the lies they'll use as long as possible. Late spring into summer may be the finest time of all for river bassing, and there's a variety of ways to fish.

The finest midseason river smallmouth lies can be anywhere from midstream to smack against a bank. Rather than searching out current edges as you would when stalking trout, look for major changes of flow in association with cover. Smallmouth river cover need not be the brambly, skeletal fingers of a downed tree thrusting into the water—although it could be. Boulders can provide bass cover and also atrract insect and minnow life. Fierce main currents

River bassing offers variety and challenge. Here Jerry Gibbs shows a catch to be proud of.

can be totally devoid of bass but, if there's a hidden ledge just out of the flow—a ledge that both slows current and provides security—you can probably find smallmouths.

One of the most isolated pocket lies I ever found was in a fairly violent section of the Delaware River. I had planned to fish farther downstream where the supports of a bridge made interesting breaks and current foils, but I had brought a new fly rod and wanted to try it here first. A wadable current ran close to shore. I walked out, stripped line, false cast, and aimed above the upper of two boils that made alternate, picture-window ovals in a troubled surface. I guessed that some big rocks were below.

The weighted chenille-and-hackle fly plopped nicely and disappeared. Suddenly, my fly rod throbbed with life. A chunky bass was instantly in the air, then rushing down current. After releasing the fish, I examined the area further. I figured there was a rock-formed cirque beneath the boils, a place where the smallie had lain.

I could not imagine that the fish would hold there all the time though, so I waded upstream along the shore and soon found an underwater sand-and-gravel bar that ran out to the first drop-off. This bar was largely responsible for the slower inshore water where I was wading. I reasoned that my bass could easily work between its faster water lie and this slower flow as mood and need dictated.

In a section of moderate-to-slow flow in a large river, smallmouths can locate anywhere across the width of the river, provided one specific type of bottom structure exists. That structure consists of channels and stair-step ledges typical of limestone areas. If the shores and surrounding land exhibit these formations, you can figure that the river bottom does, too.

If your river was utilized during the heyday of pulp-log drives, there will likely be areas where old, waterlogged timbers are stacked by current sweeps at bends or setback mouths. These giant jackstraws make top smallmouth hides. You can often spot the logs through clear water as you move along in a ca-

oe, and you're missing a good bet if you don't pull off and fish them awhile.

Of course, big deep pools, slow-moving river sections, holes and drops out of current on the downstream ends of islands are notoriously good smallmouth spots. This water can be eight, ten, or 12 feet deep. It'll hold the larger fish, but the key is to find boulders, logs, man-made structures, bars, and points—cover that the smallies can relate to.

Finally, there's bank fishing. Smallmouths locate smack against the banks, beneath undercut banks (just like trout), and just a little way out from shore if current-breaking rocks or downed trees are present. If a tiny cut exists in the shoreline and the water in it is deep enough, a fish could be there. A small point extending out underwater provides a good ambush point for predatory smallmouths. The fish typically hold downcurrent of such points and back in the eddy that it creates. But if they're in an aggressive mood and the current is not too swift, try them on the upstream side.

If you're faced with the "tough" assignment of a good-sized, easy-moving river that's punctuated with broken-water sections, some deep holes, and occasional boulders, you can experience some of the most enjoyable and relaxed johnboat fishing on earth. You can use a variety of artificials, but this situation often lends itself to flipping natural baits. Minnows are good choices, as are grasshoppers and crickets, but the most productive bait of all may be the larval stage of the dobsonfly, that finger-nipping nasty called the hellgrammite. Any smallmouth, large or small, will eat a hellgrammite—unless it's on a hunger strike. You can catch hellgrammites yourself in riffles using a small seine or hand net. Keep them in a little water in a bait can or between saturated vegetation, and fish the creatures by bouncing them along the bottom with a small split shot on light line.

At this time of year, smallmouths seem more inclined to eat bottom-oriented fish life such as sculpins or stonecats, rather than brighter, open-water minnows. This trait is especially true in rocky pocket water. Float a canoe, raft, or johnboat down an easy current and throw a small balsa floating/diving plug up against the bank, though. If a bass is there, it'll usually whack the lure. A spinner or spoon is second best in the same situation. If we bring flies in, a dressed and floating muddler or sculpin pattern or one of Eppinger's Devil Bugs will be right up there with the balsa plug in productivity against those cut banks.

Those same flies—weighted or sink treated—are great when wading in pocket water. In shallower, rock-studded water, I'd never be without big nymphs, fast-sinking fur-head mini muddlers, small wooly buggers, and Woolly Worms. Shallow, pocket-water smallmouths can be every bit as tough and fussy as trout. At times, the medium-size and smaller bass will feed wildly on caddis or larger mayflies just like trout. They'll be selective, too, so you'd better toss them what seems to suggest the real thing. You can cast emerging nymph patterns when they're keyed on a hatch, but surface angling at this time is much more fun. I still catch smallies at this time of year in setbacks and eddies on surface poppers early and late in the day when there's no big hatch going.

A lot of other trout tricks work on river smallmouths. If it's been hot and dry, the area at or downstream of a river tributary mouth often produces well. Fishing after a shower is wise and, if you're working a subsurface lure or fly across and downstream, wait until the offering has completed its swing and let it hold in the current before beginning your retrieve. That retrieve should be one of forward progress coupled with fluttering fallbacks, just the way a slightly injured creature might maneuver.

Despite the fact that they love hellgrammites and opportunistically gorge on prevalent insects, river smallies—like lake smallmouths—have an overwhelming affection for crayfish. Hot weather pushes the river bass to the bottom of their deeper holes where they'll eat for brief periods very early or quite late. If you miss those short feeding bursts or just want to fish at other periods, a crayfish is often the only thing that will work. Sometimes fishing even a declawed crayfish won't work. You need to take the approach of a master chef preparing a meal for an irritable and unremitting gourmet patron.

One warm summer day, angling compadre Al Diem and I pushed downstream in waders through skimming pods of water boatmen and water striders, trying to find a decent bass hole in a fairly low river. Earlier in the day, shallow pockets below runs had yielded small fish, but we wanted something larger. A point of land thrusting into the current carved off a section of river, slowing it into the kind of deep, rock-lined pool we needed. There was even a scoured-downed tree reaching from land into the river. We soon had our sink-tip lines carrying muddlers and big nymphs down through the water.

The bass were there—occasionally we saw one of them moving through the clear water—but nothing worked. Leaving the fish to rest, we waded back to the main river. There seemed to be only one option left. Turning over rocks, we confirmed that the river was loaded with crayfish. Armed with a few of the little crustaceans, we returned to the pool. The fussy bass would not even eat a perfectly drifted crayfish.

"Well, would you eat an unpeeled shrimp?" Al demanded.

A plan of desperation was in the works, I could tell.

Shortly, he had his muddler back on. In two deft movements, Al plucked and peeled a crayfish tail and slid the tender meat onto the muddler's hook. The muddler curved out, sank out of sight, and, in another moment, a bass had split the surface and gone into the air.

In fall, river bass are as concentrated as they are in spring—but not in the same places. Many of the setbcks and eddies are too shallow. Some of the main currents ae so slow now that they make ideal holding water. If the fish aren't there, two alternatives remain. One, of course, is the deep, slow-moving river sections. Such a spot saved me one autumn on a favorite river where even my favorite pool failed to provide action.

Resting in frustration, I looked upstream from the quiet pool to where the gradient was steep and I could see the whole river angling down through bouncy white water that made me wistful for a canoe in which to run it. I suddenly realized just how low the water was, for that entire section was so boney with rocks that not even an inflatable raft could have run it. I looked at my pool again and knew I must move.

I simply followed the river to where it could no longer be called freestone water. Just past a bridge, I saw meandering channels with grass- and rush-lined shores. I knew that, just a short distance away, the shores would spread and I'd be into a lake, but I didn't need to go that far. The smallies were in this deep and winding river section, and they ate the more brightly colored spinners and streamers they normally seem to favor in fall. In some areas, this kind of territory experiences numerous frog migrations, and those amphibians are happily devoured by the smallmouths.

River bassing in all its wonderful variations and seasonal challenges can grow on you. Said a friend of a friend who recently enjoyed his first light-tackle and fly-rod season with these fish: "I'll never fish trout again."

Now that statement is pretty strong, but it does say something for the sport, doesn't it?

How To Find Smallmouths In Lakes

Byron W. Dalrymple

Bass fishermen in general are far more knowledgeable about the largemouth than the smallmouth. That is logical. It is the former that gets the major share of attention because it is the most abundant, available, and wide ranging. The smallmouth bass is a rather *specialized fish*. It is more selective and demanding in its relation to habitat, and far less tolerant of marginal conditions. Thus smallmouth waters are scattered and by no means as numerous as those containing the largemouth.

Although lack of experience with the smallmouth may make it seem puzzling and difficult to many a bass fisherman, the truth is, its specialization is a help, not a hindrance, once you understand what it requires.

The largemouth may live comfortably in a dozen widely differing lake habitats. In a lake that has varied environments, largemouths may be in any one of them—fat and happy. The smallmouth is not that adaptable. Natively it favors lakes with very specific attributes. It has now been transplanted and established, as all bass anglers are aware, over much of the United States—but *only* in suitable waters because it can't make a go of things in environments lacking its favored features.

Transplants of smallmouth bass to the South and Southwest—in fact almost everywhere outside the ancestral range of the species—have placed it almost always in lakes where largemouths also are present, but in a few perhaps marginally. In some of these new homes the largemouths thrive. In some they have never done very well and the tilt is toward the conditions smallmouths demand. That's why, with modern fisheries knowledge, the smallmouth was tried.

Wherever the two species, by introduction or natively, are present in the same lake, many an angler assumes that consistently catching both is too complicated to dope out. They just go fishing and trust to luck. *But they assume the smallmouth is the difficult bass.*

That's not the case. Certainly one may catch both fish while fishing purposely for either. But in all lakes where both species are present, the smallmouths still cling to their selective habits in relation to habitat while the largemouths are more congenial to variety, even though favoring heavier cover such as weeds. Therefore, to become an expert on fishing smallmouth lakes, you fix in mind certain patterns and requirements of this species.

Knowing these, you can then catch them just as reliably in lakes where both species occur. Further, though you may happen to catch some largemouths in smallmouth "territory," and vice versa, by sticking to the basic restrictions the smallmouth has lived by and evolved from over many centuries, you will become an eminently successful smallmouth expert.

LAKE CONDITIONS

The lake conditions in which smallmouths become most abundant, both natively and by transplant, are quite concise. The angler must know these conditions because they tell a lot about the species.

This bass requires *clear water*. Clarity, of course, is a relative matter. Smallmouths do occur in some lakes less clear than others. But they seldom are abundant in dingy or discolored lakes, which largemouths take in stride.

The species also establishes the best populations—often of the largest fish—in *deep lakes*. This is quite a departure from largemouth requirements. In fact,

The article appeared in the March 1982 issue of *BassMaster* magazine.

Byron W. Dalrymple

Knowing the patterns and requirements of the smallmouth enables you to catch them reliably.

the largemouth thrives in scores of lakes with maximum depth of only five to ten feet, even though it also manages abundantly in deep lakes, too.

By and large, it can be said that the smallmouth is seldom able to thrive in lakes with depth less than 25 feet, and lakes with three times or more that depth are better suited for it.

It is most at home also in *large lakes*. That term, too, is relative. Largemouth fishermen have become so used to man-made impoundments of large size that a lake of a couple thousand acres is sometimes considered small.

In the North, the smallmouth is found natively in numerous clear, deep lakes of a hundred to a few hundred acres. Nonetheless, it invariably does best in lakes of substantial size. But lakes in which it has

been transplanted, if deep and clear, sometimes serve it well—even though not very large.

Cool water is also demanded. This likewise is partly a relative matter. Northern lakes where the smallmouth is native are cooler than some of those in the Southwest, for example, to which it has been introduced.

It is easy to state succinctly what "cool" means to this bass. As hordes of largemouth anglers know, that fish is at its most alert and active when the water temperature is in the 70s. They will feed eagerly in some instances at 80, and they spawn at 65 to 70 and even sometimes above.

You can deduct ten degrees and come close to the high activity and spawning temperatures for the smallmouth, say an average of 55 to 60 for spawning, and a prime-activity span of about 65, give or take two or three degrees.

An extremely important whimsy of the smallmouth is its penchant for what can be called *steep-sided lakes*. It not only does best in such lakes, but it likes to hang out along the steep places.

The spawning habits of fish, incidentally, tell a lot about their personalities. The smallmouth spawns in general much deeper than the largemouth.

It is common, as all bassers know, to discover largemouths over beds so shallow their backs almost protrude from the water. They also like to fan beds at the edge of or right in weed beds, where bottom soil is suitable. The smallmouth prefers to make beds anywhere from three feet to ten feet down or more. As a rule, it stays away from weed beds when fanning, but commonly places a bed, for example, at the base of a single sparse clump of slender reeds, which invariably grow from firm bottoms.

BOTTOM STRUCTURE

Bottom composition is another important choice. The largemouth can be found in various situations where it grubs around over mud, varied debris, submerged brush, and, almost without fail, weed beds. It also, where necessary, hangs out around rocks and gravel, but it is so enamored of weeds that it is far more likely to be discovered in abundance over bottom soils that are fertile and thus grow heavy crops of vegetation.

It is not correct to say that the smallmouth shuns weeds. Much depends on what it must put up with. It is correct to say that lakes in which this bass thrives best are infertile to only moderately fertile, thus not conducive to excessive weed growth. The bottom situations it prefers, and finds most abundantly in its favorite lakes, are rock rubble, gravel, hard sand. Large rocks of course are also *magnets for smallmouths*. But in general hard bottoms with a minimum of weed growth are their fundamental preference.

Here again, checking *spawning habits* of the two species tells a sharp bassfisherman where to seek the smallmouth. The largemouth will make do with a wide variety of bottom soils for nest building. In many lakes smallmouths refuse to spawn except where there is small gravel or firm sand. Indeed, this fact may control smallmouth populations. Sometimes one can discover spawning grounds of the two bass species in the same bay of a lake. With hardly an exception, the largemouth beds will be around weeds, stumps, brush, whereas those of the smallmouths will be on the few spots of fine gravel or sand available.

In fact, in practically any smallmouth lake during spawning time the basser who searches for patches of near-shore firm bottom of gravel or sand, or even small rocks, will find the fish without further trouble. For years, the bays of upper Lake Michigan have been prime spawning grounds for smallmouth bass. Many of the most productive areas have no aquatic vegetation whatever, just expanses of large-sized gravel with large rocks intermixed with occasional large boulders.

It probably is safe to say that, lumping all smallmouth lakes together, whether or not any of them also contain the largemouth, if an angler forgets weed beds, stump fields, drowned brush and timber, and ferrets out the far less fertile *rocky shores,* he will always be on the right track. This is true throughout almost all the midSouth range of the smallmouth and of the territory to which it has been introduced, in the Far West, West, and Southwest.

There is one notable exception which occurs mainly in the Great Lakes region, sourthern Canada, and New England. Here, in native smallmouth lakes, most of which are clear, deep, cold, and infertile, there are countless places where fallen timber along shore has made a crisscross of logs, some submerged, some not. In a few such lakes jackstraw piles of lost logs from long-ago logging days thrust into and are heaped along the bank. These are invariably smallmouth hangouts, but note well that they are seldom very weedy. It is the shade and secretive hiding places the fish are drawn to.

In fact, the smallmouth hangouts are easier to find than those of its cousin because they are fewer, less varied, and less lush. Vegetation cannot be totally discounted. In some lakes *thin stands of reeds* draw smallmouth bass, which chase minnows and take bottom-dwelling aquatic nymphs in them and, on surface, the adult insects. But if the stand of reeds is dense, it usually will not hold fish, or else, if both bass are in the lake, it will be a largemouth feeding ground.

A typical lake cove may have both sides lined with aquatic vegetation. A smallmouth seeker here will test the middle of the cove. Here there may be deep gravel bars, down as much as 20 feet. Sometimes smallmouths are simply lined up in such a situation.

If a cove has a rocky, weedless shoreline, with stair-step ledges and *crumbled rocks* going down into deep water, somewhere along it, if you find the proper depth for that day, you will almost certainly hit bass. If there is a slide of rock on shore and to the water's edge, it probably continues on down at about the same slant. This is a natural for these bass.

Look, too, for rock and gravel *shoals* that may fool you because they are not very deep—maybe two or three feet. With clear water and pale bottom you won't find bass there by day. But if the shoal runs out on a modest slant to water six to ten feet and then falls away swiftly, it may be alive with bass at evening and after. The reason?

This kind of environment is perfect for growing heavy crops of crayfish, and also certain aquatic nymphs. Both are mainstays of smallmouth diet. These shoals also sometimes attract swarms of minnows. Smallmouth diet, because the lakes it inhabits are not very fertile, is less varied than that of its relatives. Nymphs, crayfish, minnows—these are mainstays. Where they are, the fish usually will be.

While shoals and deep bars are now 'n' then discoveries, *points* are without question the most important feature of any smallmouth lake—rocky points or semi-rocky points that have large and small gravel off them. All points in these categories are particularly appealing to the bass because they are three dimensional—two sides and the end.

At different times of day, because of sun angle, smallmouth groups may lie on one or the other side of a point, and feed there. These bass are extra-shy of bright sun, possibly because of the clarity of their usual habitats. This may also influence them to stay deeper and to feed far more under water than at the surface.

A point that slips down into a mass of crumbled rock and rubble and off at a ten-foot depth, drops quite steeply, but with ledges and rocks on down, may hold fish at different depths incessantly. If there is a shady side, try it first. If a wind is blowing, try the side toward which it is blowing, or the point end if it is heading at the point. Fish the side of the lake where the wind strikes, but down fairly deep. Wind pushes forage in against such structures, and it also breaks up surface light as the water is roughed up.

Points, at some depth along their below-water portions, are the most surefire places to locate smallmouth bass. Not every one, of course, will hold fish when you're there. But these are lake features easy to spot and some of them are virtually certain on any day to show you action. No vegetation at all is necessary.

Lures bumped right along bottom do the most consistent business, once you find the depth. Occasionally lure travel direction makes a difference—a lure moving up the incline, which means you'd fish from shore or very close in—or traveling down the slope, fishing by boat from off the point—fetching a lure across a point. Bait, especially live crayfish, is a killer for this situation, or on a proper crawdad infested shoal.

Don't hesitate when probing a point to go way out off it, if the slant continues on down. Fish deep. When surface water is warm, and conversely when it is very cold, these bass are rather commonly located at 50- to 60-plus feet, off a steep drop, along a deep bar, in a deep, rocky hole.

In many of the northern home-range lakes of the smallmouth *islands* are a standard feature. Most have conifers or other trees growing on them, with the surface rocky and the slant rather steep and rocky underwater. But there are also scores of high points in these—and other—smallmouth lakes that didn't quite become islands.

They'll be indicated by a rock or two sticking up, sometimes by a bit of aquatic vegetation, often of a floating sort with stems reaching a couple of feet down to the firm base. Others are those *midlake shoals* or shallow, rocky places you make note of and avoid scrupulously so not to damage boat and motor.

If those spots fall away anywhere along the perimeter of the area to deep water, right there is a hotspot for congregating smallmouth bass. A cone-shaped island with or without vegetation atop, or that barely submerged conical knoll—these also are great finds. Bass can lie at any depth anywhere on the underwater slope, enjoying their favorite rocky cover, or they can move on down to the lake floor at the base of the island. They can rest at any depth, and they can find favorite forage over a wide span of depth.

Midlake knolls topped with a circular patch of semi-floating vegetation draw thousands of minnows and nymphs and sometimes crayfish. This is a gourmet restaurant for smallmouth bass, which can feed clear around or on any side. They move up or down the slope as light and temperature dictate.

Because these bass are light shy, and also far more skittish and wary than largemouths—again perhaps because of the "glass houses" they inhabit—they are famous for dusk and dawn feeding. Approach a point or an island—which is for all practical purposes comparable to a point—quietly at dusk and begin casting. The bass make vertical migrations sometimes two or three times daily up to and back to various depths. At full dusk, they may be right up by the edge of the submerged knoll or island.

SEASONAL RULES

By and large, because of their selectivity regarding habitat, smallmouths do not make as many and varied moves around the season as do their relatives. The reason? Their choices are few.

The basic rules are these:
- In summer, fish deep except at dusk and after.
- In fall, an excellent time, one of high activity for this bass, fish the points and coves with bars and the islands at moderate depths and concentrate especially on dull, overcast, blowsy days.
- In winter, search out the deep holes, bars, points, and island bases.
- In spring, during pre-spawning and spawning, get a fix on the gravel, hard sand, and small-rock rubble areas in water four to six to ten feet deep.

There is one spring habit of the smallmouth that should be kept in mind where the proper situation is available. Possibly because of their proclivity for clear, swift streams, these bass in some cases attempt definite spawning runs from lakes up tributary streams. They are probably following an ancient urge. In the pre-spawning weeks, and during the spawning period, it is not unusual to discover large concentrations of bass off the mouths of clear, cold streams or moving up them.

These then are the basics for becoming an expert on smallmouth bass lakes. Contrary to what numerous largemouth anglers have believed—those who visit smallmouth territory, or have this fish, by introduction, in their own bailiwick, or who have paid it little heed even though they live within its native range—this is not a difficult fish to locate in lakes.

To be sure it is more shy and less impulsive than the largemouth. But at least, sticking with its favorite lake features, it finds fewer places that suit it for consorting. A bass fisherman who thoroughly understands what kinds of places in a lake the smallmouth favors should have little trouble finding fish.

PART 3

TROUT FISHING

How Trout Feed In Streams

Dave Whitlock

Trout, char, grayling, and land-locked salmon living in freshwater lakes or streams have specific physical characteristics that govern their feeding behavior. The flyfisherman must understand these in order to succeed in catching these fish with aquatic-food imitations. Trout live in an environment that few if any anglers understand completely; water drastically alters and handicaps our senses when we swim beneath the surface. How trout—whose senses are keyed for them to survive in water—swim, see, smell, taste, hear, and feel relates directly to how they eat natural aquatic foods or accept artificial imitations. It is a great learning experience for trout fishermen to spend a few hours swimming underwater in both clear and murky trout lakes and streams. Such an adventure greatly heightens one's ability to understand trout and their unique environment.

Trout are not capable of mystical, magical, or highly intellectual reactions. They simply use their well-adapted senses in combinations that give them the best results for any given water and food situation. In murky water, for instance, their sight is greatly handicapped, but they then exploit their acute senses of smell and hearing to locate food or escape danger.

Trout see, hear, feel, smell, and taste very well. Their bodies and senses are well designed to function efficiently within the limits of their environment. But one must not compare water with our far less restrictive air environment. Water is many times denser, thus greatly altering what can be sensed. Movement is also greatly affected due to increased density and the effect of water turbulence or motion.

Trout are well adapted to live in stillwaters and flowing waters with currents up to ten miles per hour. They can swim up to 20 miles per hour for short periods and maintain a five-mile-per-hour speed for many hours. Their compact shape and soft-rayed fins and tail enable them to move through the water efficiently. Even as they inhale the water through their mouths and expel it through their gill openings, they produce a jet action that moves them through the water. Their entire body and fins have mucous glands whose secretions greatly reduce water drag and guard against injury or infection.

A trout uses its dorsal fin and anal fin as vertical body stabilizers (or keels), as rudders, and to brake themselves. The pair of pectoral fins assists in ups-and-downs or planing movements, braking, backing up, and turning slightly. The paired pelvic fins are used to some extent as secondary planers, but they more consistently serve for balance and protection against the bottom when resting on or near it. The tail (caudal fin) is used mostly for propulsion but also as a rudder, for protection, and for digging. The entire body length behind the head is a series of muscles whose strength is directed into the tail. Being predators, trout have perfect body-fin-eye coordination with their well-developed and efficient mouths.

A trout can achieve a high peak of efficiency by becoming nearly weightless through use of its internal swim bladder (or air bladder). By adjusting its air pressure, a trout can float, reach neutral buoyancy, or, by becoming heavier than water, sink. Trout can make these minor adjustments as they swim, feed, rest, or even sleep. A trout sleeps by relaxing itself into a semiconscious state, still alert to external stimuli as well as maintaining its holding position with involuntary fin and body movement. Its eyes have no lids, so it does not appear to be asleep. Sleep periods can last just a few minutes to several hours.

In flowing waters, trout move up, down, or sideways by using the current's energy against their body and the attitude of their fins, just as you would control a glider in moving air. Minimal energy need be used.

In calmer waters such as sloughs, deep pools, ponds, and lakes, trout must provide most of their movement with muscular flexes of their fins and tail. However, it is well to remember that though they use a little more energy foraging and capturing food in calm waters, they do not use as much total energy as trout holding position against a constant flow. Trout of equal age and nutritional intake in lakes will consistently be heavier bodied than their stream counterparts; but a stream trout is usually a bit faster and has greater endurance.

Trout, as most other predatory fish, are generally considered sight feeders, using their other senses to a lesser degree to capture their foods. They have excellent eyes with which to see their environment. The round lens of their eyes has a very short focal length; it can only be refocused by muscular movement closer to the retina. Trout cannot flatten the lens as we can on our eyes to obtain greatest total focal length; but they seldom need to see more than ten to 15 feet away as water clarity in most places becomes greatly restricted past those distances. Water supports large amounts of dissolved minerals, chemicals, and particles and is a poor transmitter of light. So a trout's near-sighted vision is best adapted to its water environment.

Trout have binocular (or stereo) vision directly in front of their heads at an approximate 45-degree angle, and monocular vision on each side of their head and body. Trout use binocular vision to see an object best with depth perception; monocular vision is best for detecting movement peripherally.

If the fly is on or in the water's surface a trout has a distorted view of it; this is caused by surface movement, refraction, reflection, and similar phenomena. If the fly is immediately beneath the surface film it comes *into full, clear, undistorted view of the trout's eyes* . . . a fact many anglers seldom realize as they view the same fly through the surface (which is highly distorted and reflective).

Trout see colors quite well but adapt slowly to drastic light changes or intensities. This is because the trout eye has a fixed iris that cannot adjust

A nymph-feeding rainbow.

amounts of light the way the human eye can. The trout eye adjusts to light intensity by extending or withdrawing the rods and cones on the retina; this is a slow process. Bright lights, then, are least preferred. Trout will hold in deep water or in heavily shadowed areas when such light is present. It can take as long as two hours for them to become comfortable after a drastic light change has taken place.

In deep water or on the darkest nights, trout see poorly—both colors and low-contrast objects. In such situations they shift to their other senses to locate food.

A trout hears by two methods: two ears inside its head and its lateral-line sensors. Water, due to its greater density, transmits sound or pressure waves much faster and more efficiently than air. The inner ear is used to hear high-frequency vibrations (sounds). The lateral line senses low frequency, close vibrations (pressure waves) most efficiently; it is more a true pressure sensor than a modified ear. Trout can usually tell the size, direction, and speed of a moving object up to 20 feet away with their lateral-line sensors. Beyond 20 to 30 feet, trout depend on their ears to hear with. Of course most of these high- or low-frequency sounds are identifiable by the trout, and it reacts accordingly to what it detects . . . food or foe.

If an angler wades toward a trout, the trout hears the splashing of the water and the grinding of the boot soles against the bottom. It detects the pressure wave of water movement, the angler's size, speed, and direction beneath the water with its lateral-line sensor. An insect, minnow, mink, watersnake, or other creature is also sensed, identified, and reacted to in this way. A sleeping trout depends almost entirely on its lateral-line sensor; this is its first line of alarm detection. Danger or fleeing aquatic creatures can be quickly detected by the snoozing trout, and it will awaken at once. Trout can be aroused by noisy foods or lures, as well. The sounds of aquatic trout foods or other feeding trout often trigger a trout into feeding.

Trout have a highly developed double-nostril olfactory system. They can detect a wide range of smells in very low parts-per-million concentrations. The physical nature of water transports smell extremely well. Odor becomes crucial when a trout's sight is limited in detecting desired aquatic food. I am convinced that odor is a close second to sight in determining trout-food choice.

Trout rely heavily on their sense of smell to confirm the edibility of any food object. All natural foods emit great amounts of odor. Dead or alive or artificial, the odor can be identified by a trout. Wild trout also recognize the unique scents put out by panic-stricken minnows, injured live foods, insects and crustaceans going through metamorphic skin changes, or by freshly laid eggs. Young or foolish trout or those under stress from food scarcity or high competition with other trout will abandon their smell sense, but most large wild trout use it religiously. I've seen many big browns and rainbows refuse a fly after smelling or tasting its tail. Cutthroat and brook trout have reputations for great gullibility; this may be due to their lack of concern for food odor.

It is well documented that all salmonids are put off by human or organic chemical odors that are foreign to their environment. A new fly reeking with head cement, Pliobond, varnish, paint, detergent, or dyes, as well as human hand scents might well cause trout to sneeze or cough and look elsewhere for a good mouthful. I'm sure the smell of a mink, snake, or heron has an equally traumatic effect on a wild trout.

The fly tier and flyfisher should give careful consideration to how his flies smell to a trout. Limiting offensive odors, washing flies carefully, masking such odors, or adding natural food odors will help you achieve optimum results. For example, when I fish subsurface imitations of aquatic food forms, I'll rub the fly with the bottom of a rock or a piece of vegetation taken from the stream. This not only helps eliminate offensive odor, but it also wets the fly to help it sink. There is no doubt that a fly so treated

Trout detect various vibrations: low-frequency are received by the lateral line, high-frequency by the ear.

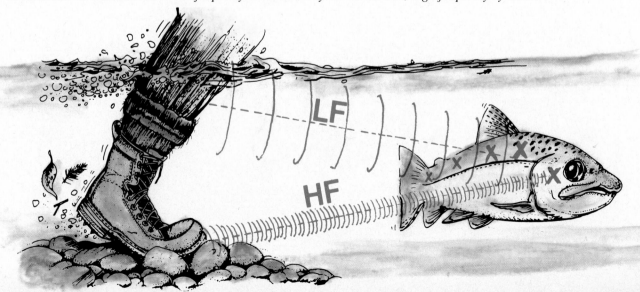

Trout live in an environment that few if any anglers understand completely. It is a great learning experience for trout fishermen to spend a few hours swimming underwater in both clear and murky trout lakes and streams.

performs better than one that carries human or chemical scents.

A trout can taste and feel sensitively with its mouth as it strikes, inhales, and closes its mouth down on its food. I've often watched a trout mouth and expel an artificial fly unencumbered by leader or drag. I tossed the fly in the water to study the trout's reaction to its taste and feel. Hard flies, and those made of plastic or enameled materials, are ejected immediately. Flies constructed of soft materials, especially natural furs, feathers, or soft synthetics, are retained longer or sometimes swallowed. The texture of a natural food or artificial is critical in the flash of time the trout retains the captured food; this is especially true for the underwater, slow-fishing techniques such as nymphing.

As trout grow and mature they become greater masters of their physical abilities and senses, at least until old age overtakes them (usually between seven and nine years). From their earliest days, most trout prefer to collect or intercept their foods. If the supply of aquatic insects or other small, slow-swimming natural aquatic food is plentiful, they will continue to feed largely on them throughout their lives. However, these smaller foods usually become less practical for large adult fish to gather in adequate quantities. So they commonly turn to larger, more available foods, such as minnows, crayfish, amphibians, and small trout. But these live foods require much more active foraging than do the smaller food forms. Adult trout can swim faster; and they usually develop stronger and more heavily toothed jaws for seizing and killing their prey.

There is usually a practical order of large-food preferences after wild adult trout abandon the insects, scuds, and smaller creatures. This is predicated on food value versus ease of gathering. Such foods as leeches, tadpoles, crayfish, sculpin, school minnows, individual free-swimming minnows (chubs, whitefish, shiners, and others), and small trout are preferred in that general order. Bottom- or deep-swimming large foods are greatly preferred over shallow-water or shallow-swimming foods, again because they are easier to find, flush, chase, and then kill and eat. The leech, crayfish, and sculpin are all extremely practical big-fish foods as each has little defense against the predator trout and dwells on or near the bottom.

The various species of trout, char, grayling, and salmon exhibit individual characteristics. The differences between wild-born trout, trout stocked as fry, and domesticated hatchery trout can be drastic also. Tame trout live by different conditioned reflexes and standards than do wild-born or stocked-as-fry fish. Knowledge of this can be of great value to the angler. For instance, brown trout and to a slightly lesser extent brook trout are twilight and nighttime feeders. Both commonly "hole up" in the daytime under objects, in beds of aquatic vegetation, or on the bottoms of deep pools, pockets, or holes. They often sleep all day and stir only as the sun begins to set. Though this is not always so, it occurs commonly across their range during the warmer months.

Rainbows and cutthroats are classic daytime feeders. They prefer to suspend themselves off the bottom adjacent to cover but not beneath or in it unless danger is present. Often they flee from their enemies rather than hide from them. Even sleeping or resting they suspend off the bottom in relatively open areas and seldom allow any major objects to pass by unnoticed.

Thus it is easy to see why a rainbow would be considered easier to take on a fly than a brown on most days. It is swimming, wide awake and ready when most of us are on the water. The brown isn't caught because it is deep, asleep, or waiting for darkness to feed. If you fished only at night you might well think browns more gullible or plentiful than the light-loving rainbows present in perhaps equal numbers in the same waters.

A domesticated or manmade "plastic" hatchery trout of either species is probably motivated to a frenzy of feeding by a man-set clock time and the sound of thousands of peasize pellets striking the water. This continues for *as long as a year* after these trout have been dumped in the water. I've taken a handful of small bits of gravel and cast it over the surface of a pool that contained stocked trout. In seconds, thirty or forty eight- to ten-inch, pellet-begging, gray-spotted forms would appear at the surface around my feet.

Such unusual environmental conditions as tailwater releases, snow runoffs, rains, droughts, storms, and temperature extremes can drastically alter trout feeding cycles. Major hatches or aquatic-food migrations can also throw normal cycles off. An alert flyfisher quickly recognizes these key changes and uses them to his advantage.

With these physical and sensory characteristics in mind let's look at several hypothetical situations to relate how a trout locates and takes its food.

Nymphing. There is a heavy mayfly hatch on a clear trout stream. A nice wild rainbow trout is hold-

ing in two feet of water just below the riffle. It has adjusted its weight so it can suspend about eight inches off the bottom and is eagerly intercepting the rising nymphs. A weighted soft-fur nymph is cast about 15 feet above the working trout and sinks about a foot before it drifts more or less straight downstream toward the waiting trout. The noise level of the dancing riffle masks its splashdown entry from the rainbow's ears. The trout senses the nymph's movement about four feet upstream and to its left with its sensitive peripheral vision. It turns toward the nymph using its dorsal and pelvic fins so it can see the nymph more clearly as it approaches. Interested now, it cocks its pectoral fins up and begins to drift back while rising upward to meet the nymph. As it intercepts the fly it watches, sniffs, and then opens its mouth to inhale the nymph. Once the nymph is captured, the pectoral-fin edges bend down and the trout begins a drifting dive back toward the bottom. Now it planes down and swims leisurely back to its holding position as it attempts to swallow the face nymph.

In this case, the trout principally used it vision, smell, and touch senses and bodily movement to locate and capture the nymph.

A night-minnow-feeding brown trout. It is two hours after dark, and there is no moon. A large brown trout is cruising around a big pool searching for its nightly prey of sculpins, crayfish, and large surface insects. The fly, a large, dark, deer-hair-head sculpin is cast across the tail of the pool. The brown hears the big streamer plop down, and it stops, tenses, and becomes silent. Next the streamer is slowly stripped deep across the bottom, sometimes swimming, sometimes bounding off rocks, aquatic vegetation, and sunken tree limbs. The brown detects from these movements the pressure waves and noises. Slowly at first, it begins to swim toward the fly.

A night-feeding brown.

Illustrations by Dave Whitlock

A brook trout feeding in high water.

The closer it gets the more accurately it interprets the fly's distance, size, and speed with its lateral-line sensor. About two feet away, the brown sees the fly's outline and surges to it for the kill. The sense of touch is next used as the brown strikes the sculpin with stunning closed-jaw blows. Something is drastically wrong! It does not give off a characteristic panic odor, blood smell, or injured vibrations. It has a horrible unnatural odor. So the brown follows the streamer, smelling its wake for several yards, then turns and swims away, seeking another, more realistic prey.

In this case, darkness restricted the trout's distance vision so it used its ears and lateral-line sensor to detect and locate its prey. But its sense of sight and touch and smell were all used in the final decision to strike but not to eat the object.

A murky, cold, rain-swollen brook-trout stream.
The 30-foot-wide stream has risen a foot only a few hours after a cold, early-spring rain. Its water temperature has risen from 46 to 50 degrees and has put a fine brook trout on the feed. The trout can barely see six inches clearly, so it holds deep in a pocket under a steep, rooty cutback just below the riffle of its home pool, listening and sniffing the stream's flow.

The flyfisherman casts a very large, black, marabou-winged, weighted Muddler on a short leader and a high-density, sinking-tip line 20 feet above the brook's lair. The big fly splats down on the water, and the trout is alerted as it picks up the entry sound with its ear. The fly sinks rapidly, dragging as it begins to swing across the stream and approach the trout. The Muddler's blunt, bulky, deer-hair head and wiggling marabou wing sets up a series of low-frequency pressure waves as it moves across the current.

The brook trout picks up this movement with its lateral-line sensor, identifies its general size and speed, and moves to its left to intercept the still un-

seen object. The waving black wing suddenly comes into view as a silhouette, and its Mylar body glints, presenting a form of vulnerable life. The trout charges with a strong tail thrust to seize the fleeing form. The scent trail of the wet, well-used streamer is that of natural origin, given to it by several previous catches of chub and trout; this masks the initial man-given odors of tying, finishing, and handling. The strike is sure and violent and the streamer crushes under the trout's bit, further confirming its reality.

In this case, the trout stationed itself safely and quietly in a deep, calm, protected area and turned on its ears and nose. The streamer was heard, felt, seen, and smelled in that order before the strike came. If the fly had been slender, small, light-colored, and dead-drifting, it would have gone unnoticed.

As you can see in these three simple examples, trout use various combinations of their body attributes and senses to find, identify, and take or reject possible food. A consistently productive fly fisher will understand these things and choose his fly designs and fish them accordingly. Knowledge of a trout's senses, the water's environmental condition, and reading the water are, therefore, the three keys to fishing the right artificial.

With all the keenly honed natural instincts and senses wild trout possess, you might feel catching them on imitations is an almost impossible task. Actually, the opposite is true. Wild trout are not difficult to catch on flies if your flies, tackle, and methods are chosen with proper understanding of the situation. Realize your mistakes as you observe the trout's reactions to your attempts to catch them: are they not biting, is it too hot or cold, are they not there, frightened, selective, or just not interested in your offering for another reason? Fly refusal or acceptance is explainable if you understand the fish. Ignorance of basic facts can handicap you for years, while knowledge of them can and will accelerate your success and pleasure as a fisherman.

Season-Long Trout In Lakes

Jerry Gibbs

It's hurry-up-and-grab-it time again. The frantic, joyous, short-lived, early-spring fishing that gives us so much trout action will soon shut off. When that happens it's the end of the year's trout fishing for too many anglers. But it shouldn't be. If you're willing to follow the year's progression in a lake, you can take rainbow, brown and brook trout in so-called "still waters" all season.

You should be willing to learn a variety of skills from casting flies to high-speed and deep-water trolling. Call it the well-rounded-fisherman approach. After that the trick is to follow the natural cycles of forage and weather in your chosen lake.

Ever consider why an angler who fishes only flies and another who uses natural bait can both catch trout in the same lake at the same time? Look harder and you'll see that there are periods when one of these methods will be much more effective than the other. Of course in some lakes trout primarily are oriented toward insects while in other waters specific forage fish give them their main sustenance. In most waters, though, a trout's diet is based on availability. Fish are opportunists. Though every lake has its special secrets, some generalities can be made. Just look at a typical year's cycle and you'll see.

The early-season or post-ice-out period finds fish in large bays and harbors. Often rainbows will be up rivers or moving down into the lake. Not all spring-spawning trout will run far up a river. If the environment permits, rainbows sometimes spawn near inlets or outlets. Brown trout are in the same kind of bays, harbors, and tributary mouths. They also cruise the mouths of the protected areas and are frequently caught off points and jetties. I catch brook trout at this time on shoals or reefs in big lakes. In small ponds, the deep water out from river mouths or deep-water shorelines is hard to beat for brookies.

Early-season trout look for available fish life—typically smelt—but they also feed on drifting spawn, and easily taken baits such as earthworms certainly won't be ignored. Trout are inshore or on reefs to look for such forage when they're not spawning. The fish also are attracted to plumes of heated water from power-plant discharges. This is easy-picking time for most anglers casting or trolling spoons, plugs, and streamer flies. Natural baits such as minnows also work. Weather is the key to when this early activity will shut off.

A long, cool spring results in an extended spawning period. This is not only true for rainbows but for the spring-spawning forage fish that attract trout. With some rain and gradual warming, trout that usually are up tributaries move down and out into the lake. Forage fish, too, finish their inshore activities and begin to depart. Cool-water baitfish are affected by warming water sooner than the trout, but it doesn't take the gamefish long to realize they'd better move if they want to eat. This is when anglers abandon trout to turn to other fish. This, however, is when phase two begins.

Before looking at midspring fishing, consider the effect of a very dry spring. Rainbows in the lower rivers or in the lake proper aren't too affected by lack of rain. Rainbows far upstream, however, may simply hold there until a good rain finally raises the water. Only then will they run downstream.

During a dry year, try this after the trout in harbors or bays have left for other areas: fish the water

Jerry Gibbs

Early spring need not be the only season for trout. Learn a variety of skills and you can take trout all season long.

around river mouths immediately after a good rain. You could hit a second contingent of fish just getting back to the lake. The same rain also can bring isolated pods of bait through bottlenecks at cove or bay mouths even though most forage (and trout) have already left. Such widely scattered spots often provide a final flurry of feeding by trout before the fish begin new behavioral patterns.

During phase two in midspring trout are on the move. The surface water temperature is not yet warm enough to drive them deep. The fish are moving toward the deeper lake areas where they'll take up summer residence, but they're a long way from being locked into those spots. This is the time they usually turn to feed on insects.

Mayflies, caddis, and midges yield some of the heaviest feeding and most exciting sport of the year. Key spots to search are quiet main lake shorelines, island shorelines, off long points, and areas some distance from tributary mouths. Growing weed beds usually hold the hatching insects and usually one type of weed holds more fish than others. Until you locate the areas in your lake that consistently hold trout on insects, you'll have to wait to see the insect emergence and the rising trout.

There'll be no doubt when the fish are eating. You'll see the gentle head and tail rises of trout sipping midges, mayfly spent wings, or flying ants. The more violent rises are typical of fish chasing escaping caddis or mayfly duns. During the hatch you can catch trout on dry flies, but an even more effective

method is to fish a nymph as an emerging insect. During the emergence it's best to work an unweighted nymph (matched to size and color of the hatching bug) on a long leader maybe 12 to 15 feet long, three to four feet of which is fine tippet. The trick is to grease all but the last foot or two of leader, then touch the nymph with a quick-sink preparation. After you have a line on a trout's direction of travel (by watching its rises), cast several feet ahead of where you think it ought to be. Allow the nymph to sink, then begin a series of short draws to simulate the nymph kicking to the surface. When the trout takes the nymph, gently lift your rod and fight him. It is a challenging game, however. And while that's how it should work, things can go wrong.

The biggest problem is getting the nymph in front of where a trout will be when the nymph finishes settling. It's similar to leading a bird with your shotgun, only in this case you can't see the bird. When you're using a light tippet and the fish reacts violently you can break off, if you don't quickly slip line. There are times in the midst of massive hatches when so many insects are either on or coming off the water that you despair of a fish ever finding your artificial. Wind and current can blow bugs and nymph husks into a slick of debris on the surface. In my lake we call it the chum line. Trout work through it, though. At times they hold their mouths open and gulping like whales engulf everything they can. It's an awesome sight. For such a situation, grease the *entire* length of your leader, but not the nymph, which will float just under the surface and, it is hoped, in line of the voracious feeder. Sometimes a true dry fly that's slightly larger than the naturals will work well.

Wind, unless very gentle, usually will wipe out this kind of fishing. So will an idiot who sees the rising trout and tries trolling through them. Trollers, however, often take trout in slightly deeper water farther from the hatch area, even when fish aren't rising there. I believe there is some form of communication between fish in a general area. I think that the activities surrounding the insect emergence are communicated to trout holding in deeper water, exciting them to feed.

If you're interested in flyfishing for trout in lakes, I recommend you read John Merwin's *Stillwater Trout,* Nick Lyons Books, Doubleday and Company, Garden City, New York, 1980.

As the weather warms and hatches slow in many lakes, trout descend and switch back to smelt, ciscoes, or other forage fish. In some cases trout must travel a good distance to reach deeper, cooler water. They tend to pause on their route to feast on available insects along the way. As they travel they're typically ten to 15 feet down. If you find them (use a depth sounder) while they're traveling, don't expect them to hit regularly. To catch them consistently, the trout should have taken at least temporary station in a specific area.

Once they've reached the deep-water areas in early summer, you can expect the fish to behave differently. The trout can begin to work fairly deep underwater bars, reefs, or islands. They also can be in nearby shorelines if deep water is nearby. Their most likely pattern will be to alternate between deep and shallow areas. Where they are will depend on the weather.

Here's the situation in one trout lake I regularly fish. In early summer the thermocline begins at 45 feet. Smelt schools are in 51-degree water at 50 feet. They suspend on a drop-off that plummets more than 100 feet. Rainbows and landlocked salmon feast on them—but not right away. The fish wait to eat until later in the hot weather. Until they start feeding on the smelt, I find most of the trout near rocky shores in 16 to 20 feet of water. A few bigger fish will be at 30 feet. Sometimes the trout will take cast, jigged, or trolled spoons in this area during the late afternoon. But the best fishing is at dusk. The west shores are in shadow first, and those are the shores I fish. As the sun sets the trout move up, sometimes to an emergence of insects, sometimes to hunt for whatever they find.

In the first situation previously described flyfishing methods will take them. When there is no hatch, try very small light spoons, spinners, or streamer flies. The water can be as warm as 70 to 74 degrees if the day has been bright and still. Conditions are ideal if there has been a little breeze late in the day to mix and cool the surface, but that has died by dusk.

Carefully watch the weather. At this time of year the surface can go from the mid-70s to 65 degrees in a very short time and this can cause a variety of reactions in insects, minnows, and trout.

Don't go home when darkness stills the surface action. The early nighttime hours can be grand for brown-trout fishing in the same rocky areas. Steep cliffs along mainland shores and islands and points extending far out underwater also yield browns. An even better period for browns can be from false dawn to daylight. Try trolling medium-running plugs, spoons, and big streamers.

Once hot weather has settled in you'll need downriggers or deep-diving planing devices to get your lures into the cool depths where the trout are within striking distance of forage. Whether you're trolling the preferred temperature zones of baitfish or going through schools of fish, alternate between the following basic lure systems: light, thin flutter spoons alone or behind dodgers, flashers or cowbells at slow speeds or streamer flies, plastic squid, seeker plugs (such as the J-Plug), and high-speed spoons at faster speeds. Work reefs, channels, between islands, deep points, and humps.

The warm calm, hazy, early-autumn days that follow wind and rain usually provide good fishing. Now the trout are returning to their early spring areas. Typically the surface temperature is in the 60s. I find trout far off shore working on schools of young-of-the-year baitfish. Birds will show you where they are. Sometimes the trout are around islands or roaming offshore shelves and plateaus. They usually haven't reached the sheltered areas of early spring close to mainland shores. You can cast for rising fish with any lure that resembles the small baitfish they'll be eating.

In late autumn the fish are in harbors, river mouths, and, sometimes, at the mouths of dead-end bays and coves. Brown trout will be moving up streams but, before they do, you often can find them rolling in wide, weedy river outlets near shorelines. Remember, brook trout spawn in autumn, too.

I guess my favorite late-season fishing is with high-speed spoons for big, smelt-fattened rainbows. The water surface is around 49 or 50 degrees and the big fish will be cruising close to the top and to shore. Beaches with some sand and weed, shores with small tributaries, and mouths of short bays are excellent now. Last year I caught most of my rainbows on Westport Wobbler spoons from Luhr Jensen (Box 297, Hood River, OR 97031). The spoons are 3⅜ inches long and the young smelt the trout were eating were a little more than 2½ inches! The best color combinations were chrome-red-and-black and chartreuse-and-orange. I trolled a little faster than I do for landlocked salmon. You can bet that while you're reading this I'll be on the water. You can be catching them, too, if you remember trout fishing's not just for early spring.

Gettin' Down

Geoff Dolbear

Rush Creek tumbles through a narrow, high-walled desert canyon connecting the two northernmost lakes in California's June Lake Loop, 50-odd miles north of Bishop, in the eastern Sierra. Native and holdover trout coming upstream from Grant Lake or downstream from Silver make this little stream the best flyfishing choice in the Loop. Usually. When I got there one spring, the water was a foot and a half higher than usual, the color of cheap restaurant coffee, and fast enough to make wading a harrowing experience.

Undoubtedly the best way to cope with such high, roily water is to fish somewhere else. Second-best is to fish another time. But when a trip has been planned weeks or even months in advance, and Mother Nature combines heavy snowpacks, cool temperatures, and late runoffs to give us a junior version of Noah's flood—what then? Sit in the cabin and sip bourbon? Catch up on the Saturday Evening Post? Or use a few tricks that catch fish in spite of the lousy conditions?

Fish, of course. That day on Rush Creek, I rigged up a heavy rod, strapped on my water wings, bade my family a tearful farewell, and ventured into the roaring torrent for what might usually be considered a frustrating waste of two hours.

But that day was not usual. For the first time, I was applying a strategy to cope with high-runoff streams. I used a six-foot 2X leader equipped with a pair of (detested) split shot six inches above an ugly Bitch Creek Nymph. I worked deep, concentrating on flow edges and sheltered pockets at bends and behind a helpful stump. And I caught several nice rainbows, including a fat two-pounder that fed us that evening.

Try as I do to avoid them, I hit high-water conditions somewhere every spring and summer. I've tried calling ahead to fly shops, monitoring snowpack reports, consulting satellite weather photos, and visiting the local Gypsy tea-leaf reader. Nothing helps. But my terrible track record forced me to learn to fish the runoff, and now I take it (almost) in stride.

MUD

When the water is muddy as well as high, fishing is generally poor. And the muddier the water, the poorer. There are several schools of thought on why this is so. One holds that trout get all the food they want from the aquatic and terrestrial insects swept into the stream as banks and bottoms are scoured by the running water. Fish don't take a fly, it is argued, when they are stuffed by the passing fare. The second school maintains that mud makes the fish sickly, or at least blunts their appetites; trout wait until things clear up before feeding again.

Both ignore the fact that bait slingers routinely catch nice trout in the muddiest of waters. I'll stake my money on the thought that trout simply can't see well in the murk, and rely on their noses to guide their menu selection. They can't see or smell artificials, so they don't take them.

OR NO MUD

One way to avoid mud is to seek out little feeder streams. These are clear more often than the rivers they feed, probably because they recover more quickly, and it takes only one muddy tributary among many to wreck a river.

Another way to avoid muddy water—on some rivers—is to fish at the bases of dams. This has worked

This article appeared in the May 1984 issue of *Rod & Reel* magazine.

When a trip has been planned in advance and nature provides high, fast water, fish anyway! With the right equipment and technique, you'll have success.

Valentine Atkinson

for me while camping and fishing around Aspen, Colorado. In '82, the well-named Roaring Fork was still in flood from the late runoff when we arrived in mid-July. Fishing with anything but a gill net would have been as futile as searching for a parking place in Aspen.

Fishing the nearby Frying Pan River was a different story. Its flow is controlled by a dam about 15 miles above where it joins the Roaring Fork at the little town of Basalt. As often happens, the lake behind the dam served as an effective barrier to the mud coming from farther upstream. The Frying Pan's flow was high, but not so high that it was unwadable. The water coming from the base of the reservoir was cold but relatively clear. I caught rainbows and brookies in the flies-only section.

Sometimes, though, we are left with no choice but to fish muddy water. When this happens, search for pockets behind rocks, logs, bridge pilings, and other obstructions. Things don't stay so riled up in these pockets; the water is sometimes a bit clearer, and trout, possibly seeking a haven from the current, can often be found here. Everybody knows this, of course, and we all search out such spots whenever and wherever we fish, but they are especially valuable when streams are high and colored.

THE LOWDOWN ON LEAD

Murphy's Law has many corollaries, one of which states: on a fast stream, wet flies, dry flies, and nymphs will all ride abou six inches below the surface—if left to their own devices. Sinking flies are lifted off the bottom by the same turbulence which slops over the floaters and sinks them. When we want to put the fly on the bottom, we're forced to add weight, on or near the fly.

Which is it to be—weighted fly? Or split shot on the leader? Depends on what we want to accomplish. It's obvious that the lead will be the deepest point on a submerged leader. If we want the fly to bump the bottom (an insect hopping a ride from one rock to the next?), then the weight must be on the fly. But if we want the fly to look like food swept along just above the stream bottom, weight should be pinched on a few inches above the fly.

(Matters of finesse aside, when the water is really sluicing along and more than knee-deep, a weighted fly is often not heavy enough. The leader must also be weighted to get the fly down.)

Lead is ordinarily applied to a leader as a string of split shot. But there are other ways, each with its own advantages. One is the twist-on, a little, flat noodle of lead that comes in a matchbook. One of these, or a part of one, can be wound around the leader at any point and crimped into place. Twist-ons are easy to carry, easy to find in your vest, and reusable.

Gourmets use the foil found on the top of good bottles of wine. Lead costs more this way, but you get some very nice wine in the bargain.

Another design, more akin to the split shot, is the Fly Rite sleeve, a little split tube that clamps on the leader. The design is sleeker than a string of beads. I haven't run a controlled experiment, but it seems that I don't hang up on the bottom as often with the sleeves as with the shot.

On streams with rocky bottoms, whatever kind of weight we use tends to catch in cracks and crevices. This often results in a lost fly, as the leader breaks either at the tippet knot or the first leader knot. A good way to avoid this is to attach the weight to a short dropper spliced in a foot or so above the fly. When the lead hangs up, a pull on the line will strip it off and return the fly to you for another weighted dropper and another cast. And make no mistake: A fly properly weighted will hang up every chance it gets. If yours doesn't, you're not getting deep enough and you need to add a little more lead— unless, of course, you're taking fish at your depth.

Hanging up on the bottom is only the No. 2 inconvenience of fishing a weighted fly. Number one is beaning the back of your head on inadvertently low forward casts. Short of wearing a crash helmet, you can alleviate the problem and/or minimize the pain by using a long rod and wearing a hat with a stiff brim in the back. You'll soon develop a compensatory casting stroke, too.

SINKING LINES

It may be unorthodox, but I use a floating line instead of a sinking in fast, high water. I find that things happen too fast for sinking lines (and especially sinking tips) to be of much help: The fly is in the water, on the bottom, and past the trout's nose in what seems like only an instant and is probably no more than fifteen seconds. With time so short, the fly must be diving actively for the bottom, not following passively behind a sinking line. If you're searching open, high water in full spate, a sinking line with a short leader, a weighted fly, *and* additional lead is best. But for probing pockets in fast water, the weighted fly/tippet gets down fast, yet the floating line avoids sunken snags.

LEADERS

My imagination was snared at an early age by images of Charles Ritz and Al McClane floating submicroscopic flies over college-educated trout, using 12- to 15-foot leaders scientifically tapered to 7X or less. From such visions came the belief, now tattooed on my brain, that all leaders must be long, tapered, and super-fine.

Well, 'tain't so. When we bombard fish with fat flies and split shot, the best leader is short and strong. Strikes in fast water can be violent, and short leaders are more easily controlled. Lefty Kreh reported several years ago that leaders as short as one foot aren't a problem with fishing sinking flies; and Charlie Brooks has repeatedly argued for four-footers when nymphing turbulent water. I use six feet of leader as a good compromise: with my combination of

A selection of flies is essential to account for whatever conditions you may encounter.   *Geoffrey Dolbear*

floating line and weighted fly, the leader must be long enough to reach the bottom, yet short enough for good control.

PRESENTATION

On a high, fast stream, presentation means just one thing—getting the fly on the bottom, dead-drift or swimming. The easiest way to do this is to cast at a quartering angle upstream and let the fly travel down and across. When the current is not too fast and the water not too deep, this time-honored method works and catches fish. But in really fast water the fly spends too little time in free drift, too much being dragged by the leader. This drag may spook the fish or pull the fly up and away from the fish.

A better way is to cast almost directly upstream, letting the fly sink as it comes past you to the fish a few yards downstream. Charlie Brooks has dubbed this the "Charlie Brooks Method." It's most effective when the slack is lifted from the water by raising the rod tip as the fly comes past. This looks (and feels) ridiculous, but what do you want—to look suave or to catch fish? The slack must be controlled in order to respond to a strike; longer casts may require a few lightning-fast strips of the line even before you begin to raise the rod tip. As you turn downstream to follow, you can carefully shake the retrieved line back out, to extend your drift.

FLIES

It was on the Owens River, just above Bishop, California, that I finally learned the importance of visibility over pattern in high water. Although it was Thanksgiving weekend, the river was in full flood. The folks who control the reservoir upstream had chosen this weekend to sluice out a few acre-feet of excess murky water. Going elsewhere was not an option since all the nearby mountain streams were closed for the winter.

Bemoaning my fate, I rigged up the usual high-water system, with enough shot to bring down a goose, and a black Woolly Worm. It got me nothing. I will pass over my trials with several other colors and go on to the good news: green worked. Once I tied on a green fly, I could almost do no wrong. When I had lost my last green woolly, I even took a fish on an ungainly, bugeyed green streamer I use for bonito in the ocean. What's more, a fellow I met on the stream, who was using what looked like a green chenille leech, was showing off a big brown that made my day look positively dull and unproductive.

Visibility is nearly always more important than pattern whenever roil water turns normally finicky trout into unselective opportunists. Visibility means big enough (sizes four to ten) to be seen as it skims past, and it means colors that the fish can see well.

The relationship between color and visibility is a topic that merits a doctoral dissertation. Mark Sosin and John Clark, in their book *Through the Fish's Eye*, devote an entire chapter to it. They report that research has proven that fish have color vision, and that shallow-water species (such as trout) have developed it more acutely than their cousins who roam the deeps. But the colors underwater depend on what colors in the light are filtered by the water. Even in the proverbial "gin-clear" water, for instance, red wavelengths are filtered out before yellow, green, and blue. That makes red flies, fished deep, look black because there's no red light for them to reflect. And in murky or stained water, the crud that makes the water look bad can be filtering out red, yellow, green, or blue. As a result, the fly you usually think of as irresistible may be totally invisible to the fish.

The choice of color depends on the condition of the water, and how it makes things look to the fish. Unless you carry a portable water-analysis laboratory in your vest, you must sort through a variety of colors to find what the fish can see. We generally do this anyway, but at least now you know one more reason *why*.

I often start with Woolly Worms because they have the bulk to be seen and a believable, buggy shape. I keep a couple of dark blue ones in my vest. (Sosin says that blue is the last color to disappear in clear water, so it's probably visible when other colors are not.) And I often tie several woollies with a red tail, as a kind of color insurance.

Shiny, silver Mylar or tinsel picks up what light there is to make a fly more visible when clarity or color are lacking. Try a couple of black Woolly Worms that have a strip of tinsel wound down the body, under the palmered hackle. Streamer fishermen, of course, carry plenty of silver-bodied flies that accomplish the same thing.

I also use black or brown Montana Stonefly nymphs and their ugly bugger cousin, the Bitch Creek. All have yellow or orange for contrast, and, tied well, these patterns are buggy enough to swat. But my favorite is the Renegade. Not the dry version that's so popular in Colorado, but a bigger, wet fly, weighted to sink. My friend Warrack Wilson ties them with head and tail collars of white or brown hen hackle and a chubby body of peacock herl. I add an invisible overwrap of fine copper wire to help hold them together when the trout become aggressive.

BE PREPARED

A former boss of mine was fond of saying "No amount of planning will ever replace dumb luck." That's as true in flyfishing as in anything else. But when your dumb luck turns sour and lands you in the middle of the spring runoff, don't forsake the long rod. Look up some clear tributaries or a helpful dam, dig out those fat, sinking flies, and fish deep. Maybe you'll find it's the trout whose luck has soured.

Spring, Small Streams, And Bruiser Brown Trout!

Doug Stange with Doug Kowles and Lee Nelson

Want to catch a huge brown? Where to begin? As always, with the fish itself. Good detectives find out as much as possible about a fugitive because they know bits of information will help locate him. Once they locate the outlaw, they may employ many techniques to actually bring him to justice.

Sound familiar? That's Doug Kowles's and Lee Nelson's F + L + P = S (FISH + LOCATION + PRESENTATION = SUCCESS) formula. Although it takes some physical effort, their formula is amazingly simple to apply. Knowing the characteristics of individual fish species allows us to locate them. Once they're located, we choose the best of many possible presentation techniques to catch them.

So what about brown trout? The brown is not a native North American fish, but was stocked into American streams in the late 1800s. In Michigan, for example, they were stocked into streams in the lower peninsula in about 1883, after the now extinct Michigan grayling had declined.

Of the three species of trout commonly sought—browns, rainbows, and brookies—browns are without question the most wary. Big browns are difficult to catch using standard "trouting" techniques, so they often grow large, even in small streams.

There are other reasons why brown trout grow large in small streams. Not only is the brown wary, it is also tenacious. Studies indicate that in many, or most, stream environments browns become the dominant fish, usually occupying the best holding positions and displacing other trout to lesser areas where predation is higher and food-gathering possibilities are lower. Where brookies and browns coexist, for example, brook trout tend to be displaced to very cold, headwater stream areas, while browns usually occupy the central and lower stretches. Where they live together in the same stretch of river,

browns usually occupy the premium holding positions—those that offer better slack-water areas or better cover.

Browns are not only tenacious in their dealings with other trout, they are also environmentally tenacious. Browns can withstand summer water temperatures approaching 80 degrees Fahrenheit. This goes hand-in-hand with the ability to survive in stream sections that hardly resemble the fast-flowing, rocky, crystal-clear stretches usually associated with trout. Brown trout also winter very well, and unlike other trout, often feed vigorously during this period.

Browns are hardcore carnivores. Sure, small fish eat plenty of small insects; so do big fish at times. As browns grow larger, however, they prefer meat. To continue to grow, energy intake must exceed energy output. Forage such as chubs, suckers, and even small trout are the answer. Big browns eat mainly fish!

Of all the trout, browns are also the most light sensitive. Big browns invariably seek out light-shielding shelter (deep pools, overhead cover, or, preferably, both) and stray away from it only during early morning and evening, after dark, or when streams are dirty after a rain. The bruisers will also charge out of cover in a flash to grab hapless prey. Indeed, because of their sensitivity to light, their desire for protective cover, and their penchant for foraging on fish, small-stream browns are almost always ambush feeders.

BIG-BROWN LOCATION

Although there are other interesting big-brown characteristics, we now have enough facts to put it all together, just as Doug and Lee did! Small trout

This article originally appeared in Volume 48 of *In-Fisherman* magazine.

(of any species) rarely run with big-brown trout for two reasons: (1) They may get eaten, and (2) they'll certainly get out-competed for prime living space. Thus, pools or areas where big browns lurk are often devoid of small trout either because they've been eaten or because they've been driven out.

Pools should be comparatively larger and deeper to support the feeding habits of a big brown. In small streams, big browns are loners during most of the year. Don't expect good, big-trout water to be teaming with small trout.

So big trout need a lot of room and a lot of forage. Plus, they can withstand high water temperatures and do very well in marginal surroundings (by trout standards). Thus, it doesn't make sense for big trout to move upstream to cooler and smaller water and smaller prey. Bigger browns are more likely to move downstream! These areas may not fulfill the average angler's vision of "trout water."

Why are big browns usually found downriver? Because that's where they're usually most comfortable. Remember, big browns are super-wary; they abhor invasions by anglers, especially armies of anglers. This doesn't mean that when noisy anglers come by they hide and come out again when the anglers leave. If possible, it means they will gradually migrate to quieter, less traveled, safer creek stretches offering a bit more depth and water color. Again, this usually means moving downstream!

Consider a typical trout stream meandering through the hills in Minnesota, Iowa, Michigan, Wisconsin, Pennsylvania, or New York. Many of these streams originate from freshwater springs. A stream's beginning has a great "trout look" to it: a narrow creek with crystal-clear, cold, fast-moving water. As the creek continues to flow, it widens slightly, but the water still runs clear and cool over rocks and gravel. This is the section where "prime" trout pools, rapids, and holes supposedly occur. This is where the vast majority of the fishing and stocking occurs because it is obviously the "best" basic trout water. Again, however, best basic trout water isn't necessarily the same for small and large browns.

Also consider that best big trout water may be different today than it was years ago. Fishing pressure is the key. Classic stretches get most of the stocking and also get most of the pressure. Again, if they can, big browns eventually move—downriver!

If a stream runs far enough, it'll reach a point where good-looking trout water ceases; the stream may even flow through open pastures. The water may be slow-moving in some places and much of the bottom will be sand/silt, deposited through a siltation process which occurs, unfortunately, in too many streams. Small trout may thrive on small organisms that live on rocks, but big trout don't spend their time and energy searching out tidbits. Big fish need big meals and the downstream environment has just the menu: plenty of suckers and chubs.

Please don't misunderstand. We're not singing the praises of marginal trout water. We're not in favor

of poor land use such as heavy grazing, clear-cutting of timber, or stream channelization to turn classic water into marginal water. Marginal water exists, often in the natural order of things. And it often holds bruiser browns that don't get fished properly.

Each and every trout stream doesn't have marginal water, anymore than each and every lake has lake-trout water. Even when only classic waters exist, however, big browns still tend to move downstream. Once they find appropriate cover, they often become quite territorial.

To summarize, Doug and Lee found the key to locating big browns was usually to move downstream, not up. They dared, in many cases, to spend time fishing water where no one else fished. And as you'll learn, even when fishing water that others fish, they spend little time fishing any one particular spot.

What do they look for downriver? Cover! Overhead cover—usually snags or logjams. Big trout need depth or overhead cover, and preferably both. Although there may be quite a distance between possible holding areas, they are easy to recognize.

LET'S CATCH 'EM

Teddy Roosevelt once proposed, "Walk softly and carry a big stick." To catch big browns, Doug and Lee suggest, "Walk far and fish fast with big baits." Let's capture the essence of Doug and Lee's approach.

Once it's time to fish, Joe Average Angler will go a-worming, a-minnowing, or a-hellgrammiting for that once-in-a-lifetime wall-bender. (You must admit a "wall-bender" is a big fish!) Joe Average may also break out the small spinners! If he's fishing good, big-trout water, he'll probably be rewarded with hand-over-fish sucker and chub action. The key is to use a *big* artificial. Fix in your mind the fishing cliche, "big fish, big bait," because it's certainly true in this instance. The diets of mounting-size browns consist mainly of suckers and chubs as large as 11 inches. Lee caught a seven-pound two-ounce brown several years ago that had consumed a ten-inch trout!

Large lures don't limit you to big trout! Even though you're not supposed to be fishing small-trout water, you'll take some small fish. But your chances for large fish are maximized with large lures.

Lee and Doug have had the most success with countdown Rapalas in sizes ranging from a CD-9S to a CD-13S. The CD-11S is their favorite, and floaters in the same lengths also find a place in their pockets. Got the picture? These guys are fishing streams that you can almost jump across with lures that can be cast a country mile. Does that make sense? You bet it does!

Besides the fact that big browns like big baits, there are other reasons for big, usually sinking, baits. In most cases, the best downstream holding areas will be snags where fallen trees and brush offer overhead cover. You'll also find a few, small, deep fish-holding pockets. In either case, the objective is to fish a small area. The large, sinking lures get deep fast, where

the browns are. However, they also allow a flip, skip, toss or a normal cast from any of fifty different unusual positions. Weaving in and out of underbrush surrounding some creeks often leaves you in a compromised casting position. Large lures also smash and crash past small twigs falling into the water, and allow fishing for five or six feet even when your line is hung over a branch. Repeat after me: A large lure is the thing!

Why walk far and fish fast? The reason to walk far is because you fish fast, so let's cover fishing fast first. Big browns are either biting or they're not biting; it's that simple. You'll either take them with a couple of well-placed casts, or you won't take them at all—at least not then. In fact, if you continue to cast you'll only spook a fish, perhaps causing it to vacate an area. You don't want that!

Get this. Big browns are like muskies; they'll often show themselves on one of the first casts into an area. Even though the fish doesn't take, big browns that aren't spooked aren't likely to move. Now you know where a big fish is!

See why you should walk far and fish fast? Walking far allows you to cover more possible areas and learn where more big fish are. Be happy with a no-fish day as long as you learn where big fish are holding!

Finding fish is important because certain weather and water conditions tend to turn big browns on. If

To locate big browns you should move downstream, not up. Spend time fishing water no one else has fished, and keep to a small area.

In many stream environments browns become the dominant fish, usually occupying the best holding positions and displacing other trout to lesser areas.

you know where fish are, once these weather conditions arrive, drop everything drop everything, take the day off, kiss the rest of the world good-bye and head for big-fish water. Doug and Lee have taken as many as three huge browns on *rainy, dark days, after fairly long periods of stable, clear weather!* Fishing is good when the water is first *starting* to color from runoff, not *after* it's already very soiled.

In a typical day, Joe Average Trouter fishes twenty pools and makes 500 casts in a three mile section of classic trout water. Doug and Lee fish twenty or thirty snags (logjams) or deep pockets, and make only a hundred casts in ten miles of marginal (but good big-trout) water. Doug and Lee are doing more walking, less line-in-the-water fishing, but more catching of big browns! Thats the essence of Doug and Lee's approach.

A ROD, REEL, AND LINE COMBO

Some streams will be in open country; others will be lined with trees and brush. You'll usually be fishing snags. Remember, your lures won't be in the water for long; it's usually cast, splash, fish five or six feet of water, and that's it. Your best bet to handle all these situations easily and still be able to wrestle a big fish from cover is a five- or 5½-foot, medium-action spinning rod/reel combo filled with abrasion-

resistant ten or 12-pound test monofilament line. If the fish run into open water, play them, perhaps even using your drag. If they don't, apply pressure and drag them out. They won't like it!

FISHING A TYPICAL SNAG

While there is no such thing as a "typical" snag, let's proceed as if there is! First, generally attempt to approach areas from downstream. Of course, this means starting your walk from downstream and working upstream. Fishing with a partner is convenient. Your buddy can drop you off and then proceed on to park the vehicle a mile or so upstream. Work your way to the vehicle and then you can pick him up another mile or so upstream.

Sneak up on good fishing water. Stay low and wear clothes that blend in with the surroundings. Polarized sunglasses will help you view underwater conditions. If possible, make your first cast to the tail end (the most down current area) of a cut or snag. Then make another cast to the rear of a snag, or the front end of a pool, and retrieve your lure the length of the pool. If a trout follows or flashes, you might make one more cast, this time twitching the plug on the way back. OK, just one more cast! But that's all! Don't let a trout associate a lure with you!

Now, sneak to a position almost parallel to, but

TYPICAL BIG BROWN WATER

You can expect most trout streams to change as they flow from their source to mouth. It's common for a headwaters to be very narrow, and flow very cold, over steep-gradient limestone outcroppings. Headwaters (*Section 1*) often hold brook trout.

As the stream continues to flow, it widens slightly and flows, still cold, over rocks, boulders, and gravel. This section (*Section 2*) has less gradient, and this results in beautiful-looking pools and riffle areas. This is "classic" trout water and often holds small- and medium-sized browns and, perhaps, some brookies and rainbows. This is stocking water.

Continuing on, the stream becomes relatively slow-flowing. By this time, siltation has occurred, the water becomes cold or cool instead of very cold, and the bottom of the stream will be partially covered with sand and silt. Nutrients and silt washed into the stream will give the water some color. While this section doesn't look like great trout water, big browns will often take up residence here, reveling in the solitude and feeding on the abundant sucker and chub populations. These are the fish and the stream sections (*Section 3*) that often aren't fished properly.

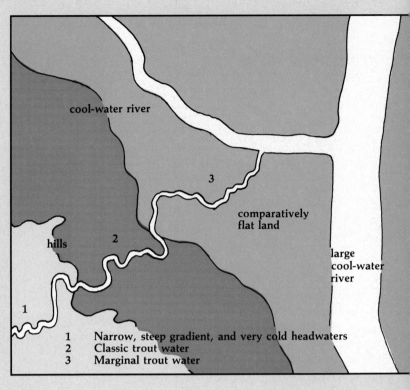

cool-water river

comparatively flat land

hills

large cool-water river

1 Narrow, steep gradient, and very cold headwaters
2 Classic trout water
3 Marginal trout water

just in front of, the snag. The spot where water washes into a snag is a prime ambush spot, so you must fish this area even if it means only being able to work a lure for two or three feet. Two or three well-placed casts should do it. If possible, let the current sweep the lure into and under the snag. The accompanying photos help clarify how to fish a typical snag.

OTHER NECESSITIES

Other than a rod and reel and a handful of lures, you should have a perfect-fitting, comfortable set of hip boots. Proper approaches are limited if you can only fish on one side of a stream. I find Red Ball Cahills by the Hampshire Company a very comfortable and durable choice.

Remember to dress for walking, not sitting. A net is an option, if you like, and a creel is nice for a few, small eating-fish. It's up to you. Make sure you have a canteen of cool water back at the car to quench the powerful thirst you work up walking during warm weather.

That brings up one final point: What's the best time of year? Doug and Lee prefer the months of April and May, although they've taken good fish all summer. The nice thing about the early season is the lack of foliage and insects.

Many anglers have been waiting for years to take a big brown from a small stream. The time's now! Hook a bruiser brown on a short line, in a small-stream tangle and you'll have your work cut out for you. But then, that's the kind of "work" we all enjoy!

It's fitting to close with the *Trout Unlimited* (P.O. Box 1944, Washington, DC 20013) organization's philosophy as it applies to trout fishing: "We believe that trout (and salmon) fishing isn't just fishing for trout (and salmon). It's fishing for sport rather than for food, where the true enjoyment of the sport lies in the challenge, the lore, and the battle of wits, not necessarily the full creel. It's the feeling of satisfaction that comes from limiting your kill instead of killing your limit. It's communing with nature where the chief reward is a refreshed body and a contented soul, where a license is a permit to use—not abuse—to enjoy—not destroy our cold-water fishery. It's subscribing to the proposition that what's good for trout (and salmon) is good for fishermen and that managing trout (and salmon) for themselves rather than for the fishermen is fundamental to the solution of our trout (and salmon) problems. It's appreciating our fishery resource, respecting fellow anglers, and giving serious thought to tomorrow."

Amen! Now lets do battle with a big brown!

MORE THAN WORDS CAN TELL

A picture's worth a thousand words! So let's let this series of photos clarify fishing for big browns in marginal trout water. You're going to be checking out the lower section of a stream. As you drove by the upstream sections, there were quite a few anglers fishing. Don't worry; that's to be expected!

Photo 1—Walk upstream, but don't waste time fishing this! Keep walking!

Photo 2—There, overhead cover with deeper water! Decide which side of the cover you can work from best. Crouch down and flip a few casts into likely spots at the back of the cover. Slip up a bit farther and do the same at the front. About five casts should do it. Move on!

Photo 3—Deeper pools deserve a cast or two. Work the tail end of the pool first. Then make a long cast or two to the front of the pool and retrieve the length of the pool. Not a likely big fish spot.

Photo 4—A man-made, necked-down area and overhead cover to boot! A dynamite spot even though you must walk ½ mile out of your way to get there.

Photo 5—A classic, big brown hideout!

Photo 6—So what if you have to work over a few branches! Hook 'em first, and land 'em second. Heavier lures make it easy to flip, skip, or cast from almost any position.

Photo 7—If it's not too tough for a big brown to live there, then it's certainly not too tough to fish. Don't be scared to toe-to-toe it with a bruiser brown.

Photo 5

Photo 6

Photo 7

Photo 1

Photo 2

Photo 3

Photo 4

Secrets Of Alpine Trout

Ron Mitchell

Alpine trout are selective feeders; at high elevations the range of food forms is small but each is very abundant.

For six days I had been in heaven. It was late September, the summer backpackers were long gone, and I had 40 wilderness lakes in Idaho's Seven Devils Mountains all to myself. I had easily fallen into a mellow routine of hiking from morning through the afternoon and camping and fishing at a new lake each evening. Now, drenched with sweat from hiking down this dusty trail, I yearned for the lake ahead, nestled below snow-splotched peaks already draped in blue evening shadow.

The trout were gorging on ants at all the lakes and, with my first glimpse of Shelf Lake through the pines, I spotted a rise. I shucked my pack on the shoreline heather and then saw a shocking sight—two men perched on a boulder looking at me.

I strolled over and met two teenagers, Larry Fouble and Harmon Fletcher from Fruitland, Idaho, who were in the process of becoming disillusioned young men. Despite the excellent fishing I had found, they had been blanked for two days.

I told them about the ants, plucked one from the lake, and showed them an imitation. Harmon squinted at the microscopic No. 22 replica. "They bite *that*? I can hardly see it. Will that little hook hook 'em?"

"Yeah, would you like to try one?" I offered.

"The trout almost hit the Rooster Tail several times," Harmon hedged, frowning. "I'll try it a little longer."

As they say, you can lead a horse to water but. . . .

I rigged my fly rod and, as I walked to a cove 80 yards away, I heard one of them call with rowdy, youthful skepticism, "Now watch him knock 'em dead."

It was a simple matter to note the general direction of a succession of rises and drop the fly six feet ahead of the trout.

"Got one!" I yelled. Both boys looked over for a minute, then went back to fishing. I released the trout and quickly hooked another and yelled again. This time they came running.

"How are you doing it?" one of them exclaimed behind me. I repeated over my shoulder the advice I'd given earlier as I released two more trout. Now both boys asked for flies. Harmon began casting his with his plastic bubble and we rigged a bubble from a piece of driftwood for Larry. In ten minutes they each had a trout.

Although I run the risk of sounding self-aggrandizing, the incident demonstrates beautifully the fickleness of trout in high mountain lakes. Ask any ten anglers for their first impressions of alpine lake fishing and nine of them will call the lakes "moody" and the fish, temperamental crazies that attack anything one moment and then suddenly reject everything.

A recent Idaho Fish and Game Department survey of fishing in its 2,000 backcountry lakes seems to buttress this traditional wisdom. When those legendary fifty-trout days were averaged in with the duds, anglers scored a paltry 2.6 trout per day—these were native trout from lightly fished waters accessible only by trails.

I fished alpine lakes for more than a decade after I turned fourteen and pretty much accepted all the above as absolute truth. One question, though, kept nagging me: Why should fingerlings planted by airplane in a 9,000-foot-elevation lake be more fickle than those in a lowland lake or stream?

I was able to probe that riddle in 1974 when I jumped on a rare opportunity to study alpine lake fishing in depth. For four summers I conducted an open-minded, objective inquiry, collecting insects and trout stomach samples from 123 lakes. I tabulated fly hatches and weather conditions and tested various fishing methods. The result was a complete turnaround in my approach to alpine lake fishing and a stunning increase in success. Much of that popular wisdom is pure malarky.

I exploded the first myth through controlled observation. The root of all evil in alpine lake fishing is the belief that if trout are biting, they are pushovers. This fatalistic attitude leads to haphazard fishing. Anglers figure any old fly, lure, or bait should do and when it doesn't, they conclude the fish must not be "on the feed." They never attempt any creative tactics nor question their original ones. The fact is, similar to sophisticated stream trout, alpine trout often display subtle taste preferences, feeding periods, and habitat favorites that must be catered to.

Examples are endless. There was the afternoon at Bench Lakes in the Sawtooth Range when small brookies repeatedly rejected No. 10 brown hackles only to immediately accept the same pattern in size 14. At Pistol Lake, ten-inch cutthroats refused No. 16 olive midges, accepting only gray No. 22s—duplicating the naturals on the water. On a September evening at Toxaway Lake, a mating flight of black ants blanketed the lake's west end and trout refused all lures but unhesitatingly slurped in a precise imitation. When its poly wings were chewed off they ignored it, too. At Cly Creek Lakes, surface-feeding cutthroats weighing up to three pounds lost interest in a formerly productive midge adult fly, opting for a cruise near the bottom, where they showed interest in only deep-drifted pupal patterns.

All too often fishermen brusquely dismiss such periods of selectivity as moodiness, never considering the all-important variable of the alpine trout's unique environment.

First of all, alpine trout are selective, though this is seldom due to wariness honed by exposure to angling pressure. At high elevation, the range of food forms is small but each is very abundant. Consequently, the trout feed on only a few food forms—the ones they are used to seeing. The angler who doesn't offer them something within their range will likely go fishless. This is especially true during heavy hatches, when trout quickly become imprinted to whatever is hatching.

Imprinting is compounded by the still, crystal water of mountain lakes. Unlike stream trout that have only an instant to inspect food sweeping by, the alpine trout has all day to read the fine print. Therefore, whatever you offer it had better be a reasonable facsimile.

Making matters even worse is the tendency of most alpine fishermen to use spinners or spoons. These simulate minnows. Minnows don't exist in 99.9 percent of alpine lakes. And while small trout are present due to natural reproduction or aerial plantings, not one of the more than 200 stomach samples I examined contained any. Sure, trout strike lures from provocation or curiosity—not just hunger—but lures seldom fool larger trout. Refusals are much more frequent with lures than with flies.

All this leads me to conclude that it is imperative to fish with flies for consistent success.

Noted fisheries biologist Cecil Heacox finds that lowland brown trout consume 80 percent mayflies, 10 percent caddis, and 10 percent miscellaneous. In similar surveys, rainbows in Western waters were found to prefer caddis. But in alpine lakes a trout's diet consists of 60 percent midges, 10 percent caddis, 10 percent scuds and water fleas (zooplankton), 5 percent waterboatmen and backswimmers, 5 percent damselflies and dragonflies, and 10 percent miscellaneous, such as ants, aphids, grasshoppers, bark beetles, and leeches. The percentages differed in lakes and by season. In some lakes, scuds and leeches formed 80 percent of the diet while, in autumn, aphids and ants amounted to 70 percent. But the message is clear: Live by worms and lures, die by worms and lures.

The "where" of fishing alpine lakes is important. Most food grows in the sun-warmed shallows and trout cruise there.

The ticket then, is to use flies and a fly rod if possible. A plastic bubble and spinning rod is an alternative, though the spin/bubble combination runs a poor second for several reasons.

One expert praised it last summer, explaining, "With the bubble I can fish dry flies on the surface or nymphs 15 feet deep."

Sounds good, but the trout are often 30 feet down. Enough weight with the bubble to fish that deep results in snags. And when your fly must alight within inches of rising trout or be lost in the crowd of insects, the bubble arriving like a returning space capsule will panic trout.

During the second summer I chucked the handicaps and matched the spin/bubble's advantages of long casts with no backcast hassle by switching to fly tackle and shooting heads. (Shooting heads are simply short flylines that allow 90-foot casts with only a 33-foot backcast including leader, as opposed to a 70-foot backcast required by regular lines to cast the same distance.) Add to the shooting head's increased range Red Ball's 12-ounce flyweight waders and six-ounce slip-on sneakers, and backcast problems all but disappear.

Anglers often neglect to arrive at lakes while fish are feeding. This has also contributed to the lakes' reputations of limits one day, nothing the next. Trout have specific hours of maximum activity and, if you're late, they won't wait.

In higher lakes of about 9,500 feet and more, trout may feed all day. Season, elevation, latitude, exposure, lake depth, and weather all affect insect activity and trout feeding binges. But generally, in sunny weather during early July, feeding begins around 9 a.m., slackens about 1 p.m., then resumes at 7:30 p.m. at the end of the lake that was first in shadow.

As summer progresses and air and water warm, trout feed earlier and later in the day until cooler weather in late August reverses the process. October finds trout feeding at midday.

The problem is that on a typical daytime hike, the morning is spent hiking in and the evening hiking out. Both are prime feeding and fishing hours. The key is to begin your hike early enough—taking into consideration the elevation gain and distance of the trail—and then either to stay overnight or come out with a good flashlight.

The "where" of fishing alpine lakes poses a problem unless you resist the stream-trouting urge to head for deep water. Most food grows in the sun-warmed shallows and trout cruise there when they are hungry, using the sterile depths primarily for rest and refuge. If the trail descends to your lake from above, pause and note any shallows, offshore reefs, underwater points, rockslides spilling into the lake, drowned timber, islands, alluvial shallows, or logjams near inlets and outlets. If you spot rises, half the battle is won.

But let's suppose there aren't any. Now you'll have to prospect for trout. If it's early season and the lake is partly iced over, work the fly slowly along the ice's edge. If the ice is long gone, amble along shore and scan for trout. Because there is no hatch in progress, chances are the trout aren't feeding on anything in particular and an impressionistic fly that suggests a variety of food forms is best. The Trueblood Otter Shrimp is a Western classic and is my favorite searching fly. It duplicates the scud (sometimes called freshwater shrimp) that inhabits about 30 percent of alpine lakes below 10,000 feet, but also resembles a mayfly nymph, caddis pupa, leech and dragonfly nymph.

The wind can alter the fishes' normal distribution in the water by blowing flying and/or drowned insects to the lake's windward shore. Ants, moths, and beetles are blown from trees along the lee shore into the water. In either case, a banquet swath of flotsam accumulates.

Spawning season also throws a monkey wrench into trout prospecting. It's July for spring-spawning rainbows, cutthroats, and goldens, and September for brookies, Dolly Vardens, and lakers.

At spawning time, trout congregate near inlets or spring seepages. In lakes lacking either, they move to reefs or shoreline shallows and build their nests. Reef spawners will take flies early but, near the end of the spawning cycle, trout are almost impossible to catch. Those hanging in an inlet's flow are intent on ascending and are oblivious to everything except salmon eggs or an egg-imitating fly—simply a No. 16 hook wrapped with a ball of fluorescent red or orange yarn.

The spawning urge, though, is often a blessing rather than a bane, allowing you to locate trout quickly. This past October, while grouse hunting, I decided to take a few hours and hike into Bear Pete Lake. I had seen a number of rises from the ridge above it on my approach but there were only a few hours of light left. I made a beeline for the inlet and peered through the willows. There must have been 200 trout milling around the mouth with about twenty already in the first pool. When I let the fly sink to their level, several rushed it simultaneously. The fishing for these brookies was too easy. Their heads were too large for their bodies, indicating that there were too many fish for the food supply. I took my limit in no time.

If the shallows fail to reveal trout, the fish are probably resting and digesting, or perhaps feeding on scuds and water fleas in deep water. They are most apt to do this in midafternoon during late July or early August. The line where extensive shallows break into the depths is a prime angling spot. Fancast with a sinking line, casting as far as you can, letting every fourth one sink about ten seconds longer than the last. Do this until you are scratching bottom with the No. 12 Otter Shrimp. If none strike, change flies, vary retrieves, and then move to another area. For reasons known only to them, trout sometimes favor one end of a lake over another.

If after thoroughly exploring a lake you get no action, might it be advisable to move on to its neighbor? The answer depends on elevation and exposure. If they are about the same for both lakes, it may be better to wait for a hatch where you are. I'd guess that if two adjacent lakes have identical exposure, there must be about an 800-foot elevation difference for them to have distinctly different feeding periods. Of course, if it is spring and spawning rainbows prove impossible, a nearby lake that has brookies may be red hot.

As intriguing as prospecting for trout can be, it probably won't be necessary if you've planned your hike to reach the lake by 9 a.m. when something will likely be hatching. Knowing the types of rises specific insects elicit from trout is the key to matching the hatch.

Midges are the most important alpine insect and the first and last to hatch each year. I can't count the times during that first summer when hundreds of trout refused everything and all I needed was a fly sold in every fly shop. These so-called "mystery rises" usually occur during morning and evening. You will need two flies and a floating flyline or bubble to take fish.

The insects emerge in the morning and the trout's response is one of leisurely sips while the school cruises. As the hatch begins, trout will take an adult imitation (dry fly). If it intensifies, the pupa works better. Matching them for size and color is crucial so, before you begin fishing, collect one with a small dip net and knot an imitation onto a 6X or 7X tippet. If the hatch is sparse, drop the fly about six feet ahead of a cruising trout—farther if it spooks. If the hatch is heavy you may have to place it within a foot of a fish to have it noticed. As a fish approaches, pull in line, causing the pupa to rise slowly.

During evening hatches, a dry fly may outfish a pupa because adult flies will also be laying their eggs and trout look for them. As the light fails, it is easier to detect a dry fly being taken by a trout than it is to see a sunken pupa. Capture an adult with the aquarium net and match it.

High-lake caddis also create fast fishing. They hatch in two different ways. The *Limnephilus coloradensis* and another unidentified species swim to shore and climb out on grass and logs to change from pupa to adult. Pursuing trout make heavy swirls near shore.

Four other caddis emerge directly into the air from the water, usually near weedy areas. Trout make heavy boils and leaping rises, often some distance from shore. The adult caddis flying off from the water or gyrating on the surface distinguishes them from midge hatches. If you can't seine a live pupa, catch an adult. If it is grayish brown or dark brown, it's one of the *Phryganea* species, so tie on an olive pupa and a dark orangish-brown one on a dropper

Be sure to get to the lake early enough to take advantage of the trouts' early feeding habits.

Photos by Ron Mitchell

to cover all bases; one of them will work. The *Chimarra* pupa is black like the adult. Retrieve these flies in two-inch pulses.

Damselflies and dragonflies are common on lower lakes and trout pursuing them cruise fast, swerving suddenly or making heavy surface boils near weeds or logs where the insects crawl out to hatch. Retrieve damselfly nymphs with a pull/jerk/jerk/pull action and move dragonfly nymphs in short spurts.

Adults of both types crash during egg-laying and mating. I once took seven rainbows weighing between two and four pounds in an afternoon at Georgetown Lake in Montana on a No. 10 blue damselfly by letting it lie motionless, then imparting occasional twitches. At the height of summer's heat this fly is especially effective.

Mayflies of several species inhabit high lakes. Trout rise vigorously over the shallows to get them. With the dip net, catch a dun (adult), match it, then cast to the rise. If the dry fly doesn't work, the trout may still be taking the nymphs.

Common in the lily-pad and drowned-timber shallows are the mottled, brownish water beetles, dubbed "waterboatmen" for their oarlike legs protruding from either side. Fish an imitation on a sinking line in sharp, four-inch jerks punctuated with pauses.

Leeches and scuds both live on the bottom and their imitations are deadly at times.

Trout eagerly take winged ants and termites in September and early October. Two sizes are best: No. 10 black carpenter ants and No. 20 or No. 22 black and cinnamon wood ants. Let an imitation sit in the vicinity of feeding trout and give it a twitch when a fish nears. Don't depend on anything but a close ant imitation.

Other terrestrials such as crickets, grasshoppers, and beetles are all periodically eaten and their presence on the water tells you what fly to use. But the tiny chartreuse aphid overshadows them all. They get blown to the water all summer and sometimes trout favor them to the exclusion of larger insects.

Last August at Otokomi Lake in Glacier National Park, I found a big cutthroat, weighing more than three pounds, cruising along shore. A school of trout nearby were feeding on big olive-bodied stoneflies and I noticed several plops near this bruiser. The fish ignored them, and my Otter Shrimp as well. Finally I stopped fishing and just observed. *Aphids.* The cutt was ignoring the juicy stoneflies and eating No. 20-size aphids, of which I had no imitation.

Of course there are those times when one has the right fly and tackle and a perfect battle plan but the trout still refuse to bite. It often happens when a strong cold front settles in, although an approaching thunderstorm usually triggers a feeding spree for a few minutes. Baffling. Admittedly, there is much about high-lake fishing that remains to be unraveled. But the angler who approaches this environment and its "naive" trout with an attitude of respect will seldom encounter the boom-and-bust fishing of folklore.

The Capricious, Predictable Lake Trout

Jerry Gibbs

The lake trout is something of a schizophrenic. Those who have fished the species in the far north or in the contiguous forty-eight states have no problem with the image of a closet *007* whose secret identity has just been exposed. The comparison would suggest flashy fight and a high level of aggressiveness—characteristics which, if applied to lakers, you may find hard to buy. Just wait. The stereotype in which the creature is held by most anglers only seasonally fits. With absolutely no slice at character, *Salvelinus namaycush* (yes, the fish is a char) is most often a lurker and a kind of prehistoric Jabba the Hutt (non-Jedi fans read Henry VIII) preferring to pop the richest condiments requiring the least effort while maintaining a total comfort situation which, for the fish, must be at some considerable depth if we're talking waters basically below the fifty-second parallel.

Equating lake trout to a flaccid toadlike creature must be based on seasonal location and behavior alone. Physically, the fish is quite handsome. Truthfully, the laker's reclusive, deep/cool-water penchant and voluptuous eating preferences produce some of the more fascinating and consistent angling for the species. To be sure, that fishing has none of the immediacy of, say, some violent contact sport; rather it is a remote-control search-and-deceive mission. If you're intrigued watching astronauts perform experiments in a no-weight environment, you should like summer lake-trout fishing.

Being one who would rather cast to his fish with reasonably light tackle, I find it rather strange to have become fascinated with the myriad techniques successful for deep fishing. Yet, the game of down

and distant can be as intense as any near-surface fishing (which we'll also consider as this progresses). Today downriggers provide one of the more efficient means of catching deep-holding lake trout, and absolutely the best means of obtaining sport with lighter tackle on fish trolled from the depths. Taken to the extreme, light tackle can mean even four- and two-pound test, possibly best fished from one of Dick Swan's so-called "noodle rods," designed to be bent nearly double by such gossamer monofilament. Swan eschews normal downrigger releases for this work, preferring to double a number 16 rubberband around his line then attach it to the 'rigger weight by slipping the band over a paperclip; the paperclip is hooked to the downrigger weight. On the strike,

The laker's reclusive nature and indulgent eating habits produce some of the more fascinating angling for the species.

This article originally appeared in the Summer 1984 issue of *Trout* magazine.

the mono cuts through the rubberband. Regardless of the method you choose, the location of fish concentrations is obviously the first concern.

Summer lake trout are precise fish, holding in water ranging from the high forties to low fifties (Fahrenheit). That's typically in the 100-foot vicinity in many of our handy lakes. It can also be from 200 to around 600 feet if you consider *Salvelinus siscowet* or the so-called "fat" as it's called by old-time Great Lakes commercialmen. *Siscowet* is a recognized subspecies with high oil content and probably the only other lake trout, although some former commercial fishermen claim a third form, the "humper" lake trout or "paperbelly," found on far offshore Great Lakes reefs and mounds surrounded by deep water.

Before the advent of reliable temperature probes and sonar for sport fishermen, lake-trout anglers got along by bumping lures on well-proven reefs and ledges via a technique called "jerking copper." Some still use the method, although monel or even braided wire line have usually supplanted copper. The real fish-finder of pre-downrigger days was the Seth Green rig, later refined into the so-called thermocline rig. This was basically a multi-lure-leader setup employing a long weighted main line from which typically five leaders were streamed. The leaders were of varied length—15 to 30 feet—and spaced anywhere from 20 to 40 feet apart along the main line. Obviously a wide segment of water was covered. A variety of means were used to keep order in leaders and line. Consider the possibilities if a fish hit on the bottom leader.

My early experiences were with a master of the system who unsnapped each leader as it came up, then dropped it around my legs. Incredibly, the mess was manageable (by him) after the fish was unhooked. Before lures were attached, the leaders were stowed on a reel powered by an old wind-up Victrola motor. I find it amusing that New York fish culturalist Seth Green who gave birth to the concept was at heart a flyfisherman, often remembered chiefly as the first man to cast 100 feet with the long rod.

Downriggers are obviously a lot easier. Coupled with electronics, they have taught us that lake trout can use a substantial amount of previously unfished water, and are often located off the bottom. More suspended fish adjacent to reefs, points, and underwater pinnacles are being located and caught. Many of them are taken in association with off-bottom forage such as alewives. Although the trout have not given up long-time staples such as chubs, sculpins, and very cold-water-oriented smelt, availability of alewives in places like Lake Michigan plays a key locational element. If the water temperature is still favorable for lakers in late spring–early summer, and alewives are present, lakers will not hesitate to move to eat them. A recording sonar becomes close to vital.

Despite periods of suspension, lake trout are still more frequently bottom-oriented fish in deeper water. Trolled lures or baits need to be presented on the money for, as earlier suggested, the laker can be a rather slothful creature often enjoying bountiful forage close by. But getting deep is not as simple as just lowering the downrigger cannonball. Forward boat movement results in a carryback effect on the weight, thus the downrigger footage counter cannot be taken as absolute unless the boat is stopped. The fact has resulted in the development of a technique called bottom bouncing in which the 'rigger weight is periodically lowered until it hits bottom, then raised a foot or two.

The method not only keeps lures in the strike zone, it causes them to suddenly behave erratically which frequently excites the trout to strike. Turning the boat, putting the engine in and out of gear, results in similar lure action. A variation is as follows: Once a fish is hooked, the next nearest lure is tripped from the release and cranked quickly up. The illusion is of a suddenly escaping baitfish, and it usually causes another nearby laker to hit.

Bouncing is best performed on relatively snag-free bottom for obvious reasons. I'll not forget early experiments—especially an episode while fishing alone. A trout was hooked while simultaneously one cannonball fouled in a niche. For a little while hysteria reigned. The action centered (literally) around the spot to which I was tethered and from which I was trying not to be swept more than cable's length in a stiff wind. New to the downrigger game, emotions ranged from rage to sheer terror not knowing if (1) the wire would break, (2) the 'rigger would be ripped from the gunwale, or (3) the boat would turn over. A thumping fish in one hand was inconsequential and the rod was soon thrust in a holder. Many circles later and a last-ditch gloved-hand-over-hand effort freed the weight. Marvelously, the fish was still there and we continued.

Though change of lure pace brings strikes, the standard troll speed for lake trout is slow, and all artificials must give maximum performance when pulled at a crawl. This is good to know for those preferring live baitfish which cannot be trolled at higher speed anyway. Even with the most painstaking presentation, lakers can force you to work unproductively for hours, unlike Pacific salmon inhabiting the same waters. Those fish, though glutted, will often strike passing lures seemingly from nastiness alone. However, once lake trout do start, an aggressive feeding period can occur with anglers taking a good number of fish in short order. Because of this, and the fact that lakers group in larger concentrations than once thought, it's wise once a fish or two is taken to work the area thoroughly, making sharp turns and repeated passes over the productive zone.

For slow trolling I've been enamored with thin flutter spoons ever since meeting Bernie Klimczak on one of New York's Finger Lakes a dozen or more years ago. Bernie was then the man behind Miller spoons. He had called me in on the radio, although

Getting lures to behave erratically will frequently cause the trout to strike. There are many techniques for that kind of lure action.

he didn't know me, to share the fast action he was enjoying. When I finally located his little boat I found the man reclining along most of its length to ease the burden of a full leg cast. He had the tiller in one hand, a kielbasa in the other. It was taking a long time for him to eat the sausage because his rod kept bouncing over as one lake trout after the other ate his lures. The paper-thin flutter-type spoons are produced by a number of firms today, of course, and are standard troll offerings for many species. For consistency I'll choose spoons of two to three inches no matter how big the lake trout.

Captain Bill Lowell (of whom you'll hear more later) is one of Lake Champlain's more successful guides and also a friend who has shared sometimes bizarre fishing adventures with me. Bill much prefers plugs when specifically fishing lakers, and he'll sometimes troll them behind flashers—those tandem blade attractors often known as cowbells. Given a choice, Lowell picks jointed plugs, particularly Rebels. Spoons and plugs each have their innings and sometimes it is a combination of both that is most successful.

Dick Streich, a Syracuse, New York, tackle representative, tells the delightful story of lure manufacturer Tom Mann's first foray into lake-trout country. Many of Tom's lures are aimed at bass fishing, and on this trip veteran trout and salmon anglers were trying to persuade the Alabaman that colors of his artificials were all wrong for northern salmonids. Unconvinced, Mann put one of his plugs on a leader behind the downrigger cannonball. He attached a six-foot leader with a flutter spoon just a little higher up on the downrigger cable. Soon, they began catching fish. Lots of fish. Mann then removed his plug and the lake trout stopped hitting. Action returned as soon as the plug went back on.

Before going further we should consider the basic positioning of whatever lures or baits are used behind cannonballs, diving devices, or just plain weighted lines. Lake trout fall into two categories—the breathers and the streakers. The sobriquets have nothing to do with unpleasant telephone callers or exhibitionists. For the most part, lake trout tend to home in on trolling weights and devices to within a hair's breadth as soon as such objects pass; the fish move in so close they're virtually breathing on the tackle—thus the name. Because of this fact and better control obtained with lures close to the trolling weight, most lake-trout anglers usually place their offerings a scant two to three feet behind the weight. Some days, though, the fish can be as skittish as brown trout—from boat traffic, sonar noise, or reasons known only to themselves. Anglers with recording depth-sounding instruments can see the paths made by fastidious lakers as they flee for the bottom and literally trace streaks down the displays of the recording units. On days of the streakers, lures trolled sometimes 100 feet behind the boat will be more productive.

Despite all the wondrous lure creations available today, there are those who steadfastly stick to various baitfish for lake-trout trolling. Specialists did and do use elaborate rigging systems for baitfish. A popular rig consists of a treble hook at the bait's tail, a leader

A selection of jigs used to catch lakers. A jigging system provides more angler participation than the usual trolling methods.

run through the vent or side flesh, and a second smaller single hook through the lips. Increased use of weight-forward walleye-oriented spinners designed to hold a natural bait, has logically spilled over to lake trout. Logically, because the walleye, too, generally demands a slow troll.

Live bait is also used in a most boring fashion throughout New England where to some, traditional fishing for *togue* consists of rowing the bait out over a shelf or feeding reef, lowering it to the bottom, then boating back to shore where the fishermen eat and bloat on too much beer. It's called running lines and, when a lake trout eats, the fishermen row back out to do battle.

In cold, deep Flaming Gorge Reservoir (Utah-Wyoming) lakers (*mackinaw* or *macks* to Westerners) are caught via the usual trolling methods, but a jigging system that provides a little more angler participation is also used. Basically, big, heavy saltwater jigs—bucktails or plastic tails—are lowered and worked once fish concentrations are located. It is much the same as jigging for landlocked striped bass.

Traditionally, captured lake trout have not been released. As with Atlantic salmon, however, the situation is changing. Lakers taken from extreme depths are, of course, more difficult to return successfully. But, some biologists and anglers have found a technique that insures a high degree of success. Once the netted fish is unhooked the belly is pushed once firmly upwards with the palm of the hand. This helps deflate the gas or swim bladder. The technique has been referred to as "burping" the fish. The trout is then aimed head low and thrust downward into the water. The momentum usually is enough to enable the laker to continue downward to its desired depth.

Wherever they're established, lake trout have be-

come a bread-and-butter fish for various user groups because of the fish's locational predictability. They are not subject to the long migrations of salmon or rainbow trout. Because of this the laker has been or is currently heavily pressured by nonnative commercialmen, native North Americans, sport chartermen, private anglers. A volatile situation currently exists in the Midwest, specifically Lake Michigan, where native North American netting efforts run head-on into all forms of sport fishing. Confrontations have occurred, trout populations have been hurt in some areas, and sport anglers continue to discover (with their cannonballs) increasing numbers of abandoned, drifting, monofilament nets which go mindlessly along still killing fish. Cooler heads on both sides continue to search for solutions.

In New York, a recent Department of Environmental Conservation (with the U.S. Fish and Wildlife Service and Province of Ontario concurring) recommendation to drop the lake-trout limit from three to one fish brought instant, aggressive response from charter captains and private sportsmen, especially those in the northeast basin around Henderson Harbor where lakers rather than other salmonids comprise the main fishery. Reprieve was forthcoming with no alteration in limits in the offing until 1986, if at all. Successful experiments in the hatching of eggs taken from naturally spawning Lake Ontario lake trout have resulted in a decision to supply this egg strain annually to the U.S. Fish and Wildlife hatchery in Allegheny, Pennsylvania. The bottom line is expected increase in natural reproduction of lake trout in Ontario.

Lake trout are pressured by a natural phenomenon other than man: the lamprey. That parasitic horror has, in fact, been suggested as one of the factors that prevented lakers from crossing the Bering Strait into Siberia to establish populations. Lake trout are the only freshwater species with such a far northwestern natural range that have not made this seemingly natural locational extension. The fish has

For lake-trout fly patterns you can't go wrong with light-dark contrast. Add flash, a somber topping, and you have a fly that's nearly irresistable.

Photos by Jerry Gibbs

remained almost entirely within distribution limits of Pleistocene glaciation. Evidence supportive of this theory shows the natural range of large lampreys and lake trout as nearly entirely mutually exclusive.

There is no question that lake trout are highly susceptible to predation by lampreys, especially in deep water when they are bottom oriented and not noted for speed and mobility. Salmon and other trout fare far better in water with high lamprey numbers. Lake Champlain is a prime example. Few Champlain lake trout are caught these days without at least one lamprey scar or attachment. Charter captain Bill Lowell regularly has runs of eight to nine fish out of ten showing lamprey infestation or wounds.

"We've been getting more lake trout plantings in recent years," says Lowell. "It's obvious that without control the parasites have more targets. You get some idea of the problem even if you're not a fisherman. In spring or fall when water's cool, lampreys can easily scatter from the surface down. They'll attach themselves to divers' wet suits. Sailboaters get them hanging to their rigs. I found a friend of mine hollering and trying to scrape them from his boat last fall."

Consensus among Lake Champlain regulars has it that something will be done about the situation when the governor's grandchild wades from the water at North Beach with a lamprey hanging from his navel. To be fair, biologists from Vermont, New York, and the U.S. Fish and Wildlife Service have been involved with an intensive lamprey study on the lake. Collected data will be presented to a technical committee composed of the state fisheries chiefs plus a Fish and Wildlife representative. The technical committee will then make its recommendation to a policy committee composed of the state fish and game commissioners and regional director of the Fish and Wildlife Service. Basically, it will be up to the two states to decide whether to treat completely or partially with chemicals or barrier dams, to take other measures, or none at all.

To date all Champlain lamprey spawning tributaries have been identified as well as juvenile concentration areas at rivermouth deltas which extend far out into the lake.

Despite my fascination with deep trolling, I'll admit that lake trout give far better account of themselves when near the surface or in shallow water. In the continental United States, that means very early and fairly late in the year. All but the most dedicated have gone on to other things by then. In the Northeast, for example, early can mean a brief period of mild weather in February or March on big lakes with open water; perhaps the start of April when open channels form in other lakes. The trout stay up through some of spring landlocked salmon trolling season in New England and are taken on spoons and flies trolled for salmon. That tells you something. No one trolls slowly for landlocks. Of late, sport fishermen using side planing boards for brown trout have noted more lake trout in their catches. Lakers can be near beaches in water as shallow as five feet during this period, but usually they are the smaller, five- to six-pound fish. The larger lake trout seem to stay on top for a briefer period in spring.

These early fish hit hard and fight with flash on the surface, though do not make clean jumps. The same is true in fall which may be a more fascinating period. Preparatory to the fall spawn, the fork-tailed trout often take on a pale-yellow or faint-peach wash on the flanks beneath their pale spots. It is more a blush of color from the blue gray that marks the fish the remainder of the year. Though the fish can spawn 100 feet deep if need be, they usually do not. Typically lake trout move upward; sometimes that corresponds with inshore. The need is for gravelly or irregular rock bottom, sometimes as shallow as five to ten feet. No redds are formed. Instead the spawn is a small group affair. Several males sweep an area of sediment. They then attend a female, the group moving slowly, eggs spilling to fall between the interstices of the bottom.

For anglers the pre-spawn period consists of hunting reefs, shoals, inshore ledges, sometimes rivermouths and rivers. Though the actual spawn can be over in a quick two weeks, the trout take some time moving to spawn sites. They remain in the vicinity of these areas afterwards, sometimes until spring. Of the lake trout that gather at rivermouths, some will move to nearby ledges, while others ascend the river a short way. While they're at the mouths, cast spoons, drift rigs (including individual eggs and spawn sacks), deep flies, spinners and jigs will all take the fish. The technique is that used for other salmonids: an up-and-across presentation, the offering bounced down to drop into deeper holes where lake trout prefer to lie. Often night fishing is best.

Where legal, night fishing can be best when lake trout actually ascend rivers from the main lake, an occurrence in some American rivers as well as Canada. For example, in Michigan alone, rivers such as the Grand near Grand Rapids, the St. Joseph, and the Leeland all host substantial runs of lake trout. In all likelihood the second week of October through the second week in November will see lake-trout river movements in the Midwest, but only last-minute local intelligence can pinpoint precise rivers and dates. It's also nice to consider that shallower fish, well-oxygenated water, and a cool temperature make lake-trout release an easier proposition than it is with midseason deep-water fish.

Although lake-trout river fishing is often associated with areas where moving water joins lakes, this need not be the case—especially across northern Canada, and into Alaska. Here the trout are often found far from lakes where rivers widen, or out of fast currents near cliffs and boulders. The species frequently becomes the change-of-pace fish and sometimes lunch fish in the far north where you're on a long series of river portages trying to locate the species for which you really came. I've had the experience many times in Quebec's Ungava Bay region while hoofing it to where the Atlantics or Arctic char were supposed to be.

Occasionally very large lake trout come from unlikely small waters in the United States or Canada, but the real stronghold of trophy lakers is Canada's Northwest Territories. Tales are rampant of the good fish (a good fish *starts* at 30 pounds) from places like Great Slave and Great Bear Lakes where relatively recent trophy limitation may help to insure a continuation of big specimens. Here, as in far northern river situations, lake trout are quite shallow. One need not troll to catch fish.

True, most of the very big lake trout from the Northwest Territories are taken by trolling. That's because most anglers use the method. Good lake trout can be taken from the big northern lakes (or rivers) casting with light conventional or spinning tackle or even flyfishing. Heavy spoons and jigs are appropriate in the lakes. You work them at bay mouths, around points, and over reefs. With the ultra-fast-sinking fly lines now available, virtually all these holding places can also be worked with a fly.

Late summer can be a prime period for flyfishers seeking a trophy lake trout, for the fish move even closer to shallow-water structures and concentrate near tributary mouths and falls. Lake trout in the swifter currents below falls tend to hit much harder than those loafing in lesser currents. Once, alternating between the lower Barnstrom Falls area and Waldren River mouth on Great Slave, I became frustrated with the distinct difference between fish at the two spots. Trout at the falls hit solidly while those near the Waldren were located a little distance off the mouth and took the fly diffidently. Most of them got off. I finally learned that for consistent hookups you had to pause briefly when one of the less enthused fish took, much like counting one second when an Atlantic salmon pounces upon a lightly dancing fly.

For lake-trout fly patterns you can't go wrong keying on the current style vogue of those in-most-demand high-fashion models. Call it a study in contrast launched by Margaux Hemingway (and imitators): a shock of vivid red set against paleness in concert with a counterpoint of darkness. Instead of lips, skin, a wave of sultry-powerful eyebrows, we're dealing with marabou, a fur, or poly, mostly white with a pinch of blood red or flame orange. Add flash, a somber topping, and you have a fly virtually no lake trout can resist. Others things work but I still go for light-dark contrast.

Timing is critical as with any species—even on waters near one another. I once flew from Great Slave to Artillery Lake where trout hordes of just a few weeks past had vanished like a sparkler dying in the night. Back at the big lake they were knocking them dead at bay mouths. Close to home in New England in late October, one favorite lake produced a surface termperature of 55 degrees Fahrenheit and lake trout at 150 feet while 20 miles distant the day before I took fish at 15 feet. The big trout didn't move shallow on the first lake until late November, when the season was closed there, but that was last year and we've been able to use *El Niño* to excuse many things, even on the East Coast.

No, lake trout will never give the electric excitement of so many favored species on a year-round basis. Still, there is a certain intrigue with a creature which survives at the final edge of what's at best a twilight world. And for many of us—including anglers not prepared to take distant journeys—the lake trout offers big fish potential on close-to-home waters nicely manageable by small boat. Without him the world of trout would be much less.

The Lure That Won't Die

Charlie Storey

The three anglers in the bright-yellow boat quickly motored past the small groups of boats already anchored 100 yards offshore in the pre-dawn light and headed toward a more secluded stretch of shoreline across the lake. The trio consisted of an expert angler, a fisherman of considerable experience and a beginner. About 25 yards from shore the engine was cut and the boat drifted to a stop. As the lake calmed, the anglers began casting to the many different likely looking spots that punctuated the shoreline. It was not long before the first trout was hooked—then another, and another.

Even though the lake was known to yield many fish, these anglers began experiencing unusual success. They decided to count each fish that was landed as long as the action lasted. Several times during the day the anglers found themselves playing fish simultaneously. Their success continued until 4 p.m., when a howling mountain storm forced them to abandon fishing for the protection of their cabin.

Their total came to 175 trout that day—a catch that many anglers would travel thousands of miles and spend a considerable amount of money for. Most of the fish were brookies and rainbows in the 16- to 20-inch range but a nine-pound hook-jawed rainbow was landed by none other than the beginner.

How do three anglers catch 175 trout in one day? And how does any angler catch one bigger than he's ever dreamed of? It helps to have accessibility to a body of water that contains a lot of big fish, and it helps to be there when they're feeding heavily but, in this situation, using a lure that looked like an irresistible meal to those trout was the clincher.

The lure that did the trick that day was a small black marabou crappie jig. But the anglers involved weren't surprised because the jig's reputation as a

A lovely specimen of brown trout—one of the smallest ever caught with a marabou crappie jib by the author.

trout lure had already been established. Its reputation is growing for other species as well.

If I were limted to one lure for all types of fish and fishing, both freshwater and saltwater, I would choose the leadhead marabou jig. Used in a proper fashion, it's the most effective lure ever devised. A jig cannot be used in every fishing situation but, when it's possible to use a jig, I rely on nothing else.

The jig was introduced to me by my best friend and fishing companion Todd Richardson. He was fishing Walden Pond near Boston on one of those days when the trout were hitting everything. Todd tied on a black crappie jig, and, to make a long story short, it worked better than anything else that day. The lure continued to work well in that area on largemouths, smallmouths, and pickerel.

When Todd later spent some time in eastern Idaho, the lure continued its spectacular performance. One day at Henrys Lake he was discourteously ejected from the lake by the anglers around him for catching—and releasing—too many large trout.

After settling in Vancouver, Washington, Todd continued to make amazing catches with his crappie jigs. Here, larger versions were effective on coho and Chinook salmon and summer steelhead.

After hearing a lot of talk, I was finally introduced to the jig in May 1979, when Todd, myself, and another companion were enjoying a three-day vacation at a popular central Oregon lake. For those three days we had a ball catching and releasing more large trout than I had ever seen. Those stories I had been hearing were confirmed and a major new dimension was added to my angling enjoyment.

Successful jig fishing requires two things: fishing the lure properly and concentrating on detecting the strike.

The marabou jig has no inherent action, so it must be supplied by the angler. The jig is fished properly by hopping it across the bottom of lake or stream, or by walking it down drop-offs. The technique is simple but requires finesse.

I was recently teaching a fishing companion the proper use of jigs. I had been catching all the decent channel catfish throughout the day. Occasionally I encouraged him to concentrate on detecting the subtle strikes of the fish, thinking that his failure to do so had been the likeliest reason for his low success. Finally, late in the day I noticed that when he raised his jig off the bottom he was whipping his rod so hard the air whistled through his guides. After instructing him to use a little less muscle, we hooked the same number of fish the remainder of the day.

After the jig is cast, it should be allowed to sink to the bottom. You will feel a slight pull on the line as it sinks. When the lure settles on the bottom and the line suddenly goes slack, lift your rod tip to raise the lure off the bottom. Remember: Don't whip it. Lift it. Try to stay in "feel" with the lure. Immediately take up the excess line as you drop your rod tip to its original position. A single turn of your reel handle should be sufficient. Again, allow the lure to sink back to the bottom. Repeat the process until the lure is out of productive water. If you're fishing from a boat, work the lure around a bit at this point by continuing the up-and-down motion or by jiggling it a little. Enough fish are taken by this last tactic to make it worthwhile.

All the materials and tools needed for making your own leadhead marabou jigs.

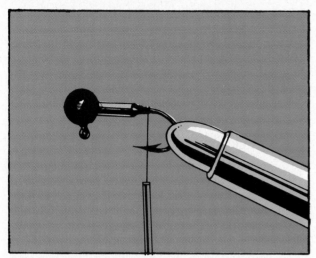

This is the bare hook with a painted head. Attach the thread ahead of the hook bend.

Next tie on the marabou tail. Be sure to make the tail very bushy for maximum effect.

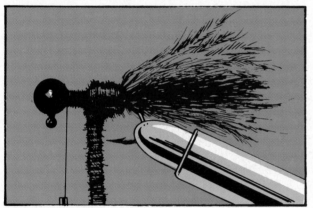

The body material goes on next. Here chenille is being used, but you can substitute yarn.

Wrap the body material forward to the head. Tie it off with a couple of half hitches, and cement well.

Photos by Charlie Storey

Total concentration is necessary to detect the strike because fish take the lure as it drops. The lure will pull a little but there is no real tension on the line. The angler must focus his attention on that portion of his line between his rod tip and the surface of the water. Any unexplained movement of the line, no matter how slight, should be instantaneously met with a *quick* upward motion. *Don't* take time to decide if what you saw or felt, or thought you saw or felt, was really the signal of a strike; by then it will be too late.

Look for three signals of a strike. The most common is a simple straight jerk on the line. You may or may not feel it, depending on how much tension is on the line and how hard the fish hits.

The second kind of strike takes the form of a circular flip of the line along its axis. This type of hit is rarely felt, even though the line goes through quite a bit of motion in the process.

The last type of strike indicator occurs when fishing directly beneath the boat. As the lure drops it seems to encounter a "false bottom" or it appears to strike bottom before it ought to. You may suddenly notice loose line coiling upon the water's surface or beginning to backlash if you're using a level-wind reel. False bottoms are never felt and always take you by surprise.

Fishing jigs in the wind is tough, unless you're using a heavy one or are fishing straight down and can feel the strikes. Any extraneous motion by the wind, water, boat, or angler makes it even more difficult to detect the strike. If the wind is blowing your boat around so much that you end up trolling the lure, the fish will refuse to take it anyway and you should try another method.

It is very difficult to fish with jigs from the shore of a lake. The angler should fish where the bottom is flat or deep which, in most cases, means you have to fish from a boat. Jigs can be used effectively from the shore on rivers, though.

Jigs may be obtained in ready-to-use form, or as pre-cast heads (painted or unpainted) that need the tail and body tied on or they may be built from scratch. If you choose the latter, remember that the most important piece of equipment is a high-quality mold. Don't skimp on price—with a cheap model you will soon tire of trimming off the lead that seeps out of the head cavity before it hardens. A good mold will turn out perfectly smooth heads every time. (The mold I use is manufactured by Do-It-Corp. in Denver, Iowa, and I purchased it through Cabela's, 812 13th Avenue, Sidney, NE 69160.) Many major mail-order companies carry quality molds, as well as other tools and materials.

Check the different lead-melting and pouring devices available and pick one that suits your particular needs. Prices and quality vary, but they all get the job done and do not affect the finished product if proper procedures are followed.

Lead may be bought or scrounged. Like any other metal, it's expensive. I've scrounged old sinkers from riverbanks for years, thinking that some day I would have a need for them. Although I've made hundreds of jigs, I still have enough for a long time to come.

Choice of paint for the heads is not especially critical. I don't know of a paint that will not chip off on the rocks or, for that matter, of a jig that will not catch fish with a lot of paint chipped off. I avoid lacquers that are extremely fragile, as I do any paint that is high-priced or takes too long to dry. Automotive touch-up paint works well and is fairly easy to find. Black is the first choice of colors.

Marabou feathers sold as fly-tying material are expensive, while marabou found in craft or art-supply stores is of good quality and is reasonably priced. I prefer chenille for the bodies and find the best selection at the local fly shop, but yarn is cheaper at variety stores or fabric shops.

The first major step in making jigs is casting the heads onto the hooks. While you are melting your lead, heat your mold on a stove burner. A hot mold will prevent the molten lead from hardening before you've poured the head cavity full. While the lead is melting, spread your hooks out on your work surface. The faster you can pick one up, the faster the entire casting operation will go. Put a hook in the mold and pour in the molten lead. Do not stop pouring until the lead has completely filled the cavity and is on the verge of overflowing. Pour quickly and smoothly so that the mold is full before the lead begins to solidify, which only takes a few seconds. When it hardens, open your mold and remove the first head, put in a new hook, and repeat the process.

Next, twist (don't cut) off the knob of lead that is left on the head after the casting operation and you are ready to paint. Dip the head in the paint, hang it up, and remove any droplets that don't fall off. Once the paint dries, repeat the process for a second coat.

With the casting and painting finished, all that remains is to tie on the marabou tail and body. Strip several strands of marabou from a feather and tie them tightly to the hook shank about two-thirds back from the head. Keep adding marabou until the desired amount is in place. Don't skimp on the marabou—it takes a lot to get a nice fluffy tail. Tie on the body material, wrap it forward to the head, and tie it off. Cecment with lacquer and the jig is finished.

The basic sizes for most freshwater jigs are one-eighth to three-sixteenths ounce with a No. 2 or No. 4 hook. On an ultra-light outfit, these can be fished in water up to 40 feet deep if you don't mind waiting a little for the lure to sink that far. When I switch to heavy tackle for salmon fishing, I use a one-half-ounce head and a No. 3/0 O'Shaughnessy hook.

Black is the basic color for trout fishing, but dark brown and dark olive green may be every bit as good. Just about any color will take salmon, but brown and purple are the colors I rely on the most. Experiment by mixing colors or adding other materials such as peacock or Mylar.

A few years ago, Todd and I decided to try fishing for lake trout on the season opener. I'm sure we looked peculiar out on that big lake with our ultra-light outfits, but we were confident and, after a couple of hours, Todd boated a four-pound laker. Soon a 14-inch rainbow was added to the fish box but, by noon, there had been no more action.

We were beginning to have second thoughts about lake-trout fishing when I felt a gentle tap and set the hook. The fish responded with some head shakes but no real fireworks. I could tell the fish was good-sized, but, with four-pound line, I was in no position to test its strength. All I could do was hold on while the fish went anywhere it wanted.

First the fish moved off slowly toward shore but only went about 50 feet before stopping and reversing direction. It passed the boat and headed toward the middle of the lake—but this time it didn't stop. I watched the line slowly disappear until the spool was almost empty. Todd cranked up the motor and we went off after the fish while I reeled in about half my line. The fish stopped, so I began pumping and reeling. I told Todd to start looking for the fish and, when he finally saw it, he got excited because the fish was bigger than we had suspected. Then *I* saw it and realized he had a right to be excited—this was no ordinary trout! Despite its size, Todd soon netted it.

The lake trout weighed 23 pounds 11 ounces on the scales at a nearby store. It's still the largest trout I've ever seen.

The marabou jigs have been around a long time and have been used regularly by many anglers. Although they may be thought of only as panfish lures, jigs are also the best stillwater trout lures ever devised and will take salmon when spinners and baits fail. Their effectiveness has been proven coast to coast and their usefulness can expand as much as the angler is willing to experiment.

Special Presentation Casts

Mel Krieger

Flyfishing, as far as I'm concerned, is preferable to any other sort of fishing primarily because the fly-casting itself is so enjoyable. There are even a number of people who consider fly-casting to be an end rather than a means, who delight more in the act of casting than in the fishing itself. There are also some fly casters who enjoy measuring their skills in tournament competition, and this small group of tournament casters has given the flyfishing world in general such notable things as the current fly-line numbering system (by weight) and the double haul. Although a few of these people are interested only in casting and competition, most of the tournament casters I've known have also been dedicated fishermen. For them, as for us, the final act required in the casting of a fly is the presentation of the fly to a fish. It is in this instant that the gap between fly-*casting* and fly*fishing* is suddenly bridged.

Another of the beauties of our sport is an almost limitless number of fishing situations and a corresponding number of methods. Most presentation methods, however, fall within the range of a few basic techniques. The basic presentation casts, in addition to such obvious requirements as accuracy, delicacy, and distance, are simple adaptations of the basic fly-casting stroke and are easily learned. As you become more and more proficient with them, you'll find yourself adapting to various fishing situations without a second thought. Take the time to practice and master these basics; they'll make all the difference in your fishing.

THE STRAIGHT-LINE CAST

This is the easiest and the most commonly used presentation cast. (Trout fishing with most dry flies plus many types of wet flies and nymphs provides a notable exception that I'll cover later.) It can be ex-tremely accurate, and the direct connection it provides between fly and fisherman offers immediate control over the fly—either for an instant retrieve or in case of an immediate strike. This direct connection permits quick and precise control of the fly, as is needed when float-fishing for trout on a western river, tarpon fishing on the flats, or sometimes when Atlantic-salmon or steelhead fishing.

When fishing bugs or poppers on the surface for bass, a Straight-Line Cast will enhance your chances of connnecting when a bass hits your bug quickly. Bass (both large- and smallmouth) often hit a bug as soon as it lands on the water (I've even had them hit before the bug landed, coming out of the water to chase it), and I've missed my own share of fish by throwing a cast with too much slack line. The bass has gulped, chewed, and spit out the bug by the time I've gathered slack line and tried to set the hook.

At the conclusion of a Straight-Line Cast, the line and the leader are both straight out on the water and directly in line with the fly. The rod tip is usually down near the water and aligned with the line, leader, and fly.

The cast is accomplished simply by throwing a good loop and then following the line with the rod tip to the water. Don't overpower this cast. If you do, the line will bounce back and slack will be created, which you want to avoid.

To elaborate on the float-fishing example I gave earlier, this is a situation in which trout are holding along the bank and a fisherman is casting toward them from a moving boat. Most strikes when streamer-fly fishing in this situation will come right at the bank or very close to it. When the fly lands

This article originally appeared in the 5th Anniversary edition of *Rod & Reel* magazine, and will be included in Krieger's forthcoming book, *The Essence of Flycasting*.

THE STRAIGHT-LINE CAST

Photos by John Merwin

THE BOUNCE CAST

next to the bank, it's usually best to be able to retrieve it immediately, and this calls for a straight-line cast. This cast is also useful in that it will enable you to cover more water. The fly can be fished back for a few feet, then picked up, and another presentation can be made quickly without having to deal with lots of slack, stripped-in line.

One of the most impressive examples I've ever seen of this was on a float trip I once took with Tom Morgan, formerly a fishing guide, who now owns the Winston Rod Company in Twin Bridges, Montana. With a streamer from our drift boat, Tom was using a straight-line cast into the bank, ending each cast with his rod pointing right at the fly. Using what he calls a "bounce retrieve," he bounced his rod sharply several times while slowly raising the rod tip. This technique caused the fly to swim in short, abrupt darts for a few feet out from the bank. A single backcast, and then Tom would make another straight-line cast into the bank. Not only did this method enable him to cover considerably more water (by not having to fool around with any slack line and stripping), but his straight-line presentation meant he was always ready for a hit. In combination with his unusual and very worthwhile bounce retrieve, it was devastatingly effective.

While the straight-line cast solves many problems, it can also create a few problems of its own. The worst is drag.

SLACK-LINE CASTS

Many sorts of flyfishing with both dry and subsurface flies require a free and natural drift of the fly. Natural trout foods—especially most insects—aren't attached to anything else in the current. Their bodies are almost weightless and they twist and turn with every subtle change of wind and water. They shimmer and shiver in or on the water in a manner that's often hard to duplicate with a hooked imitation tied to a leader. Successful presentation of such imitations requires slack in both the leader and the fly line. I am certain that the biggest mistake that most flyfishers make in fishing a dry fly is not their choice of fly (imitation), but rather that their fly is not drifting naturally.

The first consideration in getting a free, natural drift is to have a leader that is long and light enough to present the fly with delicacy and to allow a natural float. George Harvey, for many years the renowned flyfishing professor at Penn State, has been a strong advocate of a leader tippet that's light and long enough to fall on the water in a gentle series of S-shaped curves. Most contemporary leaders don't have adequate length in the tippet section to allow this. A good place to start for those of you having any problems in this area is with the so-called "Rule of Three." Divide the fly-hook size by three for the correct tippet size (i.e., hook size No. 18 divided by 3 equals tippet size 6X). And then use at least three feet of tippet material to ensure adequate slack during your presentation to the fish.

The other primary factors in getting a good drift are both a slack line and a slack leader. Failure is almost assured by a straight, tight line on the water between your rod and the fly. Every little nuance of wind and current, plus your own rod movement, will cause the fly to drag in or on the water, and a natural float has been lost. Ordinarily, this isn't something you can see for yourself from 20 or 30 feet away, but be most assured that the trout can see it all too well—and will thus refuse your offering.

Mike Lawson of Henrys Fork Anglers in Idaho has told me that he and his guides explain to their clients that they must try to present the fly as if it were not attached to the line. This is an excellent concept with which to introduce some slack-line casts. These are extremely important presentation casts that are used with not only dry flies, but sometimes also with wet flies and nymphs that require a natural, unimpaired drift. Along with the proper leader tippet, they are the basic key to successful dry-fly fishing.

THE BOUNCE CAST

Make this presentation cast so that the line and leader are fully extended while still one or two feet above the water. Use enough line speed so that when the cast stops above the water, it will rebound or "bounce" back slightly before line, leader, and fly land on the surface. That bounce creates slack in small amounts along the whole length of line and leader, and most especially in your long tippet section. This slack will help your fly drift naturally for some distance.

On a long cast, you may even have to pull back slightly on your rod after the casting stroke is complete in order to enhance the bounce. This cast also offers a very delicate presentation, since the fly is stopped above the water and then drifts gently down to the surface.

This is a presentation cast that I use often in dry-fly fishing. With a bit of practice, you'll find that you can control your line speed and timing and thereby control the degree of bounce to match a presentation situation exactly. But even a novice can develop this basic technique quickly, and the immediate results will be a better drift and more fish on the end of the line.

THE WIGGLE CAST

If the Bounce Cast doesn't give you enough slack, you can use what's called a Wiggle Cast, sometimes known as an S-Cast because the line falls to the water in a series of gentle Ss.

After the forward casting stroke has been completed and the line loop is unrolling in the air, all you have to do is shake the rod. You can wiggle,

THE WIGGLE CAST

THE PILE CAST

THE REACH CAST

jiggle, shimmy, shake, twitch, or vibrate the rod in any way you want. The result will be that those vibrations are sent along the unrolling line. When the line falls to the water, the line and leader will be in a series of bends. While the intervening currents are straightening out those bends, your fly will in all likelihood float without any drag.

This excellent technique solves a variety of slack-line situations. The amount of slack can be increased or decreased by the number and size of the wiggles. It's even possible to determine where you wish to put the slack in your line. Slack at the end of the line, near and including the leader, can be obtained by wiggling your rod early in the cast—just as the loop is being formed. Slack nearest your rod is obtained by wiggling the rod late in the cast after the loop is well out in front. Like the Bounce Cast, this one should also be aimed a little high so that the line shape can be established in the air.

With practice, this cast can be made quite accurately. You may find it helpful to allow some line to shoot through the guides while you are wiggling the rod. This will prevent your rod wiggles from pulling the line backward and shortening your cast.

Although I use it less often than the Bounce Cast, the Wiggle Cast is still an importatnt slack-line technique. The basics are easily learned, and I encourage you to practice it. As with other casts, you'll quickly find yourself adapting it to a variety of fishing situations.

THE PILE CAST

When fish are holding and rising in faster water, you may need yet another slack-line variation called a Pile Cast. Use this when you want an extreme amount of slack in the leader near the fly. While the slack is uncoiling in the current, your fly will be drifting naturally.

All you have to do in this case is aim your forward cast higher than normal—actually about parallel to the water—almost as if you're casting toward the treetops. As the unrolling line loop travels skywards, lower your rod tip toward the water. When the line falls, its tip and the leader will fall straight down, landing in a wonderful pile of slack. After the resultant perfect drift, Moby Dick will inhale the fly, and you'll be having another perfect day astream. Once again, it's easy to learn, it's fun to do, and it will occasionally enable you to take a fish that you otherwise would miss.

THE REACH CAST

Of all the presentation casts I've described, this last one is my favorite. First popularized by Doug Swisher and Carl Richards, this is not only an accurate cast, but also one of the most versatile in trout fishing. Happily, it's also easy to do.

This presentation cast can be made with any size of fly and leader. Very basically, it consists of moving the back end of the fly line to either the right or left side of the caster. All you have to do is make your normal forward cast toward the target, and, while the line is unrolling in the air, reach with your rod to the right or the left. Instead of the *line* landing straight between you and a target, the *fly* has landed where you want, but the line closest to you has been moved dramatically from where it otherwise would have fallen.

If you like, while the line is still in the air and after you've made the reach, return your rod to the straightaway position. Now when the line falls on the water, it will have a broad curve in it to the right or left, depending on the direction and extent of your reach. This could be called "mending the line in the air," since you are adjusting the line to the current's speed before the line hits the water instead of afterward. When you reach, you will likely want to let some line slide through the guides to avoid pulling the fly off target.

I find myself using this cast often and almost automatically in downstream fishing and in those situations where there are fast currents between me and the fish I'm seeking. This cast also has the benefits of a slack-line cast, since the upstream reach means the line will be dragged by the current long before the fly's drift is affected.

Just as important, this cast helps to establish good angles between me, the line, the leader, the fly, and the fish. Many people, myself included, use this cast when fishing slightly downstream. It means that even though I'm casting partly across the stream, the line, leader, and fly are in a gentle curve toward the fish, and the fly will float by the fish without drag and ahead of both leader and line—an ideal situation.

Striking the fish while you have slack line on the water is surprisingly easy, not only because of the very long movement that's possible with a fly rod, but also because of the friction of the thick fly line against the water. A sideways strike with the rod tip close to the water is frequently recommended by experienced anglers. I must admit, however, that most of the time I instinctively raise the rod on the strike, and it seems to make little difference. Both motions work well.

The key to striking a fish on a slack-line presentation (or, for that matter, in almost all fishing situations) is to be sure there is no slack *between your rod tip and the water*. You must keep your rod tip close to the water. Point the tip of your rod at the fly and keep it there!

I suppose one key word for learning these and a myriad of other possible presentation techniques is: Experiment! You'll find that even though they may sometimes sound complex, these techniques are easily learned with practice. Most people find, as they start to master these basics, that their fishing becomes both easier and more enjoyable. And, not least of all the consequences, they also catch more fish!

PART 4

PIKE, WALLEYE, MUSKIE

In Search Of The Water Wolf

John Weiss

"Hold it. Back the boat up, my plug is snagged on something," George Marsh shouted. "Isn't that the damndest thing, to get hung up on my first cast."

We were at McGavock Lake in northern Manitoba, and we had just drifted into a cove to cast along a lily-shrouded bank.

The water was too weedy to use the outboard motor, so I grabbed an oar and used it like a pushpole to maneuver the boat through the cover to retrieve George's lure. Suddenly George rocked back, and I saw his rod double over into a throbbing bend while his line began sawing at a sharp angle through the lily pads.

George's eyes widened in disbelief. "It's a big pike," he said, "at least 25 pounds."

Apparently the fish had clamped down on the plug and was just sulking under the pads until George began jerking his line to free his lure from what he thought was a snag. That triggered the northern into action. When it felt the hooks it began to lunge in one direction and then another, and the line became hopelessly wound around cover. Then the fish surfaced about 40 yards away, giving us our first good look at it. It looked like a five-foot log with cream-colored spots on it. Seconds later the fish swam three or four circles around a clump of thick lily-pad stems, began shaking its huge head violently, and broke free.

George has caught and lost more trophy-size pike than perhaps any other fifty anglers combined, and the look on his face was one of painful melancholy.

Erwin A. Bauer

There is something about the pursuit of giant northern pike that entrances fishermen.

It would have been his largest pike in more than thirty years of fishing Manitoba's finest pike waters.

There is something about the pursuit of giant northern pike that entrances fishermen. No, maybe it's a combination of things that creates the alluring effect and makes the pulse hammer.

The setting itself, where pike commonly live, is part of the experience. Just thinking of the fish creates visions of the north country—a soft lemon glow at dawn, bears patrolling the edges of spruce-fringed shorelines, the wail of loons, and everlasting evenings of blended crimson and orange.

Yet the fish themselves have the lead roles. Northern pike represent everything that is free, wild, untamable, and thrives best in the wilderness.

Will Rogers used to say he never met a man he didn't like. But few know that when he fished the north country he observed, in a similar vein, that he never caught a pike that didn't have the devil's malevolent glint in its eye and a compulsive passion for explosive madness. No wonder the Crees and Ojibwas call the fish the snake, and water wolf, and other similar names.

But modern anglers have long since learned that few species of fish are so widely distributed as the pike is and so consistently willing to engage in the pugnacious antics fishermen find so stimulating and will travel far to experience.

Pike inhabit more than three million square miles of water on this continent. But most of them that weigh more than 15 pounds are in a very restricted range. Only certain types of water steadily produce large numbers of trophy-size fish over long periods of time. This is something I've been studying intensely in recent years, by fishing and by researching everything that I could find in scientific journals that has been written about the species.

On this, the final leg of my mission, George Marsh had steered me to one of the most likely places to catch outsize pike in his native Manitoba, as other authorities had done in other regions. When I later had a chance to sort everything out, the lakes and rivers I mention here emerged on top as prime candidates—the best pike waters in North America.

With few exceptions, most trophy-pike waters are not so far north as many anglers believe. Though most pike are north of the forty-eighth degree parallel (roughly, the Canadian/United States border), they are south of the sixtieth degree parallel (the border between the provinces and the Northwest Territories).

Thousands of years ago when the glaciers melted and retreated from this territory they left behind countless lakes and connecting river systems. And from just below the cloud ceiling on a sun-splashed day they now appear as a sprinkling of sapphires upon a rich tapestry of tamarack, spruce, and green and auburn tundra. Manitoba's McGavock Lake is one of those jewels. There are tens of thousands of seemingly identical types of lakes, but it was nature's whim to inhabit this one with an inordinate number of mind-boggling pike.

The only facility for fishermen visiting McGavock is Lauri River Lodge, operated by Jack Merz.

"We've only been open a few weeks," Merz said as George and I unloaded our gear, "and already we've recorded twenty-seven pike weighing more than 18 pounds each. One fellow landed a brace of carbon-copy 23-pounders."

That week George Marsh didn't succeed in beating

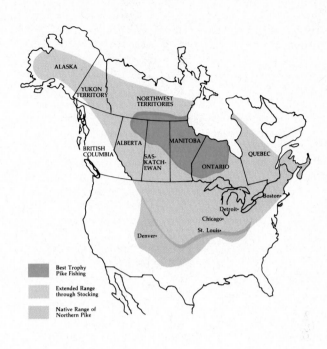

Beyond the oblong-shaped haven of trophy pike, the average size of the fish declines rapidly.

his own personal pike record, though twice he had good candidates on his line briefly. They broke off. Good fortune came my way, however, in the form of two 17-pounders and a 22-pounder.

Anglers in search of trophy-size northerns rarely eat any they catch because they realize how long it takes a pike to grow to such sizes. Canadian biologist H.H. MacKay has "aged" thousands of pike, and he has learned that 18-pound fish average thirteen years old. Anglers are increasingly being encouraged to release carefully all large fish they don't intend to have mounted.

It was just south of McGavock Lake in the Grass River Provincial Park where I caught my first 25-pounder. Third Cranberry Lake is the hotspot. It can be reached by driving north on Route 10 from the North Dakota border to the town of Cranberry Portage, and from there motorboating from any of the well-known fishing camps through First and Second Cranberry lakes to Third Cranberry.

My guide was 22-year-old Cameron Webber, and it was near the tip of a long finger of thin reeds where we first saw the big fish roll on the surface as it chased a 15-inch whitefish. But every time Cameron sculled the boat to within casting range the pike boiled the water and dived. That happened three times in as many days, and finally I decided the only way to get close enough to that fish was to wade.

"You're crazy," Webber said as I slipped over the side of the boat into waist-deep water.

After stalking the fish one slow step at a time for almost 100 yards, I began casting a two-ounce swimming minnow plug. On the third throw the pike raced toward the lure, mauled it savagely, and then began bulldogging just under the surface.

The fight wasn't a long one because I wanted this fish, and I had armed myself with heavy-duty bait-casting tackle and 30-pound-test line. But there was a scary moment when the pike suddenly reversed its line of travel, came straight toward me, and brushed against my legs as it sped on past. On the next pass, I led the fish slowly by and grabbed it firmly just behind the gill covers, which is the best way to guarantee survival of fish that are to be released. Using a landing net can defeat the purpose, since a lure's hooks often become entangled in the meshes and, while you are trying to free it, the fish thrashes around and loses much of its protective body slime. Grabbing a pike by the eye sockets is sure to cause blindness or other physical harm.

As I mentioned earlier, the finest trophy-pike fishing opportunities fall within a rather narrow geographical range. I call it a "core area." North-central Manitoba is the hub of activity, because of the nature of the species. Technically, the northern pike is a warm-water species, at least when compared with true cold-water species such as lake trout, grayling, and char. The generally accepted end of the warm-water range is the northernmost borders of the Canadian provinces. The northern half of Saskatchewan falls into the core area, as do the western two-thirds of Ontario and the northeast corner of Alberta. Beyond this oblong-shape haven of truly big pike, the average size of the fish declines rapidly.

Ontario biologists Miller and Kennedy confirmed this in a recent Canada-wide study in which they explained that the growth rate of pike varies inversely with both latitude and longitude. In other words, the farther north you go, or east or west, the longer pike live, yet they do not grow large.

Alaska, for example, is home to many pike, and in its wilderness regions you might expect to find plenty of giants. But you won't. What is generally considered to be a big pike in Alaska usually weighs six to eight pounds. The same is true throughout most of the Northwest Territories and northern Quebec. The waters there are too cold for too many months to allow pike to grow large.

Even within the core area, only certain types of water sustain the steady production of large numbers of big pike. In his book *Northern Pike Fishing* (Dillon Press, 1975) Kit Bergh described big-pike water as having a salinity level of no more than six percent.

There also must be available to the fish extensive areas of very shallow marshes and backwaters to serve as spawning and nursery grounds. In addition, a certain optimum ratio of weed growth to open water must prevail to allow big pike to establish hidden ambush stations, but yet not so much vegetation as to permit forage to escape easily and to hide. Only a small percentage of the many thousands of lakes in each of the core-area provinces meet these requirements.

Another important thing involves the pike's pre-ferred forage. Along the southernmost reaches of their natural range, pike feed heavily on panfish (crappies, perch, bluegills), rough fish (suckers, carp, shad, and small catfish), and even smaller gamefish such as walleyes, bass, and immature pike and muskies. But on such a diet, only small numbers of pike in this range reach trophy size.

In the core area, however, pike feed on forage species that promote rapid growth. The baitfish that are soft-scaled, soft-finned, and very high in protein include smelt, whitefish, ciscoes, tullibees, and lake herring.

It's not so much an angler's willingness or financial ability to travel to remote waters that determines his success in finding big pike. Instead it is his effort to learn of those lakes in the core area that have been longtime producers of trophy fish because of their favorable habitat and abundance of nutritious forage.

Tom Beaurrant, my regular fishing partner whenever I explore Saskatchewan waters, believes in this so firmly that he fishes only time-proved waters and uses only certain types of lures. When we were recently on Wollaston Lake I noticed his tacklebox contained no spoons, bucktail spinners, or other conventional lures many pike anglers favor. Instead, every lure was some type of swimming-minnow plug. Some were of the jointed, broken-back design, and others were shallow-runners or deep-divers, but all were long and slender. One lure he uses more than any other is a floating bass plug, the Heddon Zara Spook.

"Topwater plugs best represent the food big pike like to gorge on," Tom said as we worked along the fringe of a wooded midland island. "The only colors I use are white, silver, gray, or light blue to closely duplicate the appearance of baitfish such as ciscoes and tullibees."

For decades Wollaston Lake has been a consistent producer of big pike, and some anglers believe that it may yield the next world record. I began to share that opinion when Beaurrant brought aboard an eight-pounder that made me shiver. It wasn't the

I caught this 25-pound monster by wet-wading as it proved to be the only way I could sneak in close without spooking the big fish.
                                                              John Weiss

fish itself that raised my hackles, but the fact that it had wide slashes and tooth marks along the side of its body. Something very, very big had wanted that 34-inch pike for dinner.

Though I haven't fished for pike in Alberta, Kit Bergh describes the province as a "sleeper," claiming that several lakes offer the potential for trophy-size pike if an angler's timing is just right. Most anglers plan trips too early, not realizing that ice-out doesn't occur until June. Even in early July the water is still cold and the fish lethargic. Late July and all of August are the key times. By then the fish have recovered from the rigors of spawning and are trying to put on fat prior to the decline in water temperatures that begins in September. The province's pike record is 35 pounds.

It has been said there are so many lakes in Ontario that if an angler fished a different one every day of his life he'd have to fish for eighty years just to sample the ones that are the most easily accessible. But when it comes to the lakes that hold the very largest pike, narrowing the search becomes a little easier.

Generally, knowledgeable anglers concentrate on the lakes and rivers in northern Ontario, from Timigami westward to Lake of the Woods and northward to the Hudson Bay lowlands. This is where most 20-pounds-plus fish live.

To date, the largest pike taken in Ontario reportedly broke a butcher's scale, then was moved to a warehouse loading dock where six hours later its weight was recorded at 44 pounds.

Lake of the Woods undoubtedly is the largest and the most easily accessible pike haven for anglers living in the East and Midwest. I remember once when Tom Norris and I arrived at the lake late in the day and set up camp on a shoreline along what is appropriately called Monster Bay. There was not enough daylight left to go exploring by boat, so we waded and used our fly rods. We cast four-inch streamers along the edges of bulrushes not more than a few yards from our tent.

Tom caught three pike weighing ten pounds apiece before I had even assembled my tackle. Then his fly disappeared in a washtub-size patch of foam, and his reel yelped as a big fish ripped off line.

"I can't stop him," Tom shouted. In less than a minute the fish had cleaned Tom's reel of line and then broke off. We guessed that pike would easily have topped 20 pounds.

Then the same thing happened to me. A big fish zeroed in on my streamer, hit it, and headed off on a nonstop course for Manitoba. Seconds later all 25 yards of line were stripped from my reel. That fish broke off too. We spent the evening spooling new fly lines and 75 yards of backing onto our reels.

What tackle is suitable for taking trophy pike? It can be almost anything—fly, baitcasting, or open-face spinning gear—but it should have the strength necessary to boat fish that may weigh more than 20 pounds. In the bait-casting and spinning categories, most anglers seem to prefer stiff-action rods and lines testing 20 to 30 pounds. Instead of a wire leader

that may spook fish and rob a lure of action, they blood-knot a shock leader of 40-pound-test mono to the terminal end of the line.

Any fly rod that throws less than a No. 7 weight fly line is probably too light. I use the same heavy rod I use for bass bugging, a level ten-weight line, and a nontapered, relatively stiff leader of 25-pound-test monofilament that is capable of turning a big streamer over on the cast.

Spincasting tackle (with a push-button reel) doesn't seem to have enough strength for fighting pike weighing more than 15 pounds, except perhaps in the hands of a master angler. Nor do the drag mechanisms on such reels work smoothly enough to counter the frantic runs and boatside bids for freedom the largest pike make.

There are certain places in the lakes I've mentioned where the largest pike are most likely to be found. Early and late in the season, concentrate on those four- to six-feet-deep embayments that are weed choked, but only the ones that are fed by active feeder streams. Overlook bays and coves that do not have some source of water running into them. Once you find a likely embayment, fish the slots, alleys, and channels that wind through the weeds. Outsize pike, superbly camouflaged, hide in the shadows and keep watch on nearby openings for forage that may happen to venture by.

Early and late in the season reed banks are also good bets but, curiously, not dense, impenetrable ones. Look for large swatches of thick-stemmed reeds rather thinly dispersed.

In midsummer fish along the outer, deep-water edges of weeds and lily pads bordering main-lake areas. Or pitch lures across rock-capped islands that are in deep water but rise to within four or five feet of the surface. These places are typically overlooked by most anglers who mistakenly believe pike always must have vegetation to hide in. Only loners do. Yet enormous schools of baitfish often congregate over these submerged rock piles. To capitalize upon this abundance of forage, big pike frequently gather in packs of ten or more and work as a team. They first encircle the baitfish, then take turns rushing in to grab one.

Finally there is Quebec, a maybe region in which outsize pike make appearances occasionally. Though the province's pike record stands at one ounce shy of 46 pounds, Quebec doesn't fall within the core area. Because of that, only two lakes are thought of as good bets, and they are within the Mistassini and La Verendrye provincial parks.

The following Manitoba lakes are trophy-pike waters where prize pike prowl—the best of the best, according to my study—along with recommended facilities for anglers and addresses of sources that can supply information: McGavock Lake (contact Lauri River Lodge, Box 550, Lynn Lake) and Lake Athapapuskow (contact Constable's Lakeside Lodge, Box 308, Flin Flon; Athapap Lodge, Cranberry Portage; Ptarmigan Lodge, Cranberry Portage; or Paradise Lodge, Box 777, Flin Flon).

Big Rivers, Big Walleyes

Dick Sternberg

Big rivers grow big walleyes. The reason is simple: not many of them get caught. Walleyes are moody, elusive, and unpredictable— regardless of where they live. Big rivers can add even more frustrations, such as fluctuating water levels and current. But even though catching big-river walleyes can be tough, the rewards make it well worth the effort.

I do most of my river walleye fishing in the Mississippi where it forms the Minnesota-Wisconsin boundary. There a series of navigation dams breaks the river into big pools. I spent seven years working on these waters as a fisheries biologist with the Minnesota Department of Natural Resources. During those years, my crew and I shocked thousands of trophy-class walleyes in the tailrace waters in March and April. I also caught my share on hook and line.

Catching trophy walleyes was exactly what Steve Grooms and I had in mind as we sped downriver one day in April. Our destination was a sandy point several miles below one of the dams, a spot where walleyes traditionally congregate following spawning. But when we arrived, a quick glance told me that something was wrong. The water was much lower than normal for late April and the current wasn't sweeping past the end of the point the way it should to draw in the walleyes.

The problem was that the winter had been nearly free of snow. Streams that normally roared with meltwater now merely trickled. In many years, late April finds river folk building dikes and sandbagging foundations. But now the big river meandered along peacefully, well within its banks.

Steve and I decided to motor up the river to check out some other spots. The first stop was a small cut connecting the main river channel with a backwater

After Spawning
Water 50 to 55°. Walleyes move away from dam and into side channels and off of points with current flowing past the tips.

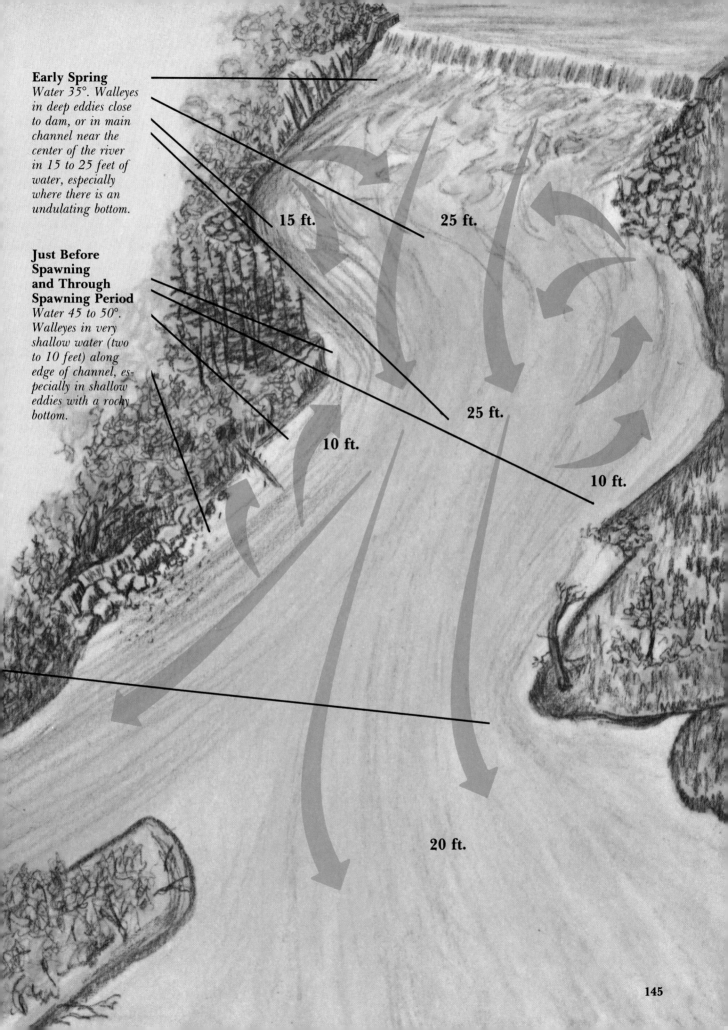

Early Spring
*Water 35°. Walleyes
in deep eddies close
to dam, or in main
channel near the
center of the river
in 15 to 25 feet of
water, especially
where there is an
undulating bottom.*

**Just Before
Spawning
and Through
Spawning Period**
*Water 45 to 50°.
Walleyes in very
shallow water (two
to 10 feet) along
edge of channel, es-
pecially in shallow
eddies with a rocky
bottom.*

15 ft.

25 ft.

25 ft.

10 ft.

10 ft.

20 ft.

lake. Again, it was the same story: The water level was too low and there was virtually no current in the cut. Next stop was a rocky shoreline in a back-water lake. We hoped to catch a few stragglers hanging around after spawning, but it was a waste of time. Two other spots on the main channel that produced at this time most years gave up nothing.

Time for a change of strategy. We decided to forget about the spots that were usually good and think about what kind of spot walleyes wanted now. I knew that walleyes look for moderate current near deep water after spawning, but now there were few spots like that around. As we motored upriver, I noticed a spot that often produces in late fall, but never in spring because the current is normally too fast. But with the low water, it looked perfect. The current gently buffeted the tip of a small point and dropped into a 25-foot-deep pool.

I positioned the boat 75 feet above the point. While Steve lowered the anchor, I tossed my jig inches from the point's tip. Almost instantly, I felt a solid tap and instinctively set the hook. After a whole day of blanking out, that walleye felt pretty good, but it wasn't a giant. My black Lab, Penny, ran to the back of the boat to make her usual grab for the fish, but Steve beat her to it and netted the scrappy five-pounder. Within minutes, Steve boated another walleye about the same size and we caught two more four-pounders during the next half-hour. Not sensational, but we felt we were on the right track.

It was almost dark when we pulled up to a tiny rocky point that I had tried many times in other springs, with little success. Much like the previous spot, the current swept gently by the tip and into a 20-foot-deep pool. We dropped our jigs over the side and began bouncing them off bottom as we drifted by the point. My depth finder read only seven feet when I felt the tap. This time the fish didn't budge. I was using a Fenwick spinning rod with six-pound-test line, so I couldn't do much about moving the

fish off bottom. As we drifted farther and farther downstream, I began to think I had hooked a big carp. But in the fading light, I caught a glimpse of the white tail spot. Just as I yelled, "It's a walleye," Steve made a swipe with the net and hoisted the fish into the boat. It weighed 10½ pounds. A day that started out as a disaster had turned into a day to remember.

LOCATING TROPHY WALLEYES IN A BIG RIVER

Accomplished river fishermen know that walleyes can be here today and gone tomorrow. It takes only a slight change of water level. You cannot expect to catch big walleyes consistently by camping out in the same spot day after day.

If the river rises extremely high, it may top the banks and spread over surrounding land. I've caught walleyes during flood stage while they were congregated over a gravel road miles from the main channel of the river.

Most trophy walleyes in big rivers are caught while concentrated near their spawning grounds. A few are taken at other times, but they are usually too scattered to be caught consistently. Female walleyes, the wall-hangers, bite best just before spawning and again about two weeks later, but fishing for them during the spawning period is a waste of time. Spawning leaves them exhausted and not interested in eating.

Before and during spawning, walleyes shy away from all but the slightest current. Their metabolism is still low because of the frigid water, and current forces them to swim, wasting valuable energy. Prime spots are slack-water areas or eddies off the main channel. You usually can spot an eddy by looking for debris on the surface.

Fishing gets tough when walleyes start to spawn. Luckily, they all don't spawn at the same time. An

Longtime walleye angler, the author displays a 10½-pounder taken on a bucktail.

The photograph at right shows an assortment of the author's favorite walleye jigs. When the water is clear, dark colors work best.

Photos by Dick Sternberg

individual female completes spawning in a day or two, but there are some fish spawning throughout a two-week period. The secret then is finding walleyes that haven't started to spawn. They're likely to be shallow and close to a spawning area.

After spawning, big females begin moving downstream, refusing food for a week or ten days. Only the small males bite during this period. But when the effects of spawning wear off, the females begin eating as if they had been starved. But by now they've moved several miles below the dam where they spawned. The areas they choose have one thing in common—current. Shiner minnows are attracted by current, and walleyes can't resist an easy meal. The current speed should be moderate. Walleyes won't hang around if it's too strong.

TACTICS FOR TROPHY WALLEYES

A properly fished jig will catch more trophy walleyes than any other bait or lure. The best type of jig and jigging technique changes as the water warms. In early spring, with the water barely above freezing temperature, big walleyes move very slowly and rarely strike a fast-moving jig. Some veteran Minnesota walleye anglers recently discovered a simple but effective jigging technique for these ice-water walleyes. It's called the "slow drag." Here's how it works: lower the jig to the bottom and let the current slowly move the boat. Resist the temptation to bounce the jig. Instead, keep the rod motionless and let the jig drag bottom.

Tipping the jig with a minnow may entice fussy cold-water walleyes to bite. But even big walleyes usually strike short in icy water. With a minnow on the jig, they grab its tail and miss the hook. To solve this problem, many anglers use a short-tailed jig such as a Lindy Fuzz-E-Grub rigged with a stinger hook. To make a stinger, tie a small treble hook to the bend of your jig hook using a short length of ten-pound-test monofilament. Then push the jig hook through a minnow's lips and impale one prong of the treble into its tail.

When the water warms to 45 degrees, the walleye's personality changes. No longer does it lethargically nip at the jig. Now it prefers bucktails or Mister Twisters that look like a bigger meal. Because walleyes are more aggressive at this time, tipping the jig with a minnow is no longer necessary. In fact, it may actually produce fewer fish because of more short strikes. Just before spawning, when walleyes move into extremely shallow water, a small jig of one-eighth ounce or less works best.

After spawning, walleyes drop into deeper water, so a heavier jig is needed. I prefer a one-fourth-ounce jig to reach bottom in 12 feet of water with moderate current. Deeper water or stronger current requires a heavier jig of three-eighths to one-half ounce. Walleyes now will wolf down almost anything in sight, but I still prefer plain bucktails and Mister Twisters.

Regardless of time of year, jig color makes a big difference to river walleyes. The best color depends on water clarity. When the water is murky, many expert river anglers swear by fluorescent colors such as orange, yellow, green, or chartreuse. Others use nothing but white.

Although I'm convinced that a well-presented jig is the best lure for big walleyes in spring, there are days when live bait works better. Some anglers insist that small minnows are best when the water is cold, but I've taken many walleyes in the seven- to ten-pound class using five- to six-inch chubs, suckers, shiners, and even stone rollers. Big walleyes are accustomed to eating big baitfish. To rig a big minnow, use a harness with one hook through the lips and a stinger in the tail. Without the stinger, you'll miss too many short strikes. Check the fishing regulations to be sure this rig is legal where you fish.

A spinner/night crawler combination often is deadly following spawning. Make your own by threading a fluorescent spinner blade and clevis on the line followed by two or three red beads and a hook. Hook the crawler once through the tip of the head.

WHERE TO GO

Big rivers in the north-central states provide first-rate fishing for trophy walleyes. My top picks are the Missouri River reservoirs in North and South Dakota and Nebraska. Next would be the St. Louis and Mississippi rivers on the Minnesota-Wisconsin boundary.

Walleyes in Western rivers and reservoirs generally run smaller. Many of these waters have been stocked only recently, and walleyes are just beginning to reach a respectable size. Those where walleyes were stocked a decade or more ago have already yielded some huge fish. A 16-pound 8-ounce giant was caught in Cherry Creek Reservoir, a small impoundment only a few miles from downtown Denver. Lake Roosevelt, a Columbia River reservoir in Washington state, gave up a walleye just one ounce short of 17 pounds in 1977. Walleyes are gaining a toehold in the Columbia system and experts feel that some monsters will be caught there in the next few years.

For the best chance of catching a walleye in the 15-pound-plus class, you'll have to go South where the growing season is longer. Each spring, huge walleyes run up the major rivers feeding reservoirs such as Center Hill in Tennessee, Greer's Ferry in Arkansas, Table Rock Lake in Missouri, and Lake Cumberland in Kentucky. In the spring of 1979, Ed Claibourne caught a 21-pound 9-ounce walleye in the Little Red River, which flows into Greer's Ferry. Some biologists believe that one of these waters will produce a world record soon. In fact, a walleye of 25 pounds 3 ounces was tagged and *released* in Greer's Ferry a few years ago. (The current world record is 25 pounds.) So if you're looking for a challenge . . .

Tough Lakes Grow Big Walleyes

Dick Sternberg

It was only 7 a.m., but the wind was already building whitecaps. Though it was late May, a light dusting of snow had fallen during the night. As I brushed the snow off my boat seat, I wondered why I was submitting myself to this kind of torture.

For two days, I had searched this northern Minnesota lake for its walleyes weighing ten pounds or more. My fishing partner had stayed with me for a day and a half, but he finally headed for home. In sixteen hours of fishing, we had hooked only three 1½- to two-pound walleyes and lost one heavy fish because of a frayed line.

Heading across the lake, I turned on my depth finder to begin sounding for the reef where I had hooked the big fish the day before. As I circled the area, my flasher signaled that another hump was jutting up to 25 feet out of 40 feet of water. This spot was worth a try. I baited up with a five-inch shiner minnow and began backtrolling around the hump. I felt a light tug, so I released tension on the line. I waited for a few seconds for the fish to take line, but nothing happened. Snugging up to see if the fish was still there, I felt only a dead weight, as if I had hooked a stick. But then I felt the telltale head shake that a big walleye makes when it feels the bait being pulled away. I set the hook.

I knew immediately that the fish was big. You can tell when the rod tip jumps a foot with each shake of the head. For several minutes, the fight was a standoff, but gradually the fish weakened. I grabbed my landing net, but it was frozen to the boat floor. It came loose with a jerk, but the bag was frozen stiff. Fighting the walleye with one hand, I held the net in the water with the other hand until the bag thawed and finally netted the walleye. It weighed 11 pounds four ounces.

As it turned out, that was the only walleye of the day, and on the next day I caught only two small ones. Sound like slow fishing? Well, that's the way it is when you're chasing trophy-size walleyes. You have to pay your dues.

Though catching big walleyes always is tough, you can do some things to improve your chances. During my years as a professional fishery biologist, I studied thousands of netting reports on a variety of walleye lakes. With only a few exceptions, I found that the biggest walleyes came from waters that most anglers consider poor places to fish. Conversely, the most popular walleye lakes usually are the worst bets for trophy fishing.

I now do much of my hunting for big walleyes in lakes that many fishermen would never even consider. Generally, these lakes fall into one of the following three categories:

LAKES FULL OF BAITFISH

In many lakes, forage fish become so abundant that walleyes have no trouble finding easy meals. Biologists often receive complaints of poor fishing in these lakes, yet fish surveys show scads of big walleyes. A phone call to your state fish and game agency might give you a lead on waters of this type. These lakes are tough nuts to crack, but they can provide some huge walleyes.

Fish early in the season before the young-of-the-year baitfish appear. The previous year's forage crop has been pretty well eaten up by early spring, so walleyes are hungry. By midsummer, baitfish hatched in spring are large enough to interest walleyes, so fishing slows down.

Fish in early morning. When food is plentiful, a

big walleye just grabs a few small fish and rests for the day. The short feeding spree usually takes place shortly after dawn. Fishing during the rest of the day is likely to be a waste of time, though there is sometimes a short evening feeding period.

Walleyes in these lakes often refuse live bait but can't resist a fast-moving lure or jig. A crankbait trolled at high speed or a bucktail jig bounced vertically off the bottom may cause a big, full-bellied walleye to strike reflexively.

LAKES WITH FEW WALLEYES

It may seem foolish to fish in a lake that doesn't have many walleyes, but these are the lakes that often yield the real wall-hangers. In the North, there are thousands of deep, infertile lakes that cannot provide a big crop of walleyes. These waters are better suited for lake trout. However, the walleyes they do provide have little competition for food and must contend with few predators, including fishermen. The walleyes in Northern lakes grow slowly, but they live a long time, sometimes more than twenty years. As a result, they grow nearly as large as the fast-growing walleyes in the South.

Many bass/panfish lakes have been stocked with walleyes, but there is little or no reproduction. Walleyes rarely become numerous, so they receive little attention from anglers. Though a fisherman occasionally catches a big walleye while fishing with plastic worms or spinnerbaits for bass, a good share of the fish die of old age.

Walleyes rarely become numerous, but reach monstrous size in the reservoirs in the south-central United States. Some reservoirs have thousands of miles of shoreline, so finding the fish is difficult most of the year. Nearly all of these reservoirs have huge crops of shad, so walleyes grow at an unbelievable rate. These man-made lakes hold the biggest walleyes in the world, but they're tough to catch. During the year, there may be only two to three weeks when walleyes are concentrated enough or are feeding heavily enough to give fishermen a good chance of connecting.

There are two peak times for fishing in lakes with low walleye populations. The first is just before spawning time when fish are concentrated in streams or over shoals. Most Northern states close the season so that walleyes can spawn unmolested. But many Southern states leave the season open year-round

Erwin A. Bauer

giving anglers the rare opportunity to catch walleyes that may exceed 20 pounds. But if you're not there at exactly the right time, the chances of hooking a big walleye are remote. Once the big ones start to spawn, they are next to impossible to catch. My favorite technique for catching walleyes prior to spawning is to cast a jig-minnow combination into current breaks or eddies in tributary streams.

There is a short period in late spring when walleyes go on a feeding rampage. Timing is critical, and the peak may vary in different lakes. In one of my favorite lakes, the peak usually is five to six weeks after spawning. In some shallow, fast-warming lakes, it may be much sooner. If you're there during this time, the chances of hooking a trophy-size fish probably are better than at any other time of year. Backtrolling with a slip-sinker rig baited with a night crawler or large ribbon leech accounts for most fish during the peak.

LAKES WITH LITTLE STRUCTURE OR CLEAR WATER

Expert walleye anglers consider lakes with bowl-shaped, featureless basins a challenge. They know that sunken islands, underwater points, and rocky reefs attract walleyes, and if a lake lacks this fish-holding structure, fishing is very likely to be tough because walleyes will be scattered.

The experts also know that fishing in extremely clear lakes can be equally challenging. Because of their light-sensitive eyes, walleyes spend most of their time in deep water and feed only after dark. Most anglers avoid waters of this type. As a result, walleyes are lightly fished and often reach large sizes.

Catching big walleyes in these lakes is not necessarily difficult, but it may require some innovative techniques. For example, the fish in these lakes often suspend in midwater, so some anglers simply turn on their depth finders and troll artificial lures until they find the walleyes. Then they anchor near the school and cast with slip-bobber rigs, weight-forward spinners, or crankbaits. When fishing in these lakes, keep alert for change in bottom type. If a lake has a bottom that is mostly mud, a patch of sand or gravel is a good place to look. Watch your depth finder for the strong signal reflected by a hard bottom.

Finding and catching walleyes in clear lakes may be the greatest fishing challenge of all. Divers have seen walleyes lying on the bottom in 40 to 50 feet of water in midday, completely oblivious to the divers presence. So it's no wonder that the fish ignore an angler's bait. But when darkness approaches, the scene changes. Big walleyes move toward shore or onto shallow midlake reefs in search of baitfish. Beginning at dark and for an hour or two after, shoal areas come alive with cruising walleyes. You can spot these fish with a strong spotlight. Walleyes are easy to distinguish from other species because their eyes reflect light much the way those of a cat or deer reflect a car's headlights.

Dark, windy days can be excellent times to fish in

Catching big walleyes in lakes with bowl-shaped, featureless basins requires innovative techniques. This angler is using a slip-bobber rig, as mentioned in the text.

clear lakes. Because light penetration is low, walleyes move into the shallows to feed just as they would at night. The fish cannot resist minnow-imitating plugs.

The three types of lakes that I have mentioned are virtually ignored by the masses, even though many are near heavily populated areas. The walleyes in them are simply tough to catch. Most anglers would rather go to a lake where they have a good chance of catching a limit of 1½- to three-pounders. I know some good fishermen who have fished all their lives and have yet to catch a ten-pounder, but fish only in easy lakes. On the other hand, I know some other anglers who love to tackle tough lakes. Though they rarely catch a limit, they take several fish exceeding ten pounds each season.

So that is the basic choice you must make—quantity or quality. Few lakes offer both. Once you find a lake that holds big walleyes, be prepared to log some long hours. You'll probably get little help from others, because the fishermen who tackle these tough lakes are the tightest-lipped bunch you'll ever meet.

And if you discover one of these big-walleye sleepers, I'll lay odds that you'll become just as tight-lipped.

Muskies Have No Virtue

Doug Stange with
Mark Windels

Thereis no virtue in muskie fishing!
Not only is the average muskie angler often scorned by his quarry, the magnificent muskellunge, but in the eyes of fellow compadres within the fishing fraternity, where such things as "compulsive fishing" should be understood, muskie anglers are often looked on as individuals driven "one step too far."

And make no mistake, one step is often a major move. A step onto the moon was "one small step for man, and a giant leap for mankind." One step can bring you into the path of a speeding semi-truck or produce a fall from a cliff. One step forward or backward volunteers you for dangerous missions in the foreign service. One step can even lead to marriage.

Life progresses one step at a time. And confirmed muskie addicts are generally seen as having taken the big one—off the deep end, where passion fades into pitiful, and where determination fades into delusion. There is no virtue in muskie fishing! So what else is new?

Yet those of you who don't fish for muskies with a passion verging on hysteria must understand. This creature—the muskie—is both typical and atypical. Sure, a fish is a fish is a fish. But by any account, muskies are "the" top-of-the-line freshwater predator. Muskie fishing is trophy fishing. Muskellunge can grow to huge proportions, given the chance— small critters aren't particularly difficult to catch, so fishing pressure and harvest affects fish size—but even then, one fish per acre is considered an exceptional population. Yet those are small-fish, or total-fish, statistics. When talking big fish, the stats should probably read one fish per 1,000 acres—in good lakes!

Let's see now. One huge fish per 1,000 acres, and

she's only feeding once every other day for perhaps one-half hour, in perhaps a one-acre area in a 10,000 acre lake. Finding a size ten hook in a basket of bucktails is easy by comparison. No wonder muskie anglers seem a bit possessed. That leads us to the altogether interesting question akin to the fabled, "What came first, the chicken or the egg?" In this case the question becomes, "Were muskie anglers odd before they began fishing for muskies, or did it happen after the fact?"

We often preach the virtues of versatility, and in 99 out of 100 cases, it is indeed a virtue. A good case can be made for approaching muskie fishing by being versatile. But surprise! A good case can also be made for not being versatile. That'll be our case here!

Make no mistake, Mark Windels, whose ideas we'll focus on, is a versatile angler. Yet when he fishes for muskies he suppresses virtuous tendencies in favor of a sure-fire, nonversatile approach that produces fish.

Perhaps we should recap for those of you too stunned to fathom the last few paragraphs the first time around. Versatility may not *always* be a virtue. There are exceptions to every rule, and Mark's found a system that applies to catching that excep-

This article originally appeared in Volume 50 of *In-Fisherman* magazine.

tional fish, the muskie. Exceptions! Exceptions! Mark's system and muskies were made for one another.

A SURE-FIRE SYSTEM?

A sure-fire system for muskies? You bet! Mark and others have been fishing it for years. There are no tricks involved and the system is simple, cheap, effective, and easy to learn. Granted, however, the system is work. Yet if you've never caught a muskie before, you can get rigged up today, and if you employ "the system" for the remainder of the season, you'll probably catch more muskies than most muskie anglers have caught in their entire life. If you've al-

ready caught plenty of muskies, we'll be bold enough to suggest that comparing your present approach to Mark's may help you spruce up your act.

To anglers who have spent hundreds of hours trying to catch "a" muskie, let alone a big one, this may be heresy. Yet Mark's system of fishing is so simple to employ that it's a wonder everyone doesn't already use it. Truth be known, however, putting the system together wasn't easy. Yet we can reap benefits quickly. It's the same with most inventions, I suppose. The light bulb took a long time to develop, but using it requires only flicking a switch. Mark's system of muskie fishing is almost that simple to employ.

While we'll talk a lot about Mark's ideas, he makes

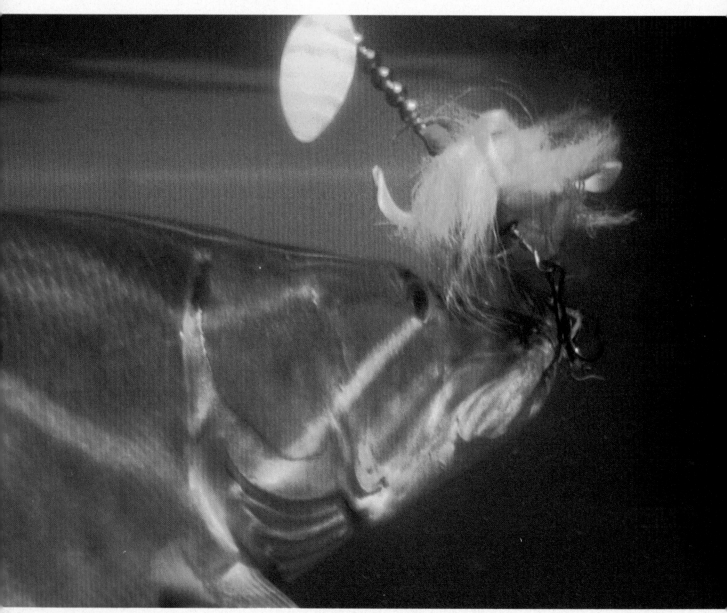

By any account, muskies are "the" top-of-the-line freshwater predator. Muskie fishing is trophy fishing. Muskellunge can grow to huge proportions, given the chance, but even then one fish per acre is considered an exceptional population.

no claim to being the sole developer of this approach. Other fishing companions helped him directly, and still others influenced his thinking, indirectly. Indeed, many good muskie anglers, who have spent countless hours in serious search of muskies and other fish, develop, usually completely on their own, personal systems somewhat similar to Mark's. Yet we believe Mark's done an unusually thorough job of developing his approach, and we're going to focus on his system and ideas in this article.

Some longtime muskie fanatics may find a few of Mark's ideas hard to swallow. Even if you disagree with his methods, however, we think you'll be a better angler for having your personal methods tested. We do want to emphasize, though, that Mark didn't initiate this article; we did. Mark is not trying to convert others to his system of muskie fishing; we are. Why? Because it's so darn effective. So if any of your pet theories or methods are criticized and you're offended, don't blame Mark; blame us. Yet if you don't learn something and fail to appreciate some of Mark's ideas, don't blame us; blame yourself.

PERCENTAGE MUSKIE FISHING

Mark seldom fishes jerkbaits. Fishing them is too slow, and their hooking and holding percentage is too low. Mark seldom casts crankbaits; they often foul with weeds, thus completely ruining a precious cast. Mark seldom spends more than a moment in any one spot, even when a big fish is known to inhabit the area. He's fishing for active, aggressive fish, and if they're not active enough to take now, in a few casts, he'll come back several times later. But he will not spend time fastidiously picking on one spot or fish. Mark does not ponder lure color; it's a mere trifling and usually makes no difference. Mark does not worry about thin leaders. He uses the heaviest leader made, as a safety factor; besides, aggressive fish just don't care. Mark does not switch hands when he casts; it takes time away from fishing.

Mark covers a lot of water looking for aggressive fish. He fishes with *bucktails*, lures he feels have the highest hooking and holding percentage, can be cast easily in all situations, and can be worked at a variety of depths and in a variety of ways. Mark does sharpen hooks and has perfected his figure-eighting. He knows that even when he's doing things right, he'll only get so many chances at a big fish. Everything must be right—all the time!

Of course, there's more. But that's the idea. Mark's approach is best described as "percentage muskie fishing." Of course, we usually attempt to play the odds when we fish. But in too many cases, our catches, especially in terms of consistency, prove we're not.

There is a tendency for this to be particularly true of muskie anglers. Too many addicts insist on placing the muskie on a pedestal. The legend and lore surrounding the fish is wonderful, but it doesn't mean exotic methods are called for. Soaking a sucker in the same spot for hours, casting to a particular fish

for days, even choosing to fish a plug like the jerkbait; these are particular techniques for specific instances. But Mark feels these methods should hardly be employed often. Why? They're not *efficient* fishing methods. They may apply to fishing for an individual fish on certain occasions, but they should not be the basis of your attack. If they are used at all, they should be used less than five percent of the time.

The basis of Mark's percentage system is fishing *fast,* all the while looking for *active, aggressive, feeding fish.* Such fish are usually shallow and associated with definite, easy-to-recognize structural items: weeds, rock bars, stumps. Muskie fishing is not so much a game of tricky location as a presentation battle and an endurance test—a test where playing the odds can make all the difference in a lifetime of fishing where only one or two, once-in-a-lifetime chances may arise. If cats can have nine lives, muskie anglers can at least extend their fishing lives two-fold by using time on the water wisely.

In essence, the idea is to make more casts and cover more water (good water), because in theory and in practice, more fish will see your presentations. The more fish that see your presentations, the more chance some of them will be aggressive biters. The more aggressive biters caught, the more likely some will be big fish. Percentage muskie fishing is an intelligent numbers plan, and therefore also an intelligent plan for big fish.

So you knew that already? Sure you did. Fish fast and cover water, right? That's logical. But a thousand things in life are logical; there's a human problem with putting logic into practice. Mark's system is a total approach based on logical conclusions tested in actual practice. Mark knows that he has only so much fishing time, and if he's using this time wisely, he can expect to catch muskies, some of which will be large. Everything is based on playing the odds. Every fishing practice is evaluated in that light. While his system may not be for everyone, it works.

One key point before going on, however. Most confirmed muskie anglers do eventually begin fishing for *big* fish: first a 20, then an upper 20, eventually a 30, a 40—most addicts would kill for a 50. For someone like Mark to use a system, it must be more than percentage muskie fishing; it must be percentage fishing for big fish. To this end, Mark spends much of his time on water he feels has the ability to produce a big fish. The fact that big fish (and what constitutes big varies by individual) can be a once-in-a-lifetime occurrence, even when you're doing things right, is a central issue—or should be—in a serious muskie angler's plan of attack.

Everything must be in your favor at all times, lest you louse up a precious, not-often-given "chance." Doing homework to find new waters with big fish potential, or taking the time to look back at the typical size of the big fish coming from certain waters, is also part of a total percentage plan. In a sentence, fishing for big fish becomes fishing big-fish water in an efficient way, with lures that have a chance to

LITTLE THINGS MEAN A LOT

Photo 1—*A good, sturdy net with a hoop diameter of at least 3½ feet is a must to efficiently land a keeper. Clubbing is not a reliable landing method.*

Photo 2—*Releasable fish should not be netted. Bring them alongside the boat and remove hooks using a Baker Hook-Out Tool (Baker Manufacturing, P.O. Box 28, Columbus, PA 17512).*

Photo 4—*Windels Tackle Company makes an extra-heavy leader with a quality swivel and a sturdy snap attachment. One or two will last an entire season, but more important, you will not lose a good fish because of a broken wire leader. There is no indication that muskies are turned off by sturdy leaders attached to bucktails.*

Photo 3—*A compound-pressure wire-cutting tool can be used to cut hooks to quickly release a deeply hooked muskie. The tool can also be used to cut hooks from you, should the unthinkable happen and you be impaled by a treble hook still attached to a thrashing fish.*

Photo 5—*A reel such as the Garcia 7000, with a wide diameter and a large-capacity spool, makes retrieving lures easy on the arm. But keep the spool filled to capacity (the bottom reel). Mark is certain that line color does not make a difference in bucktail fishing. However, he readily agrees with fishing a color you have confidence in.*

attract, hook, and hold a once-in-a-lifetime trophy, as well as plenty of other fine fish that happen along. To Mark, that means fishing big-fish water with bucktails.

WHY BUCKTAILS?

A good craftsman knows it pays to use the right tools to do good work efficiently. Knowledgeable fishermen use lures as tools and must choose the right lure to put more fish in the boat. The right lure for a given species at a given point in time usually varies.

Even though versatility is usually a virtue, Mark has a strong case for choosing the bucktail spinner as the basis of a muskie fishing system. In the Midwest and western Ontario, more muskies are caught on bucktail spinners than any other lure. In the East, bucktails aren't popular due only to tradition. They do catch fish there, as Al Lindner can attest after fishing Eastern waters, where trolling is the norm. Let's take a look at why Mark feels bucktails are "the" bait for muskies.

Bucktail spinners get their name from the whitetail deer hair tied to the lure. The long, white hair on the underside of a deer tail is long enough for tying large creations, and since it is white, it can be dyed various colors. In the water, bucktail fluffs out, pulsating to life behind a churning spinner blade. Bucktail hair is durable and usually does not mat, as is the case with some synthetic materials. However, the term *bucktail* is generally applied to spinners tied with synthetic hair, rubber, or other materials, too.

Spinner blades vary among manufacturers, but in general, Mark feels a large blade is called for. The purpose of any blade is three-fold: (1) to give off vibrations that fish can sense, (2) to produce flashes of light or color, and (3) to churn water to make the deer hair pulsate attractively. Small blades may serve a purpose earlier in the muskie fishing season. But a wide choice of blades isn't necessary, and goes against part of Mark's percentage plan for muskie fishing. In this case, don't worry about having ten different blades on hand and changing baits often; pick one you know will do the job and fish it. And that's the point: Fish it, and then fish it some more.

How the blade or blades are attached divides bucktail spinners into three categories. Straight-shafted bucktail spinners are assembled with hooks, a weighted body, a clevis, and a blade on a straight piece of wire. All original bucktail-spinner designs were of the straight-shaft variety. In the last decade, however, bucktails have been built on bent-wire forms similar to spinnerbaits for bass. Bent-wire designs fall into two categories: (1) surface buzzbaits, and (2) subsurface baits.

The three designs add to the versatility of bucktails. The straight-shaft design is generally stronger since there are no bends in the wire to fatigue and break. The safety-pin design is more weedless and can be fished in heavy vertical cover such as reeds. Mark does not feel there is a real need for fishing a surface buzzer; a straight-shaft spinnerbait can be fished near the surface, providing the same effect with better hooking odds.

The bodies of bucktails are commonly made of brass or lead to add weight for casting or trolling. Bucktails without enough weight have great air resistance and often cast poorly, especially into the wind. Too much weight, however, results in hard splashdowns and causes hair to wear down and mat.

WHERE THE BIGGEST MUSKIES HAVE COME FROM

Who knows where lunker muskies lie? Your guess is as good as anyone's. Certainly huge muskies still exist in areas of the Great Lakes; indeed, each year a few fish approaching 50 pounds are caught. The Georgian Bay portions of Lake Huron are particularly noteworthy; the Moon River is a notorious producer of big fish. Wabigoon Lake near Dryden, Ontario, has produced several 50s during the past few years, and there are bound to be other Canadian waters where a few monsters lurk. Down-South waters also have the potential to produce big fish. Ditto for classic muskie waters in the northern United States. All you have to do is find 'em and catch 'em.

While it's purely speculation where lunkers lie today, it's not so for past catches. Larry Ramsell provided the accompanying map pinpointing the areas where the top twenty muskies came from. Curiously, the 45- to 50-degree-latitude range that has produced most of the largest muskies also produces most of Europe's huge pike.

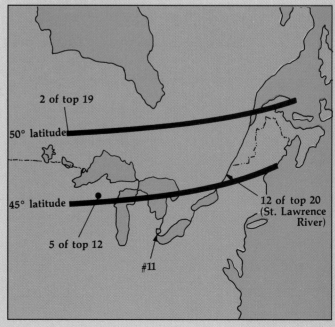

A BIT ABOUT BUCKTAILS

Are bucktails the best all-round bait for muskies? Mark certainly thinks so. Bucktails spinners are easy to cast and work in a variety of situations, create the illusion of being a large bait even when they are not, and hook and hold well. Plus they're good lures to figure-eight.

Bucktails can be divided into three categories: (1) straight-shaft baits, (2) surface buzzers, and (3) bent-wire sub-surface baits. The straight-shaft design is usually stronger: there are no bends in the wire to fatigue and break. This design applies to most fishing situations and should be thrown a majority of the time. However, in heavy weed growth, especially emergent weed growth such as reeds, a bent-wire design is more weedless. Mark sees no use for a surface buzzer because submergent baits can be worked bulging the surface and offer better hooking features.

One widely accepted theory is that small lures are better during the spring. Big muskies are rather unavailable to anglers after spawning; they seem to disappear from the shallows. But smaller male muskies often linger in the shallows and cruise shorelines. To these smaller muskies, a small lure is acceptable.

Many muskie anglers also feel that jerkbaits are a superior bait during the fall. Mark thinks some anglers believe this results from improper presentation. Because water temperature is cool in fall, fish are less active and swim slower. A jerkbait is automatically retrieved at about half the speed of a bucktail because reeling is only done between jerks. Thus, the speed of retrieve for most jerkbaits is ideal for cool- or cold-water fishing in spring and fall; yet no more ideal than a slowly fished bucktail. A bucktail angler must consciously slow a retrieve—not an easy task after burning it through warm water all summer. To slow a bucktail down, switch to a reel with a lower gear ratio or remove about 50 yards of line to reduce your spool diameter. Bucktails fished slowly work great in the fall.

THE QUESTION OF COLOR

The merits of particular colors are heavily debated in muskie circles. Few would argue that black bucktails account for the most muskies. But it is correct to point out that more muskie fishemen use black bucktails. Still, the fact remains that black works.

Black is highly visible. A muskie below a black lure will spot it against the sky background as well as, or better than, any other color. High visibility seems to be the only logical reason why black has built a reputation as "the" color for bucktails. Yet Mark has equal success with white, brown, red, yellow, purple, orange, and chartreuse bucktails. Some lakes do seem to have a most productive color; however, angler confidence in a color is probably the most important consideration. An angler confident that black will do the job will be more alert and fish more aggressively when using black.

Each year Mark fishes a popular muskie tournament on Deer and Bone Lakes in western Wisconsin. These small lakes get heavy fishing pressure all season long, and at tournament time 140 contestants pound every acre of water. Anglers who think they have to fool a fish with an unusual color (or some new lure) should note that the tournament is generally won by an angler tossing a black or yellow bucktail.

Color may be a key on some bodies of water. Most experienced anglers have probably seen instances in fishing for walleyes, bass, trout, or salmon where it was. Yet Mark's contention that muskie anglers seldom catch enough fish during a day, week, or even a season to establish a true pattern for any one water, is probably true. Thus, all the more reason to toss a color—any color—you have confidence in. A tactic Mark relishes is to catch a fish, remove his bucktail, and give it to his partner. Mark then picks out a bucktail of contrasting color and proceeds to catch fish on it. Spending time worrying about bucktail color is definitely not part of Mark's percentage muskie fishing plan.

Then there's the subject of blade color. While silver is the overwhelming favorite, Mark leans towards using fluorescent-colored blades. He finds it easier to make eye contact with his bait while casting and retrieving. Eye contact is important in order to stay alert for strikes or follows. It is also necessary for proper figure-eighting. Of course, in dirty water, fluorescent blades are definitely the way to go. Fluorescent orange shows up especially well. But these blades catch fish in clear water, too.

WHY BUCKTAILS WORK

Muskies usually feed on whatever is readily available and of suitable size. To a point, "The bigger the bait, the bigger the fish" seems to be true when it comes to muskie fishing. Yet muskie anglers are limited in lure size largely by the rod, reel, and line needed to fish big lures.

Big muskies probably select large meals to minimize the amount of energy expended in feeding. It's probably the selective feeder that takes an occasional big meal, and then goes off feed for a while, that grows to trophy size. These hawgs may not even consider a fast-moving, small snack. Of course, with millions of anglers tossing small spoons and spinners at anything that will hit, big fish (exceptions) will continue to be caught on small lures.

Compared to big plugs and jerkbaits, bucktails don't seem large. However, reel both through the water and notice how hard the bucktail spinner retrieves. The churning blade pushes a lot of water and gives the impression that the lure is larger than it is. For this reason, Mark feels that bucktail spinners with blades creating the most resistance and giving off the most vibrations are the most consistent fish getters.

It is impossible to figure what percentage of a given muskie population is located on a shallow flat, along a breakline, or suspended in deep water at a given time. However, Mark feels that muskies on comparatively shallow water flats, or on or along breaklines, are the most accessible to anglers. Fish located in such areas are easy for anglers to find, and they are more likely to be aggressive, feeding fish. Bucktail spinners are the most efficient type of lure for working shallower water.

Why are bucktail spinners so efficient? There are many reasons. Speed up the retrieve or hold the rod tip higher to keep the lure near the surface, or count it down and use a slower retrieve if you desire a deeper retrieve. Running depth is often fixed in other lures, or requires some modification each time you wish to vary the depth. That takes time away from fishing and reduces your chance to catch fish. Not so with bucktails.

Bucktails are also efficient because they travel in a straight line. An angler making eye contact with the lure can move the rod tip to maneuver a bucktail through tall weeds. Erratic-running plugs are not good baits for weed beds. Retrieves with weeds on the lure are generally wasted, further reducing percentages for catching fish.

Many lures also have one optimum retrieve speed. Bucktails generally work at all speeds. Even at high speed a bucktail is easy for a muskie to catch because it travels in a straight line. Lures with erratic actions result in a higher percentage of missed strikes. Such lures often hang up on the outside of a muskie's mouth. Hooked fish often free themselves in the struggle, or are torn off when an angler sets the hook.

Percentage muskie fishing calls for covering lots of water quickly to contact aggressive fish. Acres of shallow water can be worked quickly and efficiently with a bucktail spinner.

The "figure 8" presentation must also be considered, since it plays an important part in casting for muskie. Figure-eighting is a last-ditch effort to turn a follow into a strike. The basic key to figure-eighting is to *never* stop the action of the lure. When a fish

A FIGURE-8 PRESENTATION THAT WORKS

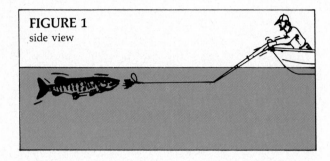

FIGURE 1
side view

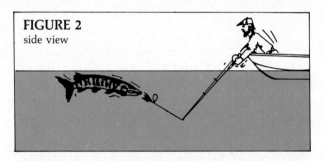

FIGURE 2
side view

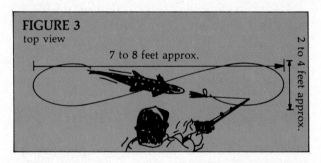

FIGURE 3
top view

7 to 8 feet approx.

2 to 4 feet approx.

FIGURE 4
side view

spinner is an ideal lure for figure-eighting since lure action can be maintained through the corners of the 8. Effective figure-eighting is difficult with a jerkbait.

A following muskie provides one of the most exciting moments in fishing. Of course, a boatside strike resulting from a properly executed figure 8 is even more exciting. But too many anglers have no idea how to properly execute a figure 8. While there is no "one" way to perform a proper figure 8, Mark has a method that definitely works.

Mark believes that most muskies in a positive feeding mood are going to strike away from the boat. Muskies are curious critters, however, and neutral fish are likely to follow a bait, often so close that their nose will touch the back end of a lure. The purpose of the figure 8 is to trick the muskie into striking the bait on impulse. Said another way, an angler must attempt to change the mood of a fish from neutral to positive for just long enough to get the fish to hit.

Always be alert for a follow. Once you spot a follow, put the rod tip into the water as in FIGURE 1, and continue reeling at the same, or preferably, a slightly faster speed. Reel the leader right up to the rod tip and *maintain* lure speed as you push the rod into the water (FIGURE 2) and begin moving the rod in an 8-shaped pattern on a horizontal plane (FIGURE 3).

Execute the figure 8 about three or four feet below the water's surface—as deep as possible while still maintaining eye contact with the muskie and the lure. Maintain lure speed in the turns, never letting the spinner blade miss a beat. Make large, round corners (two to three feet wide) on the end of the 8 to give the muskie room to turn and follow. When the muskie gets in good position behind the lure, as in FIGURE 3, begin to speed up. Concentrate on keeping the lure out of its reach. This often changes fish mood from neutral to positive.

As the muskie starts to *aggressively* chase the lure through the figure 8 and is positioned right behind the lure (again, as in FIGURE 3), completely change the direction of the bait, bring the lure up, and back towards, and over the muskie (FIGURE 4). Done properly, the muskie will raise up and intercept the *escaping* lure. The really nice thing about this maneuver is that muskies almost always grab the lure in the corner of their mouths, making hooking a sure thing. If the muskie misses, push the rod and lure back down and start figure-eighting again.

FINAL POINTERS

● Never stop the lure; change a muskie's mood by keeping the lure ahead of the fish.
● If the fish disappears, keep figure-eighting; it'll probably return.
● If you figure-eight slowly, hoping the fish will take the lure, it probably won't.
● Try to make the fish think the lure is trying to get away. When he really wants it, you won't be able to move it away fast enough.

follows behind your lure, maintain or speed up your retrieve (don't slow down) until your lure almost reaches your rod tip. Then, without breaking stride, smoothly push your rod into the water and move it in the pattern of the number 8.

Make your 8s very large, and move the lure fast—as if you are trying to take it away from the muskie. Your lure should be deep in the water, but always visible, so you can watch for the strike. A bucktail

PART 5

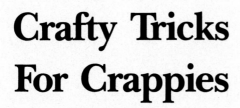

PANFISHING

Crafty Tricks For Crappies

Gary Nelson

A gushing creek empties into the lake at your feet as an early spring sun warms your back. The birds are your only company. You toss a little white jig into the lake's inlet and in a few minutes you beach the first crappie. Then comes another and another. Each cast, without exception, brings you a fish.

You've just taken part in the early spring ritual of catching inlet crappies—a little-known crappie-getting technique known to only a handful of anglers.

INLET FISHING

"I've had many successful days at a feeder stream, especially in the spring," says Gary Korsgaden, a Fargo, North Dakota, tackle salesman, fishing-school director, and part-time fishing writer and guide.

"The feeder streams bring warm runoff water into the lakes. The crappies move into these areas earlier than they do elsewhere," Korsgaden notes. "Medium- to large-size feeder streams, which are at least three to four feet deep, are best. Small aquatic insects and minnows will be in the inlet, but the crappies primarily are moving in because of the warmer water."

Korsgaden fishes the inlets in the Northern states during April. This date gets earlier as you go south. "I wait until all the snow has melted in the higher areas," he says. "Then the water starts flowing."

Korsgaden fishes right at the stream mouth or in the lake water immediately adjacent to where the water empties. He finds that a minnow hooked on a small jig works best. "I use a small jig such as a yellow-and-white crappie jig or a Bass Buster marabou jig. The best marabou jig is yellow and white, weighs about one-sixteenth ounce and is tipped with a small minnow. Pink works well in cloudy water. I use a small bobber three to four feet above the jig. It's best to cast right up into the shallow-water areas and work the jig back with short little hops on the bobber."

You can fish for crappies from either the shore or a boat. Korsgaden, however, finds that they're more accessible from a boat. He also notes that crappies occasionally swim up into the feeder streams. When fishing the streams, he casts without a bobber, letting the lure and minnow drift along with the current around the brush into the inside bends and through other crappie cover.

Korsgaden says many of these fish weigh a pound to 1¾ pounds, and he adds that catching a limit of crappies this way can be pretty easy because not many people know about this type of fishing.

FISHING DURING THE SPAWN

The spring spawning period provides top-notch crappie angling throughout the country because the fish congregate in the shallows. Every angler, however, can increase his catch and possibly take the heftiest fish he'll ever catch by heeding the advice of Mike Colvin, a fisheries research biologist with the Missouri Department of Conservation. Since the late 1960s, Colvin and his co-workers have been studying crappies, and a lot of their research has been conducted during the spawning period.

One of Colvin's observations might help fishermen quickly locate the depth of the spawning fish. "The

Crappies are more accessible from a boat than from the shore, as this angler on Lake Dardanelle, AR, can attest.

clearer the water, the deeper they spawn," says Colvin. "In a turbid or murky reservoir, crappies usually spawn very close to shore in very shallow water. In clear water they spawn much deeper."

To find the exact spawning depth, Colvin uses a Secchi disk. This is a white disk about eight inches in diameter that is lowered into the water until it disappears. "A basic rule of thumb is that the fish will be spawning at the same depth where the Secchi disk disappears, or possibly two or three feet deeper," says Colvin. A lake's clarity can change from year to year and thus, so will the spawning depth.

To make a Secchi disk: Cut an eight-inch circle from a piece of sheet metal and paint it white. Then punch a hole in the center of the circle and attach an eyebolt through the hole. The size of the hole is determined by the size of the eyebolt you use. Attach a string to the eyebolt so you can raise and lower the disk horizontally in the water. The disks also can be ordered from Wildlife Supply, 301 Caff Street, Saginaw, MI 48602.

The spring spawn is the best time to catch the largest crappies of the year because females weigh more than usual due to their egg-filled bellies. Another observation of Colvin's will help you find fish: "Males are in the preferred depth before the females so they can build nests. Females will be at about the same depth, but in more open water. They may be as close as 20 to 30 feet. Then, when the males are ready, the females come in and spawn, and the males guard the nest."

The studies showed that the youngest, and therefore the smallest, crappies spawn earliest and that white and black crappies have similar spawning habits.

Colvin adds that crappies will nest on almost any type of lake bottom, though they usually like to find exposed root hairs or similar material.

Anglers will find a water thermometer to be useful. "Spawning begins when the water temperature reaches about 54 degrees," says Colvin. "It will continue until the water gets up to about 70 degrees. This is the temperature of the water at the nest site, so it's not necessarily the same as that at the surface. The water usually is a little cooler where the fish are nesting. And there's a kind of peak in the spawning activity. The bulk of the spawn occurs when the water is from 58 to 64 degrees."

DIFFERENT TACTICS FOR DIFFERENT CRAPPIES

Do black and white crappies differ enough to justify using different fishing techniques? Mike Colvin doesn't think there is a great deal of difference between the two fish. "While white crappies predominate in Missouri, we also have varying numbers of black crappies," says Colvin. "There probably is some difference, but we haven't noticed it in our studies. We have seen both crappies spawn in the same areas. And we see anglers catch them in the same kinds of areas."

Applying the results of the behavioral research done on crappies by Colvin and his associates can help you catch more fish. For one thing, anglers should move around a lot while they fish because crappies are travelers. "If you found fish in one submerged brush pile a few days ago," Colvin says, "they may not be there today. We have seen fish that have moved a considerable distance from where we tagged them. The farthest a fish ever traveled was 35 miles. I'm quite confident that fish was the exception rather than the rule, but we've seen many fish move from one to five miles from the area where we tagged them."

Colvin advises that anglers fish lakes that are open and cover-free. "We know, of course, that crappies like to congregate around some sort of structure," he says, "but we have found that structure doesn't have anything to do with how many crappies there are in an area."

Colvin notes, however, that when brush or trees are put into a cover-free lake they may draw lots of fish.

THE RIGHT LURE

What's the best crappie-catching lure around? "I find two lures extremely successful," says Dan Gapen, a lure manufacturer from Big Lake, Minnesota. "Number one, I use a $\frac{1}{32}$-ounce or $\frac{1}{16}$-ounce white or black rubber jig tipped with a very small crappie minnow. This combination is deadly on schooling crappies whether I'm casting or vertically jigging a brush pile.

"Normally crappies, which are minnow feeders, prefer white, yellow, pink, or chartreuse. Thus my first choice is white. I've found, however, that when these lighter, normally more successful lure colors fail, switching to a black jig works well."

Gapen says that the lure should be worked very slowly in either a rolling jig type of retrieve or, if you're fishing vertically, by slowly lifting and lowering the jig between four and 12 inches. "Also," he says, "tie the jig onto the line so it sits horizontally. It's a key to successful crappie fishing."

Gapen notes that in spring, a crappie's mouth isn't as sensitive as it is during the rest of the year, and a fish may take a rubber jig, hold onto it, and then swim off.

Gapen believes that "clear, open water generally requires light-color lures. If you're going to use an L-shaped spinner on the jig, it should be extremely small. A No. 00 spinner blade would be good. When there's a lot of structure, I vertically fish a rubber jig."

For murky, open water, Gapen likes to use a chartreuse-color lure with a flashy No. 0 or No. 1 spinnerbait. For murky, snaggy water, he attaches a No. 0 jig spinner to a rubber jig. He says he doesn't like to use a spinner unless it's necessary. "A plain, straight jig-type lure will outfish a jig/spinner lure any day of the week if the angler is knowledgeable.

"Live bait, in the minds of many anglers," adds

Gapen, "probably is the best way to catch crappies during midwinter and midsummer. But during early- and mid-spring and during a forty-five-day period after the first heavy frost in fall when the crappies' mouths are less sensitive, I believe anglers can do well if not better with jigs."

While most crappies are caught below the surface, fish can be taken by topwater anglers. You often can spot these fish by looking for the rough patches that appear on an otherwise smooth lake top.

"I see crappies surfacing in many rivers and in a lot of lakes, particularly late in the evening during the heat of summer," says Gapen. "Schools of crappies that normally travel at a depth of 20 to 25 feet during late July and early August will feed at the surface right in the middle of the lake or river just before sundown. Most anglers have no idea what they are, and spend fruitless hours casting surface plugs or tossing a too-large popping bug at them."

Fishing the feeder streams as Korsgaden does yields many crappies weighing a pound to 1¾ pounds. He finds it easy to catch a limit this way.

Photos by Gary Nelson

Gapen says that the surface fish are eating nymphs or feeding on minnows that are feeding on nymphs. "I have cut open these crappies," he says, "and found them full of insect larva."

Gapen takes these fish on a plain brown Muddler fly or a ¹⁄₆₄-ounce nymph jig called the Nymphet. Gapen says that an extremely small dry fly that matches the hatch will work, too.

STRUCTURE AND HOW TO FISH IT

What's the best crappie-holding structure? First an answer from a Northern angler, then from a Southerner.

Gary Korsgaden, who fishes in the clear, deep, natural lakes of the North, likes to look for crappie cover in a lake that has good walleye and largemouth bass populations, reeds around the shore, 30 to 50 feet of water, and a creek feeding into it.

"To find the crappies," says Korsgaden, "I look along the sunken islands and bars and cabbage-weed beds. For this type of fishing I use a graphite rod, four-pound-test line, and a jig and minnow—Bass Buster jigs or one-sixteenth-ounce marabou jigs. I cast the jig and count it down—'one thousand one, one thousand two'—until I hit crappies."

The shallow, murky, wood-strewn reservoirs typical of the South call for a different approach. Joe Lacy of North Little Rock, Arkansas, is president of the National Crappie Association. The organization was set up to promote crappie fishing. You can write to the association at Box 9531, Little Rock, AR 72209.

Lacy's most reliable crappie cover is underwater hardwood treetops that are invisible from above.

"Once I catch a crappie, if I can catch the sun just right, I'll be able to see this structure beneath the surface," says Lacy. "From then on, I keep going back to that place. I look for hardwood trees, particularly oak. They don't deteriorate as badly as tupelo or coniferous trees."

Lacy's tackle may seem old-fashioned to some anglers, but it's extremely effective for hefting fish from this snaggy water. He uses a cane pole rigged with eight feet of 12-pound-test line and a sliding cork. A few feet above the hook or at whatever depth he finds fish, he ties on a two-inch piece of 20-pound line to act as a bobber stop. Enough split shot is clamped above the hook to keep the top of his cork nearly submerged. This way, he says, a crappie feels little resistance. For bait, Lacy hooks on a two-inch shiner, or if the water temperature is moderate, he'll fish a plain Beetle jig. If the water is cool, he'll tip the jig with a shiner.

To fish lots of cover, Lacy fishes a submerged treetop for only five seconds and moves to another spot if nothing happens. "By the time I count to five, that minnow's right in the crappie's face," he says. "It's going to hit my offer or it's not."

Using this method one October day, Lacy took home one of his best catches ever—an easy limit that included four three-pounders.

Big Bluegills

Joe Ehrhardt

Joe Ehrhardt believes that, ounce for ounce, a full-grown bluegill puts up more fight than any freshwater gamefish.

Adult bluegills—especially one-pound-plus beauties—are the most pugnacious of all panfish. I consider them the "bantam-weight" champions of sport fishing. Ounce for ounce, a full-grown bluegill puts up more fight than any freshwater gamefish I know of. If you're passing them up, you don't know what you're missing!

The following article is a simple guide to successful panfishing. No high-priced tackle or electronic gadgets are required; light spinning gear will do just fine. If (when!) you decide to make big 'gills a regular part of your fishing, an ultra-light spinning outfit will enhance the fun even more.

As with all gamefish, there are certain peak times of the year to catch numbers of big bluegills. Since the bulk of my fishing takes place on natural lakes, the examples we'll discuss center around fishing in lake environments. However, you folks who fish rivers and reservoirs can certainly apply the same locational principles and techniques to the waters you fish.

EARLY SPRING

Good early season bluegill fishing often begins shortly after ice-out, which generally occurs anywhere from late March through early May on most northern natural lakes. After a few warm, sunny days, or following a warm rain, shallow water sections of a lake warm slightly and begin attracting aquatic life—especially bluegills.

My first choice for a good early season area is a small, soft-bottomed, wind-protected bay that's five feet deep or less. In general, the smaller the bay, the better. These soft-bottomed bays generally become thickly choked with weeds during the summer months, although they sport little growth this early in the year. As the days pass, the sun will warm the bay and clusters of lily pads will begin poking their stems toward the surface. Microscopic plants and animals, nymphs, insect larvae, and tiny minnows become active. This typically initiates major food-chain activity, creating perfect conditions for drawing bluegills into the shallows.

Similar early bluegill activity takes place in man-made channels, if they're available. In many regions, property owners dig channels to provide access to the main body of water. These areas warm early, and attract panfish soon after ice-out.

Bluegills are typically at least a month away from spawning at this stage, so their behavior is food-oriented, rather than spawning-related. Fish that enter the warm shallows are far more prone to feed than those that remain in deeper, colder water. Thus your best odds for catching early season fish are in the shallows.

This article originally appeared in Volume 49 of *In-Fisherman* magazine.

Early season, shallow-water fishing offers several challenges. Fishing shallow, muck-bottomed bays in a slow, easy fashion requires a suspended bait, since an on-the-bottom offering could be hidden by mud. Yet you must also use a heavy enough rig to be able to cast at least 60 to 80 feet to avoid spooking fish in the typically clear water of spring.

The best way to accomplish this is with a long spinning rod, 4-pound-test monofilament line, and a plastic "bubble." Notice I didn't say a large, round, red and white *bobber*. Instead, I use a ³⁄₁₆ or ¼ ounce *clear plastic casting float*. Its clear appearance won't spook fish, and adding water inside it adds weight, making the rig easy to cast. I prefer not to add any type of sinker since it tends to hamper the bait's natural action. A lure or bait suspended about three feet below a bubble is deadly!

A number of lures are attractive to early season panfish. A tiny panfish popper is a real favorite among bluegill anglers. You don't need a fly rod to fish a feather-weight popper, since a plastic bubble and spinning rod lets you cast as far as you want.

For best early season results, *take it easy*. Your bait should imitate the food the bluegills are accustomed to eating. For example, no unlucky insect that's fallen into the water races by at high speed!

Easy does it. Cast out and let the "bug" lay still for at least thirty seconds. Slightly rattle your rod tip to pulsate the tiny popper as though it were an insect struggling on the surface.

If a bluegill misses the lure, don't panic! Just let it lie there. An aggressive fish will usually come back several times before it gives up. On some days, a closed-cell floating rubber bug does a better job of hooking fish, so switch baits if you feel it's necessary. Work it similar to the popper. In any case, if you don't catch a fish by the time the lure is halfway to the boat, you're probably in barren territory. Reel in and cast again.

Fly-rod trout lures also work well for early season bluegills. Some anglers prefer a small streamer or nymph. Flyfishing requires considerable expertise, so for beginners, and especially young children, I suggest sticking with spinning gear.

Popular winter live baits like waxworms, "spikes," mousies, red worms, etc., are effective all year long. But these tiny grubs have one common feature: Shortly after ice-out, they usually attract too many *small* fish! We're after *big* ones!

Strange as it sounds, my first choice in live bait for early season, *large* bluegills is a four-inch-long nightcrawler! I use a tiny No. 10 Aberdeen hook, and hook the worm *once* through the body about one-half inch behind the head. The point of the hook will show, but that's OK. A large bluegill will usually take a big worm by the head. When your bubble goes down, you've got 'em! The nightcrawler continues to be a good bait for big bluegills up until summer arrives (July in my home area of Wisconsin).

Before we proceed, I'd like to mention two more early season bluegill options. Bulrushes and reeds also attract early season bluegills, although the fish usually don't spawn there in the lakes I fish. Bulrushes often grow on a bottom that's too soft, and reeds on a hard sand/gravel/marl bottom that's too hard, to allow successful spawning. Yet when these plants grow in two to four feet of water, feeding bluegills often relate to them in early season.

To catch fish in these tall aquatic "grasses," you must first place your bait close enough to interest them. In most cases, that means *in* or *tight against* the weeds. A cast only a few feet outside reeds or rushes is often a waste of time. Do it right!

SPAWNING TIME

All fish proceed through a number of seasonal transitions as the year progresses. Anglers who adapt to the changing conditions are usually the most successful. Failing to follow the fish as they change location is one big reason why few people catch big panfish throughout the year.

As the water temperature warms, the bulk of the bluegills drop back a bit deeper, spreading out away from very shallow, early season hotspots. They continue to feed, and slowly begin repositioning near the areas where they intend to spawn. They're often hard to contact "in bunches" until they actually move into their spawning sites.

In the upper Midwest, most panfish spawn during May and June. Males select nesting sites, set up "housekeeping," and begin building nests. Prime spawning areas generally have a *fairly hard* bottom consisting mainly of gravel, sand, or marl, covered by a light layer of sediment. When these conditions are not available, they'll select the next best hard or semihard bottom option. They cannot, however, spawn successfully on silt.

Male bluegills create spawning beds by fanning out an area with their tails until it is clear of debris. The number of nests built in an area is determined by the size of the local bluegill colony. A "bed" area looks like so many large, clean, 12-inch platters set closely alongside each other.

Spawning begins once the water temperature becomes sufficiently warm—usually in the high 60s (degrees Fahrenheit). Females are attracted to the nests, and after a brief courtship are induced to lay their eggs. Spawn and milt mix and settle onto the clean nests. Under normal conditions, the eggs hatch into fry in several days.

The average female bluegill reaches sexual maturity in about four years. An eight-ounce female can produce from 10,000 to 12,000 eggs, with Wisconsin DNR records showing some large bluegills to have carried as much as 38,000 eggs at one time.

Many anglers believe that catching bluegills off spawning beds is poor sportsmanship. However, unlike most fish, bluegills are incredibly prolific. Many fisheries biologists believe it is nearly impossible to hurt good bluegill populations significantly by hook-and-line methods, and I agree (with the possible exception of a small body of water being fished by many intelligent anglers).

Don't feel guilty about fishing for spawners. Any good spawning bed may have several dozen fish using it at any one time. It would take an exceptionally experienced (and lucky) angler to catch a significant fraction of the biggest bluegills without spooking the others. In most lakes, few of the best beds are even fished!

As a general rule, you'll find mainly smaller bluegills using shallow-water nests that you locate by eyesight. Heck, anybody can catch *them!* Bigger bluegills, however, tend to make their beds in less obvious spots, often as deep as eight to ten feet. Thus the biggest 'gills must be located by *probing*. This is a key locational factor for big fish. Don't underestimate it!

To catch the biggest spawning bluegills, concentrate your efforts on shallow flats immediately adjacent to the first major drop-off. Maneuver your boat *very slowly* along the drop-off, casting up onto the flat. Use a single-hooked nightcrawler as described earlier, and a split shot or casting bubble for weight. Once again, I prefer the plastic bubble. I open it up and add enough water to *barely* sink the bait to the bottom. Most bubbles sink at about one foot per second when they're filled with water. By counting, "one thousand, two thousand," etc., until the bait hits the bottom, you'll know how deep you're fishing.

Cast the night crawler out, let it sink to the bottom, and reel it in *very slowly*, with frequent pauses. Meticulously working the deepest edge of the shallow flat should eventually put you on a deep spawning bed. Once the worm is dragged through a nest, a big bluegill should pick it up. They're not really feeding, but rather simply clearing the nest. I like the medium-sized, four-inch 'crawler better than smaller baits for this condition. Smaller baits definitely play second fiddle to the 'crawler when it comes to eliciting this "clearing" response.

Done properly, you can usually take eight or ten large bluegills from a bed area without moving the boat. Remember, however, that bluegills will not move far from their nests to take a bait. If you're on the money, this is usually your best shot at taking numbers of very large bluegills during the entire year. Since all bluegills do not spawn at the same time, the prime "big-fish" fishing often lasts a month or more until all the bluegills have spawned.

SUMMER BEHAVIOR

As the season progresses into summer, larger bluegills often move to areas along deep drop-offs, out to sunken islands, or perhaps even suspend over deep, open water. Location varies from lake to lake, and is largely determined by the location of the available food. Big bluegills become a mystery at this time of the year for most anglers.

In addition to 'crawlers and artificial lures, sum-

TYPICAL BLUEGILL SPAWNING BED

Big bluegills often spawn in "beds" containing four to ten, or even more, individual nests spaced so closely together that they nearly touch. Shallow beds are easily located—you can see them—but they seldom attract the largest fish. Big bluegills often nest as deep as eight to ten feet deep in clear water lakes, and it takes considerably more effort to find their spawning areas. Once you do, however, you can often catch several nice fish before the others spook.

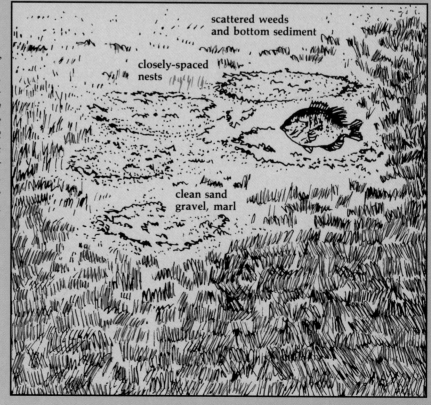

scattered weeds and bottom sediment

closely-spaced nests

clean sand gravel, marl

QUALITY BAIT—QUALITY BLUEGILLS

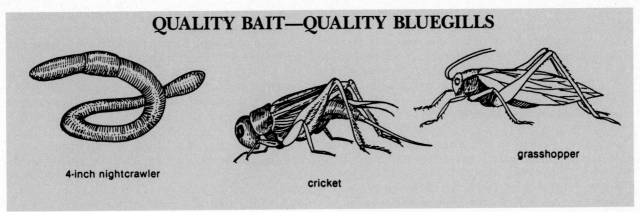

4-inch nightcrawler **cricket** **grasshopper**

It's a fact: No self-respecting trophy bluegill would hit a sad mess like a piece of night crawler, threaded on a jumbo hook, hanging beneath a beach ball bobber. Arggh! Like Rodney Dangerfield, give the poor bluegill a little respect!

A bluegill trip with Papa Joe is a real eye-opener. He carries so many boxes of assorted creepy and crawly baits that they say, "Joe brought the zoo along again." However, you never know when a bit of experimenting will pay off.

Carefully hook a four-inch night crawler about a half-inch behind the nose with a light wire, No. 10 Aberdeen

hook. Looks almost good enough to eat, doesn't it? Thread a slightly larger No. 8 Aberdeen hook through a cricket, dragonfly, or grasshopper and out behind the head. Hey, not bad! Son-of-a-gun; there's more to bluegills than a bobber and a worm, isn't there. You better believe it! If you're after the big guys, pay them all the attention and respect you'd give a walleye or bass. Otherwise, you'll only end up with a batch of wafer-thin mouthfuls, instead of frying-pan-sized fillets.

mer bluegills are partial to aquatic nymphs, and any of the grubs or larvae used for winter fishing. A small, one-inch-long crayfish will do a good job of luring large bluegills to the hook and keeping the small ones away! For best results, hook these small crustaceans through the tail from the bottom up.

Oversize bluegills also have a great fondness for tiny minnows. When adult fish are after minnows, they often cruise over deep water, perhaps ten feet below the surface. They're tough to locate and hold on in open water, but they're there.

If you spot suspended fish on your depth finder, try drifting across open water with your bait about 15 or 20 feet deep. Experiment with different-sized sinkers a few feet above your bait, and take the wind into consideration, when you work different depths. I'll try this approach, particularly if I believe there is a mayfly hatch occurring from a mud bottom, although I definitely prefer fishing along drop-off areas.

Later in the season, worms and small minnows get stiff competition from crickets and grasshoppers. A windy day can really get the big bluegills going. It blows grasshoppers onto the lake; they float around struggling, and the 'gills will be looking for them. I once cleaned a large bluegill whose stomach was crammed with grasshoppers—yet the glutton couldn't resist mine!

When fishing with crickets and grasshoppers, *don't* use the common method of hooking them beneath the collar. You'll miss too many strikes. Instead, insert a long, light wire Aberdeen hook into the insect's rear, thread it through its entire body, and bring the point out just behind the head. You won't miss any

short strikes, and big 'gills will nail it even though the 'hopper is dead.

FALL BLUEGILLS

During autumn, and into late fall, big bluegills once again move back toward shallower water. If you can stand the brisk weather, and are a bit patient, you'll enjoy some jumbo bluegill fishing.

Most small baits like larvae, grubs, nymphs, etc., will take fall fish. However, I've had good, late-fall results on a 1/32-ounce jig, either with or without a plastic body, and baited with a wax worm. Fish this set up with a plastic bubble over the tops of the weeds, along their edges, and into pockets.

In some lakes, good, big bluegill fishing lasts all the way 'til ice-up. Sometimes I break thin ice to get out to my big bluegill spots. You'll probably have little competition and good action if you're willing to experiment.

I'd like to close with a thought. Float fishing is *not* obsolete. Whether you use a spinning rod and a slip bobber, or a humble cane pole, float fishing is one of the better methods of offering baits to slugish bluegills—particularly when the water is cold. And, as we've shown, successful float fishing is both an art and a science, not just "hangin' a piece of worm under a bobber"!

I have had a lifetime of bluegill fishing and have never tired of it. If you "get to know" the bluegill, you'll find him a sporting "game" fish that you'll enjoy. And when you get on the big ones on light tackle, you'll have all the fight and excitement you can handle.

Pandemonium Panfish

W. Horace Carter

Speak in hushed tones. Set the bait bucket down easy. Don't scrape the oars. Kill the motor. In other words: Be quiet!

That's standard behavior for most anglers fishing from a boat. But Billy and Tommy Vaughan, a father-and-son fishing team from Elloree, South Carolina, say that the best way to catch a lot of fish is to simply cause a commotion. And the incredible numbers of crappies and bluegills that they take with their offbeat method are proof positive.

These veteran panfish anglers have the know-how and know-where to catch legal limits of gripper-size flatfish virtually year-round. They are certain that the system they use to put panfish in the boat will work on any lake or river that contains a respectable population of these species.

Billy and Tommy fish primarily with jigs. They punch their metal boats right into the grass and weed beds, slip the outboard engine out of gear, and let it idle. As the water churns about, they'll drop tiny red-head jigs through the froth to the bottom.

Fishing such heavy cover is certain to bring some hang-ups, especially when a good-size bream gulps down the jig and heads for the tangles. But the Vaughans have constructed some gadgets that eliminate a lot of trouble and delay when this happens, such as the "holy rod": a ten-foot piece of metal conduit bent at a 90-degree angle about 15 inches from one end. When they stop the boat in the thickets to fish, this homemade apparatus is used to jiggle out a hat-size opening so the sinkerless and bobberless hook and line will slowly sink to the bottom.

They've also made a "jig retriever," another piece of conduit with a small forked end. When the jig hangs up, they straddle the monofilament line with the fork, push it to where the hangup is, and free the jig. Few panfish anglers take to the water with a holy rod and jig retriever, but they are as important to Billy and Tommy as their poles and lines.

The Vaughans use 14-pound-test monofilament and a lightweight jig with a red head. The jig is tied to the line at a right angle. This father-and-son team seldom loses a jig and line and almost never fails to catch all the fish they want.

Billy has been fishing the swamplands of upper Marion all the way to the dam for more than thirty years. Tommy, his 28-year-old son, has been pulling in the crappies and bream for twenty years. They live in the Stumphole Landing section of Santee-Cooper and few guides or other flatfish anglers have the consistent record of success that these two sincere and talented fishermen have.

"We use nothing but jigs year-round for crappies," says Billy, a large, quiet man. "The No-Alibi, Challenger, and Teeny Bopper and the split-tail black, red, white, or yellow grubs made by C. M. Bait Company here in Santee are the best jigs you can buy for our kind of crappie fishing. But Tommy is making his own type of jig now, one he calls a 'Rooty Tooty 309.' It catches just as many fish as the regular jigs in the tackle shops. His jig has a red head, yellow skirt, and a No. 4 Eagle Claw hook. We use the 1/16 and 1/8-ounce sizes of both the homemade and commercial jigs.

"Our crappie and bream fishing style will work anywhere, not just here in the South Carolina Low Country. Waters in Florida, Georgia, North Carolina, Virginia, Louisiana, and Mississippi are almost identical and we can catch fish in any of these waters."

"In muddy water we'll fish darker jigs," says Tommy. "In clear water, light-color jigs are best. We do

Photos by Robert C. Clark

not see any use in buying minnows just to watch a cork move around and around, when it's possible to catch the fish quickly with a jig."

These unique crappie anglers have some other innovations and ideas that are inconsistent with most fishermen's ideas on how to catch fish. But the Vaughans insist that their techniques are adaptable to any lake or river.

The Vaughans generally use an eight- or nine-foot stripped-down fly rod—no reel, guide, or tip section. They tie a line to the end just long enough so the jig will sink within a few inches of the bottom and the rod end is six inches above the surface. They catch their fish in anywhere from 18 inches to 12 feet of water. The four-foot depth in the swampy areas is best.

"From March 15 until October we fish a great deal in the deeper water around submerged logs, trees, and stumps. We catch few fish around the standing timber," Billy notes.

But the Sparkleberry, Indigo Flats, and Broadwater swamps are where these veteran anglers catch most of their fish in the four-foot depths. They usually fish these waters from fall through February.

Contrary to what many avid anglers have preached over the decades, the Vaughans do not believe that you can spook either the crappies or the bream that they fish for in Santee-Cooper.

"We never cut our outboard engines off," says Billy. "We run our metal flat-bottom boats right up into the floating grass islands that are too thick to put a hook through. We then use our holy rods to work out a hat-size hole so our line and jig can go down. The water pump, the exhaust, and the vibration shake the grass and water around us. We believe that this racket and water motion disturbs the freshwater shrimp, potbelly minnows, and insects that are hiding in the grass. They scramble out of hiding and the crappies and bream strike them. The fish will chase our jigs right along with the baitfish and other food supply that has been dislodged.

"Making noise in the boat or in the water only helps this kind of fishing. Even catching one and letting it flutter on the way up and on the surface attracts others. They know that the fish has found food and others will come running.

"If you ever get hooked on catching crappies with jigs, you'll throw your minnow bucket away. You'll catch more fish, and we think it's more fun than using live bait. Sometimes you don't feel the fish hit your jig, you just see the line go slack on the way down. Just yank with your wrist and you'll have another nice black or white crappie."

Billy and Tommy fish an average of at least 225 days a year and each generally catches his thirty-fish limit. The fish average from one to 1½ pounds, which means each of them is landing more than 6,500 pounds of fish a year.

What do they do with so many fish?

"Well, in addition to eating a lot of fish ourselves," says Billy, "we frequently get together with our neighbors for fish fries. You can eat up a lot of fish when you just invite all the friends in the neighborhood."

And the two offer good examples of Southern hospitality. They have even built a nice entertainment cabin a few yards off the water where they can put up a number of tables and feed a large group of people indoors.

"You have to remember that crappies and bass are not inclined to stay in the same place day after day," says Billy. "They will move around and you have to find them. If you are fishing every day or two, you'll know where they are. But if you miss a week or so, then you have to work harder and longer to find where they are holding.

"We don't have as many large crappies here now as we once did but there are still plenty of fish. When the water was about 5½ feet low in Sparkleberry Swamp during the 1981 winter months, we experienced the best fishing we had in seven years. It gave us access to more areas where the fish had schooled. We once landed a 3½-pound crappie—our largest—and recently took a 2¾-pounder. I know there are other big ones out there in those vast swampland waters.

"When you are fishing in the open, a little wind helps. You'll get more bites, but I do not believe in the sun and moon tables that say there is a best time and worst time to fish each day. I don't think it has anything to do with how many we catch. A southwest wind is the ideal wind to fish here. The day before a front moves in is also a good time to fish, but two days before the front is very poor. Two hours before a thunderstorm hits is also a productive time.

"When I am not fishing, and when the water is down a few feet, I go out in these flats and fasten a stick to the submerged logs and stumps so I can find them out there now," Billy says while pointing to hundreds of markers sticking out of the water.

"We don't hunt for bedding crappies or bream.

We just find places where they are schooled up and looking for food," Billy explains. "Tommy often fishes from one boat and I from another but we may be fairly close together. The crappies are so aggressive and bunched up at times that we have caught as many as ninety-six in a five-foot-square area over a period of two days. We did that last December—not a spawning month here.

"The gator grass is plentiful in the upper portion of Marion and it is full of freshwater shrimp and popgut minnows. When we run our boats up on this grass, the curious crappies just swim right in to inspect the area and gulp down the food we dislodge with our boats.

"My advice to other crappie and bream fishermen is to always fish the shady side of logs and stumps. When you are fishing early and late, you'll always have more luck on the shady side. If there's a current present, you'll always do better by fishing the upstream side of the log or stump, not the eddy side."

"Our style of fishing is hard work," says Tommy. "You don't have to keep a cricket moving for bream but we always keep the jig moving for crappies. We keep the pole in one hand and the throttle of the outboard in the other.

"In April and May there are bream and crappie tournaments held here on Santee-Cooper. I've entered several of them. I always placed in the top ten and was first in four tournaments."

The Vaughans represent two generations of panfish anglers at Santee. They are not guides and fish only for their own pleasure and for neighborhood picnic tables. But it would be hard to find more panfishing expertise among the hundreds of people who call the banks of this watery wilderness their home.

PART 6

JUST FOR LAUGHS

Ode To The Lake Trout

Jerry Pabst

As I relaxed in my seat, contemplating the bright, beautiful morning sun, I thought I saw the port downrigger rod twitch slightly, but nothing more happened. A minute went by, and the rod twitched once again. I quickly snatched the rod from the holder, expecting the release to trigger, and the drag to screech out in response to the surge of a wild Chinook salmon. But nothing happened. Perplexed, I thought maybe the line had picked up some floating seaweed, or was being bumped by a school of alewives.

Standing, with the rod in my hand, I sensed the slight trace of a tug on the line 80 feet below. Jerking the line from the downrigger release to check it out, I slowly began reeling in a heavy, dead weight. Pumping the rod and laboriously reeling, I winched to the surface, to my utter surprise, a nice-sized lake trout.

Wonder of wonders, the trout hadn't even opened the release, and we had towed it around on the downrigger for at least five minutes. To my chagrin,

I had landed a 16½-pound lake trout—the largest I've ever taken, and a big fish on any body of water. Yet my only reaction was, "big deal."

Lake trout, in my opinion, rate only fair as a food fish. As a sport fish, I figure it rates somewhere between seaweed and clams.

Dragging five pounds of lead on wire lines over the bottom, in order to hook and haul up unresisting lumps of fish-style protein, is not the type of action (I feel) makes anglers rush to the waterways. Boring—boring—boring!

For those who persist in purposely trying to fish for these "sluggards of the deep," I propose to open the *"Jerry Pabst Lake-Trout Fishing Clinic."* Students will be instructed in all phases of lake trout fishing, such as:

This article originally appeared in Volume 54 of *In-Fisherman* magazine.

1. How to troll slow enough and not attract nesting gulls.
2. How to boil trout, and get enough oil to run your car for a month.
3. How to tell the difference between a live and a dead lake trout. (Live ones still have lampreys on them.)
4. How to hook the bottom consistently to reduce boredom.
5. A surefire remedy for insomia.

If your world has become unbearable and pressure prevents sleep, go lake-trout fishing. It will put anyone to sleep. You need not worry about anything exciting happening.

HOW TO FIND LAKE TROUT

Drive out onto the lake, after taking at least one-half bottle of No-Doz to fight off the urge to sleep that hours of boredom are bound to produce. Lake trout like deep water, so move out beyond all the other boats and turn your graph on. If you don't see anything, that means there are lake trout around. You won't see them because they sleep in the mud and will not be picked up by the graph. No other fish will appear, because they are repulsed by the poor hygiene habits of the lakers.

The surefire way to check an area for lake trout is to cut your engine, and listen for snoring. Make sure your crew is awake, since you don't want to confuse fisherman snores with lake-trout snores.

HOW TO CATCH LAKE TROUT

Make a lot of noise in your boat. This will not wake the trout up, but will partially rouse them, and they will begin to yawn. Put a spoon on the downrigger about two feet behind the ball, and lower the downrigger weight until it hits bottom. Raise the weight,

and drag it along several inches over the bottom. If you do this long enough, and get those fish yawning enough, you will eventually snag one in the mouth. Lake trout never strike a lure intentionally.

You can detect the attack of a laker because the downrigger wire will start to sag back, due to the weight of the sleeping fish being pulled along. Quietly work the release loose, and begin winching the trout to the surface. This will not wake the fish up, so just take your time. Slide the trout carefully into the net, swing it aboard, and remove the hook. Notice the fish is still asleep.

If the fish is large, pictures are in order. Place two fingers beneath the trout's gill covers, and hold it high. Snap the shutter. The shutter snapping usually wakes fish, which responds by messing up your shoe. This is the only thing a lake trout does really well.

THE FINAL EXAM

The final exam is a real toughy. Students are taken to a lake, and confronted with three rods with lines in the water. These lines are connected to:
1. an old boot
2. a 12-pound lake trout
3. a pair of panty hose

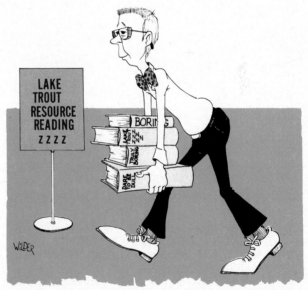

The student must correctly identify which rod has what on it. If he has done his homework, the successful graduate knows that the rod offering solid and determined resistence is the old boot. He also knows that the panty hose are the only things that come up easier than lake trout. Therefore, by process of elimination, he can deduce the presence of the rod holding the 12-pound laker. (There is no known way to detect the presence of a fighting lake trout without employing this process of elimination.)

For further information on lake trout in the Great Lakes, contact the U.S. Fish and Wildlife people. Ask for the pamphlet titled, "Truly Boring Things to Do."

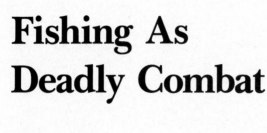

Fishing As Deadly Combat

Joel Vance

There's an old joke about a guy who has one terrible thing after another happen to him until finally he throws up his hands, looks to the sky, and cries, "Why me?"

And a booming voice reverberates from the clouds: "I don't know, Jones—there's just something about you that ticks me off."

As I stood with a popping bug dangling from my sternum, I was tempted to cry out, "Why me?" but was afraid the thunderous answer would be: "Quit your griping—it gives you something to write about."

The pendulous popper was a fairly typical Vance fishing outing (I once caught an 80-pound collie and found they can jump higher than a tarpon). I was fishing for bass on a small mid-Missouri pond, shirtless against the summer heat. Somehow a back cast—as perfectly executed as if Lee Wulff had been manning the rod—went astray, and the bug leaped on my unprotected chest with a tiny scream of rage and sank its fangs through the skin over my breastbone.

I found out that day how tough the human covering really is. I might as well have been trying to pull the hook out of set concrete as to pull it out of my skin. That was my first move—just rip the thing out, figuring I wouldn't lose more than a quart of blood. But chest skin is tougher than chrome-tanned elk hide and all I did was stretch it out until I looked as if I were wearing an old baggy sweater with two brown buttons.

Next, I decided to try the trick where you loop a piece of twine around the bend in the hook, press the shank down, and give a sharp jerk (there was a jerk involved in this business, but he wasn't very sharp). The theory is this maneuver defeats the barb. You've seen the magician cut a girl in half with a crosscut saw? Far less painful and disfiguring. And that also works . . . if you're a magician.

The bug was lodged high enough that I could just see it by tucking my chin down and looking cross-eyed down my nose. I couldn't work on it directly, but found that if I looked in my rearview mirror, I could see what was going on—in reverse. Moe, Shemp, and Curly Bill performed with consummate grace compared to the way I fumbled around trying to make left be right.

But I got even. Fishing equipment hurts me—but I hurt it. As soon as I was able, I broke a fishing rod. There is no rod so stout that I can't break it. You put line guides and a reel seat on a telephone pole, and I'll show you how to break it. I have more broken rods than Carter has pills (or peanuts) and have done them in with ever new and inventive ways.

Part of the problem is me, part of it is car doors, and part of it is my dog. Apparently there is something hypnotic and compelling to the dog about the gently-bobbing tip of a fishing rod in a moving automobile. The rhythmic movement of the rod titillates the chew muscles of the dog. And they go for the tip, even as an attacking wolf goes for the throat.

Dogs are not without their uses in fishing, however, especially to the fly tier. The average dog is a hairbag whose major contribution to the family is to aggravate asthma, bronchitis, and dust pneumonia. He turns rugs from whatever color you want them to whatever color he is, and generally demonstrates, winter and summer, that Nature has endowed him with far more hair than he needs. Why not put this otherwise wasted, free-floating resource to good use?

Reprinted, with permission, from *Outdoor America*, the magazine of the Izaak Walton League of America.

Illustration by Hobe Hayes

I tied dog-hair flies for quite some time. (I'm tempted to say they worked especially well on bowfin, which are called dogfish up north, but far be it from me to make a joke out of anything so serious as fly-fishing.) It got so my resident dog, a multi-colored collie, began to whine piteously every time he saw me coming with a pair of scissors and a creative gleam in my eye. He looked as if he had been gnawed by enormous moths.

As well as tying flies, you can get involved in making your own fishing lures and save a great deal of money. Of course, the lures don't work, and what you save in money, you lose in sanity. A friend once gave me a handmade lure that was lovely—baked-on enamel, carefully carved, a real work of art. It sank like a lead hippopotamus and had all the action of a dead shoat dragged through a muck hole.

And, while I'm on the subject of fishing lures, let me mention one little-known use for lures. Along with attracting fish, lures can be used to catch trees—especially big ones.

Foresters have a hard time finding national champion-sized trees. Big trees hide in the woods and crouch down when someone comes along with a transit and a tape measure.

Shucks, I can find the champ of any given tree species in five minutes. Just let me cast fishing lures at random. You may not believe this, but I've seen trees big enough to provide lumber for an entire seven-room, ranch-style home jump eight feet or more to one side or the other to flag down one of my lures. This is true. Fishermen never exaggerate.

We haven't talked yet about fishing line and I'd rather not. It brings to mind endless loops and snarls leading nowhere. Dante had it all wrong. Hell is not

ice and fire and easy stuff like that. It is you—poor lost soul—sitting in a bass boat, with fish rolling and slurping in a feeding frenzy, endlessly picking at a backlash that will not come free for all of eternity.

The line goes on a reel, and reels have contributed to the fitful nervous tremors that shake my poor broken psyche. The first fishing reel probably was a stick on which Proto-Angler wound his rough sinew or whatever passed for fishing line. Now, the only thing more complicated than a modern fishing reel is the inside of the control console at Kennedy Space Center.

My approach to fixing things is to kick them. This seems to work marvelously well with television sets, but apparently is not written in the repair manual for fishing reels.

Someone made the mistake of giving me a set of small screwdrivers, and when one of my sons recently came to me with a fishing reel that had developed gastritis, I got out my tool kit. The family scattered like startled snipe, for they had been there before.

With the exhilarated rapture of Cro-Magnon man brandishing a rock and shouting, "Tool!" I descended on the helpless reel.

Boy, let me tell you, when you lift the lid off one of those suckers, tiny springs, microscopic screws, and indescribable shreds of metal and plastic fly all over the room, like shrapnel from an exploding grenade.

The reel got fixed all right, and the repairs cost only 87 percent of the price of a brand-new reel. Don't ever let them tell you Vance is a Bad Daddy.

We come, finally, to the tackle box, repository of the terminal weapon, the fish-getter. I admire conscientious fishermen whose tackle boxes look as neat as a spinster's hope chest. My tackle box has all the charm of a nest of adders.

Somehow, water always gets in it, and the hooks rust, leaving not only ugly stains in the lure compartments, but dull hooks. Invariably, plastic worms make love to my most treasured and expensive plugs and turn them into gelatinous globs that further encrust the lining of the tackle box. The whole effect is that of a sump pit at the city dump.

Most anyone can backlash a reel, but I backlash fishing lures. I can nest any three fishing plugs, ganged with treble hooks, as far as possible from each other in the tackle box. But when I open it, the three of them have clasped their barbed hands and untangling them would baffle the world champion at Rubik's Cube.

Yes, it has been a dreary story, this tale of fishing, fishing equipment, and me. But this story only begins to touch on the distress and disappointment I've endured in the name of fish. I could recount other stories that would put the silver dust of age in your youthful locks.

In fact, let me tell you about the one that got away . . .

The BASS Classic Caper

Patrick F. McManus

You make a lot of enemies in my business. Word on the street was that some guys in Montana had put out a contract on me because of the last job I did there. Sure, the contract was for only $3.98 but times are tough and people will take any work they can get. While I was riding the bus to work, a hit man tried to take me out by tying a plastic bag over my head. He apologized for not being able to afford bullets. I told him to forget it and gave him a buck for making an effort to stay off welfare.

When I got to my crummy office that crummy Monday morning, my crummy secretary was soaking the mail in a bucket of water. A lot of guys have dishwater blonde secretaries. Maizy is dishwater all over.

"Anything of interest, Maizy?" I asked.

"Naw, just the usual ticking package and lumpy envelopes marked 'Handle with Care.' "

I wandered into my crummy private office and flopped down at my crummy desk. I felt like a cigarette. It was an odd sensation, and I wondered if maybe I should consult a nerve specialist. Then the phone rang.

"McManus here," I answered gruffly, all business.

"Mr. McManus," drawled a voice soft and Southern as cheese on hot grits, "this is Renee Wheatley in Montgomery, Alabama. I work for Ray Scott."

Ray Scott! The man was a fishing legend! Some years ago he had invented the bass in his basement during nights after work as an insurance agent. He became so obsessed with the fish that he started to devote all his time to it. Rapidly, his basement began to fill up with bass. Then his wife told him to get his bass out of the house and start making some money. So Scott did. He started promoting professional bass-

fishing tounaments and organized the Bass Anglers Sportsman Society or BASS. Both were a big hit with anglers around the country, and it wasn't long before Scott's basement began filling up with money.

Renee's melliferous voice interrupted my recollecting. "Mr. Scott has requested your presence at the 11th Annual BASS Masters Classic in Montgomery."

"That's a tough assignment," I said. "I'd be going up against the top bass fishermen in the country."

"Mr. Scott believes you can handle it. He knows about your, er, uh, talent."

"But why?"

"I can't tell you that. Mr. Scott just wants you to come down here and do, uh, your thing at the Classic. Oh, by the way, he said he thought it would be best if you traveled incognito."

"Forget that, baby," I said. "I'm gonna fly."

Odd, I thought after hanging up. Ray Scott had a reputation of being a bright, honest, rich human being. Now he was pulling me in to do a job on the contestants in his own BASS Masters Classic. I had been in on some weird capers in my time, but this was the weirdest.

Just to be on the safe side, I decided to pack a rod. Then I decided it might be even safer to pack three rods—two casting and one spinning.

I told Maizy not to expect me back for at least a week.

"I see you're goin' to Alabama," she said.

"What makes you think so?"

"The banjo on your knee. It's a dead giveaway."

This was originally executed as one drawing. The "3" in the signature refers to the 3 "Nina"s that appear in the drawing as a whole.

I was getting careless. In my business, little slip-ups like that can cost a man his life.

The six-hour flight to Montgomery gave me plenty of time to bone up on the 11th Annual BASS Masters Classic and try to figure out what Ray Scott was up to.

One thing was clear: I'd be going up against forty-two of the best bass fishermen in the world, guys like Roland Martin, Bo Dowden, Jimmy Houston, and Bobby Murray. Most of them made their living as bass pros, fishing anywhere from 150 to 300 days a year. It was said that every one of them went over a piece of water like a human sieve.

I had been told that some of the contestants even thought like bass. That seemed unlikely. I know quite a few people who think like bass and they don't even fish.

It was much more likely the bass pros would be to fishing what Einstein was to physics. They would have reduced catching bass to a mathematical equation. They would extract bass from the water with the regularity of a metronome and the precision of a computer. They would be tough. I began to worry that the old magic might not work against this kind of competition.

About the old magic. Many years ago I discovered that I had a psychic power over fish. Merely by showing up at a lake or stream, I could make the fish stop biting. If I rigged up and made a few casts, the fish would fall into a catatonic state and sink to the bottom, where they would remain as immobile as lox on a bagel until I took leave of the place. Scarcely would my departing epithets have ceased echoing among the distant hills, however, than the fish would arouse from their stupor and churn the water to a maelstrom in their frenzy of feeding.

Soon my friends refused to fish with me. As my reputation for shutting off fishing began to spread, local anglers began pleading to have my intended fishing destinations included in televised fishing reports so they could go where I wasn't. News of my reservations at fishing resorts brought more cancellations than an epidemic of botulism. It wasn't long before angling groups around the nation were trying to get me banned from their states as a dangerous substance. I felt like an outcast.

Then a peculiar thing happened. Other fishermen began looking upon me as a challenge. They would make bets that they could catch fish even if I was in the vicinity. Guides would stake their reputations on the promise that fishing parties would catch fish regardless of my being along. I beat them all. But I must say it is a pitiful sight to see a grizzled old fishing guide, tears streaming down his cheeks, pleading, "Cast into that—*sob!*—hole one more time. I *know* there's fish in there!"

Finally I went into the business of shutting off fishing on a full-time basis. I called my firm "The Empty Creel," and handed out business cards with the motto, "This rod for hire."

But why was Ray Scott bringing me in to shut down the 11th Annual BASS Masters Classic?

I knew that Montgomery was Scott's hometown. It seemed unlikely he would want to disgrace himself in front of the home folks by putting on a BASS Classic in which no bass were caught. Ordering another Scotch from the flight attendant, I decided to check the rules for the tournament.

"Holy cow!" I shouted, and downed the Scotch in a single gulp.

"What is it?" the passenger in the seat beside me yelped. "One of the engines on fire?"

"Nothing so mundane as that," I replied, prying the man's fingers loose from my leg. "I just discovered what Ray Scott is up to!"

Having given the tournament rules the once-over, I had no trouble imagining the following scenario:

Scott and his head henchmen, Harold Sharp and Bob Cobb, are sitting around a table working up the regulations for the tournament.

"As you know, I don't want this BASS Classic to be too easy for the guys," Scott says, chuckling evilly.

"Gee, the rules are pretty stiff already," Cobb puts in. "A limit of seven fish, none under 14 inches, no scouting the water a month prior to the tournament, only ten pounds of tackle allowed, no trolling. . ."

"And if a contestant is even a minute late for the deadline, points get taken away," says Sharp. "If a fish dies, points are taken away!"

"It's tough enough, bass—I man, boss," Cobb blurts.

"No, no," mutters Scott. "Still too easy. I got it! We won't allow them to use landing nets! Can't you just imagine them trying to land a six-pound bass by hooking their fingers in its mouth! Henh-henh!"

Sharp and Cobb glance at each other, blanching. "No landing net? But. . . ."

"Still too easy," says Scott. "I want this to be the toughest bass-fishing tournament ever. Let's see, maybe we could make them balance on a pogo stick while fishing blindfolded. No, that would be too obvious. Wait! How about bringing in that fellow, what's-his-name, McManus?"

"No! No!" Sharp and Cobb shriek in unison. "We could all get arrested for that!"

But Scott has already leaped from his chair and is striding off, gleefully rubbing his hands together. "Yes, yes, McManus is what we need here. Henh-henh, henh-henh!"

That was probably how it had happened, all right. Ray Scott hoped to get the 1981 BASS Classic into the *Guinness Book of World Records* as the toughest ever!

The jet banked over Montgomery and I peered down at the beautiful Alabama countryside cloaked in forests and sparkling with lakes, creeks, and rivers. Wondering if the bass down there had yet detected my presence, I was consumed by the wonderful, glowing feeling that comes from the sense of my own great psychic power. The other passengers were staring at me strangely. It took a moment for me to realize I had been going, "Henh-henh, henh-henh!"

The Classic consisted of two practice days and then three days of the real thing. I didn't go out the first practice day but stayed at the hotel, just to see if my presence in the general vicinity would affect the bass. That afternoon I wandered down to the Montgomery Civic Center, where the day's catch of bass was to be weighed. I had no trouble keeping my enthusiasm in check. After all, what kind of drama can you expect from weighing a bunch of bass?

I had underestimated Ray Scott.

Right there in Montgomery, Alabama, he produced the world's first bass-weighing spectacular! Thousands of spectators crammed the bleachers. Television crews manned their cameras. A hundred reporters and photographers jostled for position. Strobe lights flashed. A huge overhead screen provided the audience with a televised close-up of the action. And the fish scale! Where I had expected one of the little spring-loaded jobs, there was this magnificent electronic device that flashed out the pounds and ounces and fractions of ounces for the entire audience to see at the precise, existential, electrifying moment that each bass was weighed. One could not help but feel humble in the presence of it all.

Ray Scott himself, nattily attired in a brilliant green sport coat and white cowboy hat, served as master of ceremonies. A consummate showman, he worked the crowd up to such a feverish pitch you would have thought he was preparing them for gladiators to bound into the arena and have at one another with sword and ax. Instead, the crowd awaited only a few dozen weary bass fishermen and their catch, if any. If I hadn't been so caught up in the excitement, I would have succumbed to astonishment.

One of the more interesting wrinkles of the show was that the bass pros and their press partners remained in the boats while being towed to and from the Civic Center. I wasn't sure whether this was common fishing practice in Alabama or if Ray Scott had just invented it for the Classic. In any case, the sight of fishermen being towed through town in their boats gave the proceedings just the right touch of levity, or so I judged from the number of pedestrians collapsed on the sidewalk in fits of laughter. What was astounding, however, was the thunderous applause given each boat and its occupants as they were towed grandly into the arena.

I was nervous. The magic didn't seem to be working against these pros. Then Ray Scott called Jimmie Houston up to the microphone and asked him how many fish he had caught and released.

"Only seventy-two," Houston said.

I shuddered. *Only seventy-two?* Then I noticed that Houston was squinting. He's from Oklahoma. It's a well-known fact that Oklahomans can't tell a lie without their eyes twinkling. Jimmie was squinting to cover up the twinkle! He was lying!

I eased up behind Bobby Murray, who was talking to a grim Roland Martin. "There ain't no damn fish out there," Bobby whispered. Roland nodded in agreement.

Sure! In spite of all the razzle-dazzle put on by Scott, the simple fact was that pitifully few fish over 14 inches had been caught and some of those had stretch marks. Boat after boat had come in without a single bass. True, only the reporters were allowed to bring in bass on the practice days, but it was evident from the expressions on the faces of the pros that my old magic was working. And I hadn't even drawn a rod yet.

The next day I went out with bass pro Harold Allen from Batesville, Mississippi. Harold seemed like a pleasant enough fellow at first, and we chatted amiably as we were towed in our boat down to the launch site. We were in the first flight of fifteen boats to line up across Lake Alabama to await the starting signal and the race down the lake to find the best bass water. I took the opportunity to study ole Harold. Even much later, after I analyzed the situation, I concluded that there was nothing in his easy-going manner that in the least suggested homicidal tendencies. Then a peculiar thing happened.

Ray Scott stood up in a boat and recited a prayer over a portable amplifier. I can't recall the words of the prayer exactly but it had something to do with everybody returning *alive and unmaimed!* Well, that certainly caught my attention. I turned to ask Harold whether the prayer was just a formality and discovered it wasn't. He was crouched over the steering wheel, his eyes all gleaming and terrible, and his bearded countenance contorted in a monstrous grin.

"W-wait," I started to say. "I want out!"

But it was too late. Harold pulled the trigger on the Merc 150 and shot us 20 miles down the lake. I opened my mouth to tell him to slow down but my cheeks filled with air and began beating against my ears like toy balloons in a gale. Occasionally Harold would flatten our trajectory enough to get us under bridges, but then he would open her up again. The depth finder was recording low-flying ducks. Smaller birds zipped past like tracers. And then, suddenly, just as I was reaching over to get a grip on Harold's windpipe, we sank back into the water.

"That fast enough for you?" Harold asked, having returned to his old amiable self.

"Phamf glimp," I replied calmly, forcing a smile. I had to force the smile because one of my lips was still hooked over an ear.

Harold was as fine a fisherman as I've ever seen. He fished hard all day, taking time out only long enough to disentangle me from my backlashes or tie one of his lures onto my line.

"The Lord should love me for this," he would mutter.

Harold Allen turned out to be one of the nicest human beings you could ever expect to meet, and I began to feel bad that I had shut off the fish for him, because I surely had. He got only three or four strikes all day and landed a single miniscule bass. Then, late in the afternoon, he did a strange thing.

With only an hour left of the last practice day, time with which he might have tried to find a "honey hole," he started driving the boat up a river. Giant beech trees lined the river on both sides, and the sun, low in the West, sent rays of orange light filtering through veils of Spanish moss and streaming across the water. Here and there we would catch a glimpse of a field of cotton in bloom, golden in the sunlight. I couldn't figure out what Harold was up to, for the river seemed an unlikely place for bass. Finally, Harold stopped the motor and let the boat drift with the current. He sat there quietly, looking around, not even picking up one of his rods. I began to get nervous again. Then ole Harold spoke.

"Beautiful, ain't it?" he said.

Well, I tell you, I was dumbfounded. Here was a professional bass fisherman with a $40,000 first prize at stake, and he used the last hour of the last practice day simply to enjoy the scenery! I had never seen anything so dumb. Clearly, Harold lacked the killer instinct. I decided not to waste any more of my power on him. After all, I had already saved some power by withdrawing it from a 21-year-old kid from Georgia, Stanley Mitchell, who obviously was just too young and inexperienced to be a real contender in the tournament. I knew Ray Scott wouldn't want me wasting power on contenders who wouldn't stand a chance anyway.

The rest of the tournament went about the way I had expected. There was much heated discussion among the bass pros about the inactivity of bass in the lake. Some thought it was because of a cold front that had moved through. Others claimed it must be because an upstream dam wasn't releasing water into the lake. But Ray Scott managed to keep tempers under control by throwing cocktail parties every night, along with sumptuous feasts and floor shows.

One night he even went so far as to make all the bass fishermen and outdoor writers dress up in tuxedos and listen to violin music. He probably thought it was a good chance to instill a bit of culture into both of these groups, but it didn't work. If you haven't seen a bunch of bass fishermen and outdoor writers trussed up in tuxedos and still wearing their cowboy boots and cowboy hats, you have saved yourself from one ghastly spectacle. It looked like a bad collision between a symphony orchestra and a gang of cattle rustlers. The catastrophe was too much even for Ray Scott. Afterward he let the guys wear what they wanted and replaced the violins with belly dancers, country-and-western singers, and rock bands. A man like Scott doesn't get rich by pursuing hopeless causes.

I had only one close call. While quaffing at a cocktail party, I was recognized by Roland Martin, who hadn't yet caught a single limit of bass. Roland knows of my reputation for shutting off fish. I could see the light dawning in his eyes and thought he was about to blow my cover. But Roland is a gentleman and humanitarian and allowed me to escape undetected. Afterward, though, he fished listlessly, with the attitude of a man who knows there is no hope.

I won't even try to describe the grand finale Ray Scott staged for the weighing of bass on the last night of the Classic, except to say that a presidential inauguration or world series seems pallid by comparison. And here I had thought I might go all the way through life without hearing a crowd burst into a deafening roar over a bass that blipped out on electronic scales at three pounds four ounces. When I saw what appeared to be a six-pounder headed for the scales, I ran for the nearest exit, fearing that the ensuing tumult might bring down the roof of the Civic Center.

I packed and went home. Ray Scott should have been pleased by my performance, since most of the bass pros agreed they had never had a tougher time catching fish. On that score, the 11th Annual BASS Masters Classic would be a shoo-in for the *Guinness Book of World Records*.

I had only one regret. The two top-money winners were young Stanley Mitchell from Georgia, who came in first, and ole Harold Allen, who came in a close second. I thought the very least they could have done was divvy up their prize money with me. But you know how it is with bass fishermen.

A Reel Man's Guide To Bassin' And Wormin'

Rex Gerlach

It has been said that *Real Men Don't Eat Quiche* and *Real Women Don't Pump Gas*. Well, it is high time that real bass fishermen struck back. You know, real bass fishermen—the ones who use worms whether they be plastic or alive. If someone else wants to run something other than a reliable worm past the basses' noses, and then release the few fish he catches, that's his business. But my idea of a good time is to catch enough bass to have a good fish fry. The best way to do this is to fish with equipment that offers an odds-on chance of catching something. But before we do this we must first repair some of the damage done to the language of fishing by the "great bass-fishing conspiracy."

Let's start defining the correct bass-fishing terminology and restore some clarity and dignity to what used to be an explicit cultured area of the English language.

Henceforth, all artificial lures will be called "lures," and true "baits" referred to as "live," "dead," or "organic," depending on your persuasion. Artificial lures will no longer be called baits, whether they be "crank," "spinner," "stick," "buzz," or otherwise.

All "sticks" and "hawg haulers" will be restored the dignity due a "fishing rod" or "casting instrument." People who call fishing rods "poles" will be deported and covertly flown to Outer Mongolia where they will spend the rest of their lives cultivating bamboo for split-cane rods.

What is now being erroneously called "string" by certain bass anglers, will henceforth be called "fishing line." "Toads" will now be permitted to hop around without being mistaken for large bass, which in the future will be known only as "lunkers" or "dandies." The same thing goes for "hawgs."

In our new bass-angling utopia, "spooning" will once again mean necking, instead of dragging a wobbling spoon in front of a school of bass caught swimming between two points of land, in what will no longer be referred to as a "suspended" condition. One suspends mobile art. Bass, which we are seeking, tend to swim.

The second phase in our return to the methods and language of the bass-fishing majority is to study how to catch bass the easy way—using worms.

First a bit about worms. Worms come in two shapes: round and flat. They are found living both on land and in the water. Those used most by anglers—night crawlers and angleworms—may also be alluded to as "garden hackle" in deference to fly-fishermen who are not purists.

There are more kinds of plastic worms than those found in the natural order. Some of these are round, others ovate, and they are molded with no tails, flat tails, or curled tails. The latest craze in plastic worms are those with auger-shaped tails. A few plastic worms even have holes in their tails. Those with curled, auger or, holey tails wiggle more than those with no tails or with flat ones.

When fishing for bass with live worms, you will quickly discover that bass prefer juicy worms to stiff, dead dry ones. Throughout nature you will find evidence of the preference of creatures for juicy foods, including men, who obviously enjoy juicy fruit and juicy chewing tobacco. This is especially true of real bass fishermen.

Of the two types of fishing worms, live worms tend to be juicier than plastic worms. However, one can enhance the illusion of juiciness in plastic worms by selecting only the softest types and either injecting air into their bodies or applying scents and flavors to them.

The nice thing about fishing with worms is that all of them will catch bass at one time or another.

Bass'n Man Language
Stick or hawg hauler for throw-un
Bass'n duds
Bass'n throne
Depth sounder
Stick-up

"Nailed 'em"
String
Super Bassfinder
Deluxe IV Rig
Baits (crank, stick,
spinner, buzz) box

Toad
or hawg

Got bit
(previously
a bump)

Live bait

Scented and flavored
plastic worm

Submerged
structure

A strike
(previously
a nibble)

Honey hole,
strike zone

Good spot

Big bass

Fisherman Terminology
Fishing rod for casting
Fishing clothes
Boat cushion
Anchor rope
(depth finder)
Dead tree

Monofilament
Boat
Tackle box
"Hooked 'em"

Snags

Illustration by Frank Brugos

But since there are so many types of plastic worms, one can avoid confusion by restricting the number of sizes, styles, and colors carried while fishing.

My personal worm selection reflects this careful selectivity. The only colors I carry are smoke, smoke with silver flake, root beer with gold flake, crawdad tricolor, brown, red, black, dark blue, light blue with purple stripe, green with red flake, watermelon, purple with fire-tail, black with fire-tail, brown with orange fire-tail, clear with silver flake, chartreuse with gold flake, and purple with yellow fire-tail. I carry this restricted selection only in four-, six-, and eight-inch lengths, and in the following flavors: strawberry, licorice, and grape. I leave my box of 12-inch worms, in those same colors and flavors, at home, except when fishing in Texas where everything is bigger, including the bass.

In bass fishing, presentation is what counts and, henceforth, as we venture forth fishing for bass with our worms, we shall refer to the act of propelling worms into the water near bass as "casting," not "thowun." One "casts" a bait or lure. One "thows" a baseball or football.

Before casting to bass, however, we must first locate them. Incredibly, the bass-fishing conspiracy has attempted to convince us that bass are located near "structure." To the contrary, bass are found in the vicinity of "cover." Structure is what is built by carpenters, stone masons, bricklayers, and concrete pourers and, from now on, may be referred to in the context of bass fishing when it is submerged, thus providing cover for bass.

The classic types of cover consist of submerged cliffs and rocks, stumps, trees, truck tires, brush, weeds, and coil springs from beds that have accidentally fallen into the lake. Cover is also provided by points of land, underwater humps and ledges, and floating vegetation such as lily pads. Docks and moored boats are also good bass cover. Henceforth, no partially submerged tree, stump, or piece of brush will ever again be called a "stick-up," because that only happens when someone points a gun at you and unlawfully demands your money.

Bass are kind of like cats. They prowl predictable seasonal beats, except when they do otherwise unexpectedly, which I must add is quite often. In the spring they are most often found in or near the shallows, more in the shallows if spawning time is imminent. Prior to that, however, they frequently will be found feeding on forage fish and crayfish near points of land and underwater humps. But please note, one does not refer to the forage fish as "baitfish" until they are impaled on a hook or swimming in a bait shop's holding tank.

Spawning is usually accomplished in the extreme shallows, in nests constructed mostly in coves and creek mouths along the northerly shores of the lake, which provide the prerequisite 60-degree or warmer water sooner than most other parts of the lake.

During the heat of the summer, bass often remain in cooler depths during the daylight hours, swimming into the shallows to feed during the twilight and nighttime hours. They do not go on a "bite," as some contend. They "feed." And, furthermore, one does not "git bit," at least not by bass.

When bass feed gently and one misses setting the

hook it is referred to as a "nibble," not a "bump." French bass fishermen have also been known to call these light nibbles "beumps," which is regrettable.

On the other hand, when a bass "strikes" one's lure with vigor, it is said to have "struck" the lure. Bass have no hands with which to wield a hammer, therefore, they cannot be said to have "nailed" it.

In the fall, as the lake's surface cools, bass are once again attracted to schools of forage fish that have also gravitated to the cooler waters. However, during the fall and winter months, they will also be found feeding on crayfish in deep water, frequently near submerged rocks and along rocky dam faces. Worms, crayfish, and their artificial counterparts are frequently effective under these conditions. However, I feel obligated to point out that a pork-rind crayfish affixed to a jig will no longer be referred to, even in jest, as a "jig 'n pig."

Large bass invariably inhabit cover from which it is virtually impossible to extract them with hook-and-line methods other than by using live night crawlers and plastic worms. Small bass, or "school bass" as they are sometimes called, are easier to catch than big ones. That is why they are so eagerly sought by tournament bass fishermen, who are not permitted to fish with live worms, which provide great attraction to large bass.

Actually, those who use live and plastic worms show a high degree of intelligence because they catch more and larger bass on these worms than are taken on other types of lures. It could be argued that, because night crawlers and plastic worms are superior baits and lures, those who use them are superior anglers and, therefore, superior people.

Of the dozens of ways to rig and fish night crawlers and plastic worms, most are quite effective. But there are several techniques that deserve special mention. Among the most effective are the "Texas rig," "Carolina rig," "split-shot worm," "fly-lined worm," and the "threaded night crawler." In the interest of national unity we shall refrain from renaming any of the above rigging methods, although several certainly deserve it.

There are two ways to "thread" a night crawler. One is to insert the hook under its thorax, which is the short enlarged segment of the worm's body. This allows the worm to wiggle actively, thus enticing bass into feeding. A less mobile rigging method, though far more weedless, consists of running the leader through the worm's alimentary canal—which is messy but nonetheless effective.

Both plastic and live worms can be rigged with the hook point exposed or with it buried in the worm's body. The Texas rig is probably the most universally popular of the latter methods. Burying the hook point in the soft plastic material makes the rig practically snag-proof. If this is done incorrectly, it also makes the worm fish-proof.

In the Carolina rig, a large sliding sinker is put on the line, then a small split ring is attached to the line's end. To this a two- to three-foot leader is attached, then a worm hook, which is usually rigged Texas style. Sometimes air is injected into the worm body to increase its buoyancy. When retrieved, the sinker kicks lake-bottom debris and mud into underwater clouds, which allegedly attract bass to the trailing worm.

Most often, anglers fish a natural or plastic worm using some sinker weight to take it down to where the fish are. But too much sinker weight detracts from the attractiveness of the worm. The trick is to use enough weight to get the worm down and to maintain good feel contact with the lake bottom without affecting the mobility of the worm or creating excessive resistance when a fish picks it up. This is the only really tricky aspect of worm fishing—balancing lure weight to the conditions at hand. When a worm is fished without sinker weight, it is referred to as "fly lining," a practice that will cease immediately!

Until now, sinkers have gradually become known as "worm heads." Henceforth, they will only be referred to as "sinkers" because the other expression is offensive to those anglers of the female gender who refuse to pump gas.

In "split-shot worming," a round, seamed, soft curly tailed worm is attached Texas style to a light wire hook. The hook point is lightly inserted into the worm-body seam on the curly tailed side. When this is retrieved steadily through the water, the worm body remains straight while the curly tail waggles, thus attracting bass and prompting them into strikes, not bumps. A split-shot sinker is clamped on the line some 2½ feet above the hook.

Retrieving worms of all types is as easy as rigging them. The rigged worm is cast out, allowed to sink to the bottom, then retrieved very slowly, allowing it to wiggle enticingly over lake-bottom contours and obstructions. Movement is imparted to the worm by slowly reeling in or by slowly lifting the rod tip. Stopping the retrieve for a moment will often prompt a bass into picking up the worm. A little tension should be kept on the line during the retrieve so vibrations caused by nibbling fish can travel through the line to the rod and be felt.

When fishing live night crawlers, use the least amount of sinker weight practical to maintain feel contact with the bottom. Let the worm lie there and writhe. Then slowly move it to a new writhing position. Once the worm has become soggy and dead, replace it with a lively one. Soggy dead worms are not as effective as lively ones.

When you finally do git bit, reel in the slack and nail 'em! Haul that hawg away from the structure as fast as you can. Put the mean on 'em. Hot dang! Git the gaff! You done caught a toad!

Ray Bergman, wherever he is, will be pleased that I have restored bass fishing to its former dignity.

Index